WITHDRAWN

Mennonite
Peacemaking

Foreword by
John A. Lapp

Mennonite
Peacemaking

From Quietism to
ACTIVISM

Leo Driedger
& Donald B. Kraybill

HERALD PRESS
Scottdale, Pennsylvania
Waterloo, Ontario

Library of Congress Cataloging-in-Publication Data
Driedger, Leo, 1928-
  Mennonite peacemaking : from quietism to activism / Leo Driedger and
Donald B. Kraybill.
      p.   cm.
  Includes bibliographical references and index.
  ISBN 0-8361-3648-9 (alk. paper)
    1. Peace—Religious aspects—Mennonites—History of doctrines.
  2. Mennonites—Doctrines—History. I. Kraybill, Donald B.
  II. Title
  BX8128.P4D75   1993
  261.8'73'088287—dc20

                                                            93-36827
                                                                CIP

The paper used in this publication is recycled and meets the minimum requirements of American National Standard for Information Sciences—
Permanence of Paper for Printed Library Materials, ANSI Z39.48-1984.

PHOTO CREDITS: p. 18, *The Martyrs Mirror*; p. 33, from the Anabaptist Heri-
tage Collection of Jan Gleysteen; p. 55, Mennonite Library and Archives,
Bethel College, North Newton, Kan.; p. 38, p. 60, p. 82, p. 97, p. 130, p. 132,
Archives of the Mennonite Church, Goshen, Ind., Mennonite Central Com-
mittee Collection; p. 108, *Elkhart (Ind.) Truth*, courtesy Archives of the
Mennonite Church; p. 159, p. 160, *Kitchener-Waterloo Record* Collection of
Photographic Negatives, Dana Porter Library, University of Waterloo,
Waterloo, Ontario N2L 3G1; p. 182, Mennonite Central Committee photo by
Cindy Sprunger; p. 210, National Campaign for a Peace Tax Fund photo by
John Eisele; p. 212, Mennonite Central Committee photo by Howard Zehr;
p. 264, Mennonite Central Committee. All photos are used by permission, all
rights reserved.

MENNONITE PEACEMAKING
Copyright © 1994 by Herald Press, Scottdale, Pa. 15683
    Published simultaneously in Canada by Herald Press,
    Waterloo, Ont. N2L 6H7. All rights reserved
Library of Congress Catalog Number: 93-36827
International Standard Book Number: 0-8361-3648-9
Printed in the United States of America
Book and cover design by Paula M. Johnson

1 2 3 4 5 6 7 8 9 10 00 99 98 97 96 95 94

*For Guy F. Hershberger and
Frank H. Epp, faithful
and persistent peacemakers*

Contents

Foreword

Mennonite understandings of peace and peacemaking have always been dynamic and sometimes the source of considerable controversy. Some observers have viewed the debate as obscurantist, and even some participants in the conversation have viewed it negatively. This lively volume describes a particularly fertile epoch—the past fifty years of discussion and development regarding peace, that identity-forming conviction.

Just as striking as the swirling crosscurrents are the deeply held commonalities. At every significant historical juncture, the concerns for ethical integrity and a Christlike witness have been present. Without such communally held commitments nurtured over time, there would be no church with a definable tradition. The commonalities and the crosscurrents, the challenge of new issues and changing circumstances, have together generated conspicuous growth and vitality.

Leo Driedger and Donald B. Kraybill have written a fascinating and unique volume exploring what they call the "restructuring of Mennonite peace convictions." Part one of *Mennonite Peacemaking* uses a narrative-analytical approach to examine the theological and ethical issues evident in formal documents and the writings of Mennonite spiritual leaders (some of whom were extensively interviewed).

As sociologists, the authors in part two mine the voluminous data accumulated from church member surveys and reported in *The Mennonite Mosaic* (Herald Press, 1991). Using these data, Driedger and Kraybill provide access to the concerns and perceptions of ordinary Mennonite and Brethren in Christ people.

This rich combination of research methods provides a solid foundation for understanding how one Christian tradition has wrestled

9

with the meanings of obedience to God's call in twentieth-century North America.

No one book, above all this type of wide-ranging volume, is complete in itself. The authors readily admit that their work is neither comprehensive nor fully systematic. Are there missing or underplayed crosscurrents?

The tension of the sectarian impulse versus social responsibility is a major motif. But this is never simply an issue of polity or ethic. Andrew Greeley and Martin Marty have observed that some groups are "people becoming a church" and others are a "church becoming a people." Such transitions, including the changing character of Mennonite communities from subsistence to affluence, add significant context to the intellectual debate. In addition, we should ask how the organizational and institutional development of the church interacts with the crosscurrents described here.

The authors forthrightly categorize the various theological frames of reference within the Mennonite family. Less clear is how fundamentalist, evangelical, mainline, and liberal Protestant as well as Roman Catholic theologies have made a coherent Mennonite ethical statement less and less possible. Add to this impact learnings from biblical scholarship and missiological experience. Without a strong sense of boundaries and highly conscious borrowing, we need to ask if it is possible to constitute or reconstitute a coherent theological-ethical tradition after the severe buffeting inflicted by pluralistic modernity and postmodernity.

Though this book cannot answer all such questions, it represents an important step in the self-understanding so essential to wise discipleship and faithful church life. Mennonite peacemaking is always more than theological conviction or ethical practice. Mennonite peacemaking cannot be reduced to an ideological program or political strategy. Mennonite peacemaking is rooted in an understanding of God who invites godly living. Mennonite peacemaking is an attempt to embody the character of a loving deity in a community of mutual regard and forgiveness. At its finest, Mennonite peacemaking is a sign of God's reconciling will for all people and all creation.

The depth of analysis makes this a pioneering volume. I suspect that the crosscurrents and debates over the Mennonite peace testimony will become even more acute in the future. The story here is reasonably hopeful, but there are those who rather gloomily suggest that the Mennonite center is not holding. They hint that the impact of secularity and the disintegration of consensus threaten the continuation of a definable alternative tradition (except among the more traditional "Old Order" varieties of Mennonites).

Driedger and Kraybill insist that if we remember who we are in God's call, struggle faithfully to incarnate Christ, patiently wait for the wisdom of the Holy Spirit, and covenant together in common purpose, there will continue to be vitality and renewal in Mennonite peacemaking.

—John A. Lapp, Akron, Pennsylvania;
Executive Secretary,
Mennonite Central Committee
August 1993

Authors' Preface

Peacemaking has been central to Mennonite life and identity. Mennonites, however, have not always been peaceful. They have had their own share of tribal squabbles which sometimes led to division and schism. Nevertheless from their beginnings in 1525 many Mennonites have persistently sought to follow the teachings of Jesus—turning the other cheek, going the second mile, and loving their enemies.

Such convictions have led Mennonites to reject participating in war. They have thus gained a reputation as peacemakers that has often shaped their public identity for better or for worse. At times they have been esteemed as peacemakers who chart the paths of virtue; at other times they have been despised as social parasites unwilling to bear their share of national defense. In any event, in their nearly 500 years of history peacemaking has been central to Mennonite self-understanding and public identity.

Publication of this volume marks fifty years since Harold Bender's "Anabaptist Vision" and Guy Hershberger's *War, Peace, and Nonresistance* appeared in 1944.

Mennonites today are scattered around the world in some sixty countries. This volume tells the story of peacemaking among North American Mennonites who for many years lived in rural communities outside the cultural mainstream. A doctrinal belief in separation from the world, forged by years of persecution in Europe, bridled many Mennonites from a full embrace of the larger social order.

The typical mode of peacemaking in these segregated rural settings often took the form of "nonresistance"—an absolute rejection of the use of force that permeated virtually all social relations within and without the community. Beyond rejecting military service, the ethic of quiet nonresistance eschewed political participation and sought to avoid conflict and the use of the law in personal and economic relations. The sectarian impulse to create a separate community anchored on the values of humility and nonresistance was partially realized in farming communities that characterized much of the Mennonite experience in North America until the mid-twentieth century.

The vibrations of industrialization and the jolt of World War II shook Mennonites out of their rural shelters. Uprooted from rural homesteads, seeking higher education, entering professions and engaging in worldwide service activities, many Mennonites joined the mainstream of social life in the last half of the twentieth century.

The process of modernization levied a dramatic impact on the mode and style of Mennonite peacemaking. In the mid-1950s the quiet and meek of the land began debating their responsibilities in the larger social order. Some of them became strident activists in the 1960s and 1970s. Others entered public office and became active in politics. The following pages tell the engaging story of how the timid were transformed into activists.

The story divides into two parts. The first section of the book traces the legacy of nonresistance and its centrality to Mennonite identity. As Mennonites were exchanging plows for professions in the 1950s, theological "brokers" were shaping the transformation of Mennonite peace convictions. We chart the dialogue of these brokers, who were often responding to change agents already embodying new expressions of peacemaking.

The story then turns to the role the civil rights movement and the Vietnam War played in converting the meek and mild into the active and strident. Many agents of change took the lead in forging new understandings of peacemaking in the 1960s and 1970s. At the end of the first section we profile the surge of peacemaking language and activist projects in the 1980s and beyond.

The second part of the volume taps the responses of some 3,000 Mennonite church members for a description of contemporary Mennonite attitudes toward peacemaking, military service, and political participation. This rich source of data, from five Mennonite and Brethren in Christ groups, allows us to plot a current profile of Mennonite understandings of peacemaking. It also permits us to measure the gap between the intellectuals and rank-and-file members.

Our story ends with an overview of new peacemaking initiatives as well as our reflections on the significance of this transformation that has so dramatically changed Mennonite ways. The engaging saga not only tells the story of a people but also raises key issues about the impact of modernization on a traditional religious minority.

This is *not* a comprehensive nor systematic social history of Mennonite peacemaking. With broad strokes we provide a sweeping overview of some of the key issues and turning points in the story of Mennonite peacemaking. We have selectively focused on certain decades, events, players, and issues which in our judgment significantly shaped the restructuring of Mennonite peace convictions. A thorough and comprehensive study of Mennonite peacemaking remains to be written.

Hopefully our foray into some of the issues and transformations will be suggestive for those who pursue the story in a more comprehensive and thorough fashion. The importance of ecumenical influences, the theological debates between fundamentalists and progressives, the forces that gave rise to peace activism, as well as the complacency of peace convictions among many Mennonites, are a few of dozens of topics that need further exploration. Hopefully our modest initiative will spur more systematic investigations of these issues by others in the future.

Our partnership began in the summer of 1991 when Leo Driedger was a fellow in the Young Center for the Study of Anabaptist and Pietist Groups at Elizabethtown college. This afforded us daily opportunity to reflect on the legacy of Mennonite peacemaking and outline the scope of the project.

Our unique backgrounds complemented our efforts to tease out the nuances of diversity in the complex story of Mennonite peacemaking in North America. Leo Driedger, a Canadian, is rooted in the Dutch-Russian Anabaptist heritage and brings a General Conference Mennonite Church perspective to our work. Moreover, living in Winnipeg, Manitoba, amidst the world's largest concentration of urban Mennonites, he espouses an urban view as well.

Donald B. Kraybill, by contrast, brings a Mennonite Church perspective that flows from the Swiss-South German Anabaptist tributary. Raised in a rural setting in the eastern U.S. and now living in a small town context, Kraybill provides a different set of interpretive lenses.

We are grateful to many colleagues who have assisted us in numerous ways. Donald F. Durnbaugh, Ervin Stutzman, Robert S. Kreider, and J. Denny Weaver offered critical feedback to an early draft of several historical chapters. Paul Toews generously suggested resources related to the Mennonite Brethren and gave wise counsel on the first half of the book.

We benefited from the constructive counsel of John R. Burkholder, Diane Driedger, Judy Zimmerman Herr, James Juhnke, John A. Lapp, Edgar Metzler, and John H. Redekop who read the entire manuscript. J. Lawrence Burkholder, William Janzen, C. Norman Kraus, Albert J. Meyer, and Linda Gehman Peachey read sections of a working draft of the manuscript.

And to all those who generously shared of their time by granting us interviews we owe a special gratitude: J. Lawrence Burkholder, John R. Burkholder, Gordon Kaufman, William Keeney, C. Norman Kraus, Robert S. Kreider, John A. Lapp, Al Meyer, Paul Peachey, Titus Peachey, Cal Redekop, Hedy Sawadsky, Mary Sprunger-Froese, Gene Stoltzfus, and John Stoner.

The project has benefited from the support of the Young Center for the Study of Anabaptist and Pietist Groups at Elizabethtown College and from financial grants from the Mennonite Central Committee and the DeFehr Foundation, Inc. of Winnipeg. We enjoyed excellent support services from numerous persons who assisted at various stages of the project. We especially thank Michael King, Herald Press editor, who ably steered us through all the turns of the publishing process.

Howard Kauffman aided us in accessing the Church Member Profile data. Dennis Stoez, staff member at the Archives of the Mennonite Church, and Irene Lehman, MCC archivist, were particularly helpful in assisting our research. Research assistants Stephanie Hackenburg, Erin Keefe, Joy Kraybill and Anne Weidner provided superb assistance with data analysis and editorial work. Brenda Troutman and Darlene Driedger in their always efficient and cheerful manner supervised the many rounds of word processing. We are truly grateful for the help and assistance of all of these persons.

—*Donald B. Kraybill*
Leo Driedger

PART I

Historic Challenges

This Jan Luyken etching from the *Martyrs Mirror* has become an important symbol of historic nonresistance. Fugitive Anabaptist Dirk Willems turns to assist a guard who fell through thin ice while trying to capture him in 1569. Willems was captured and executed.

CHAPTER ONE

The Legacy of Nonresistance

Conscientious objector Irvin Burkhart was denied U.S. citizenship in 1938. Born in Canada in 1896, he was baptized into the Mennonite faith at thirteen years of age and entered the United States in 1919 to study at a Mennonite college in Hesston, Kansas. After marrying Gladys Loucks and serving as a Mennonite pastor, Burkhart taught biblical studies at Goshen College in northern Indiana. In September 1937, as war clouds billowed in Europe, he applied for U.S. citizenship.

The application form asked, "If necessary, are you willing to take up arms in defense of this country?" After citing historic Mennonite beliefs and describing the formation of his own convictions, Burkhart wrote, "One who believes sincerely that war is wrong under all circumstances and contrary to the Word of God, would out of moral necessity and intellectual honesty be compelled to refuse the bearing of arms, since there are no alternatives to the dictates of conscience."[1]

On December 5, 1938, the Superior Court of Elkhart, Indiana, denied Irvin Burkhart citizenship. Judge Conley concluded that an alien who would not bear arms could not be naturalized. After a nine-year legal battle, Burkhart received citizenship in 1947 when the U.S. Supreme Court favored admitting conscientious objectors as citizens. Burkhart was not alone. Other Mennonites—Martha Graber Landis, John and Anna Klassen—had also been denied citizenship because they refused to bear arms.[2]

Military interests have often shaped conceptions of citizenship in

Europe and North America (Giddens, 1987:233). Military conscription at times becomes, in essence, the price of citizenship. Pacifists are deemed unworthy citizens, or at best, second-rate ones—freeloaders who refuse to pay the costs of citizenship. Those who reject violence understandably threaten political leaders who assume that their ability to govern and defend national interests rests ultimately on a civic consensus that legitimates military conscription.

The tie between citizenship and conscription sometimes forms a fundamental friction between peace churches and nation-states. The power of the state ultimately rests on raw coercion—even lethal force when required. In stark contrast, Christian peacemakers advocate suffering love and the rejection of force—even in the face of death. In Yinger's (1970:457) words, "The final concern of the state is self preservation, whatever the means; the final concern of religion is salvation, whatever the costs." Military conscription thus often pits the desires of the state against the virtues of pacifism as the two social orders—anchored on opposing values and purposes—collide.

States which conscript citizens must persuade them that dying in military action is a necessary duty—a noble sacrifice for the rights of citizenship. It is the stuff of national heroes. Peace churches on the other hand must convince their members that participation in military service mocks the essence of Christian faith and betrays their Savior, who taught the love of enemies. The willingness to die for country, the highest sacrifice in the patriotic realm, becomes a sad transgression in peace churches. Not surprisingly, they have often excommunicated wayward members who entered military service.

Thus the most sacred value in the civic realm turns on its head—and becomes the most profane in the peacemaking tradition. In the political realm, citizens may be asked to die for the cause of the country; in the religious order, for the cause of Christ. The inherent rift between the state and peace churches is more than polite dissent; it is an inversion of ultimate values. Military defense, atop the hierarchy of national values, skids off the list of peacemaking priorities.

Many religious groups have accommodated to the larger culture by turning defense of the country into a Christian duty. Indeed, the religious duty to defend the country often becomes a common ground of agreement between church and society. Christians may challenge government policies on all sorts of other issues—abortion, discrimination, pollution. But when it comes to war, mainstream churches and the state agree: Christians have a moral duty to muffle their criticism and fight. As churches clarify their ties to states with conscription, they also define their stance toward the larger culture. In other words, the willingness of a religious body to participate in military service serves as a basic barometer of its accommodation to prevailing social values.

Although conscription may have symbolized the price of citizenship for American citizens throughout much of the twentieth century, the tie has dissolved with the advent of a volunteer army. The Persian Gulf War offered a taste of a high-tech limited war which cost citizens of the U.S. and Canada little in terms of taxation, conscription, or personal sacrifice. Juhnke (1991:58-59) suggests that such wars, which no longer pivot on conscription and which make few sacrificial demands on citizens, pose a new challenge for Christian pacifists.[3]

Mennonites have espoused peaceful ways since their inception in sixteenth-century Europe. Although adult baptism sparked the initial breach between Mennonites and civil authorities, Juhnke (1989:32) notes that military service has long since replaced baptism as the flash point in church-state conflicts for Mennonites in North America, especially in the United States. The peacemaking posture of Mennonites has often defined their relationship to government as well as to other religious bodies. It has earmarked their North American identity in countless ways and defined them as a conspicuous socio-religious minority. Indeed since the mid-1930s they have been publicly identified as one of the historic peace churches.[4]

Tracing the Nonresistant Legacy

What happens when the members of a religious minority swim into the cultural mainstream? Do they discard peaceful ways and begin paying the price of citizenship as they achieve a comfortable niche in the larger culture? Our study of Mennonite peacemaking explores the inherent tension between the responsibilities of citizenship and the convictions flowing from a pacifist heritage. We begin with a brief overview of the legacy of nonresistance.

Defenseless Christians

The simple words of Jesus, "Resist not evil," found in Matthew's gospel (5:39) have shaped Mennonite identity and praxis over the centuries. The English rendition of this verse in the King James Bible gave birth to the word nonresistance among Mennonites in North America. The concept of suffering love, however, had been harbored in Mennonite hearts from the beginning of their movement in sixteenth-century Europe. Named for a sixteenth-century leader

Menno Simons, Mennonites trace their religious roots to the Anabaptists who broke with the Protestant reformers beginning in 1525.[5]

Anabaptists (re-baptizers) sprang up in Switzerland and in Germany as well as in the Dutch-speaking Low Countries. In the years following 1525, Anabaptists also fled to areas such as Moravia to avoid persecution. Considered religious heretics and political insurgents by civil and religious authorities alike, Anabaptists faced persecution and torture. Thousands died for their faith—burning at the stake, drowning in rivers, starving in prisons, and losing their heads to the executioner's sword.[6]

Although the dissident movement was fragmented in its early years, most Anabaptist leaders emphasized the authority of the New Testament Scriptures, obedience to the literal teachings of Jesus, adult baptism, the separation of church and civil government, and a disciplined community separated from the larger society. Seeking to follow the teachings of Jesus, most early Anabaptists rejected violent ways.[7]

However, without centralized leadership or a unified creed, various interpretations of nonresistance surfaced. First generation Anabaptists held divergent views regarding the use of the sword by Christian magistrates and civil authorities. Anabaptists in the town of Münster resorted to violent insurrection. But even in the early years the majority of Anabaptists rejected the use of the sword. In any event, by the 1560s nonresistance had become, in the words of Brock (1991a:100), "a dogma of the Anabaptist movement" for the second generation.[8]

The first theological confession of Swiss Anabaptism was formulated in 1527 at Schleitheim. This statement of "Brotherly Union" placed the use of the sword, "outside the perfection of Christ" (Yoder, 1973:39-40). It called Christians to learn from Christ, "who is meek and lowly of heart" and forbade them to use the sword in warfare or serve in the office of magistrate. A sharp dualism between church and world also permeated the Schleitheim statement.

Over a century later Mennonites adopted a formal confession of faith in 1632 at Dordrecht, the Netherlands. This influential statement which Loewen (1985:24) calls the "mother of Mennonite Confessions" has shaped the tone and content of subsequent Mennonite confessions. It remains operative even today in the more conservative Mennonite and Amish communities.

The Dordrecht Confession contains an article titled "Defense by Force." Based on Matthew 5:39 and other New Testament verses it rejects revenge and advocates overcoming evil with good.

> With regard to revenge and resistance to enemies with the sword. . . . Our Lord Christ as well as his disciples and followers have forbidden and taught against *all* revenge. We have been commanded to recompense no man with evil for evil, not to return curse for cursing, but to put the sword into the sheath. . . .[9]

The Dordrecht taboo of forceful defense was not novel. The defenseless posture had become a trademark of the Anabaptist movement—in the writings of Menno Simons, in the interrogations of Anabaptists by the authorities (*taüferakten*), in public debates that pitted Protestants and Catholics against Anabaptists, in Anabaptist hymns, and in numerous editions of the martyr stories called *The Sacrifice of the Lord*, first published in 1562.

European Anabaptists had used the German words *gewaltlosigkeit* (abstaining from the use of force), *wehrlos* (defenseless), and *wehrlosigkeit* (defenselessness) as well as their Dutch language equivalents to signify the rejection of force.[10] According to Lowry (1990:36-42), the term defenseless (*wehrlos*) first appears on the title page of a 1631 edition of an old Anabaptist martyr book.[11]

Defenseless appeared in the title of van Braght's (1985) massive *Martyrs Mirror* first published in 1660 as well as in the title of the English edition in print today, *The Bloody Theatre or Martyrs Mirror of the Defenseless Christians*. Although in many ways it is a violent epic, Lowry (1990) calls the response of the martyrs in the 1,200-page *Martyrs Mirror* "a mirror of nonresistance."

Defenselessness and nonresistance have shaped the heart of Mennonite theology over the centuries. The terms capture a cluster of Jesus' instructions in the Sermon on the Mount (Matthew 5)—"resist not evil . . . turn the other cheek . . . go the second mile . . . give away your coat . . . love your enemies . . . bless them that curse you . . . do good to them that hate you." Nonresistant theology also flows from Paul's writings in Romans (12:14-21)—"bless them which persecute you . . . recompense to no man evil for evil . . . avenge not yourselves . . . for it is written, Vengeance is mine . . . if thine enemy hunger, feed him . . . be not overcome of evil, but overcome evil with good."

Anchored on these and other Scriptures, nonresistance became the Mennonite mode, par excellence, of coping with evil. Rejected were revenge, retaliation, coercion, physical force, and of course participation in military service. Although the concept became embedded in Mennonite history and practice the word *nonresistance* slipped into common parlance in the second half of the nineteenth century, as

Mennonites in North America laid aside the German language for English—a transition that stretched well into the twentieth century in some midwestern and Canadian Mennonite communities.

Denominations in the Mosaic

Over the centuries Mennonites have branched into several subgroups and denominations based on ethnic and national heritage as well as religious belief and practice. By the last decade of the twentieth century, Mennonites were scattered in some sixty countries around the world speaking up to eighty different languages. Various migrations and aggressive mission endeavors throughout the twentieth century had propelled the diaspora. Mennonite church members numbered nearly 925,000 worldwide in 1993, with some 381,000 living in North America.[12]

Our study of peacemaking focuses on North American Mennonites—especially those that participated in the 1989 Church Member Profile (CMP) of five Mennonite and Brethren in Christ denominations.[13] These groups represent the bulk of mainline Mennonites in North America. The more conservative Old Order Mennonite and Amish groups lie beyond the scope of our study.[14]

Before sketching the story of Mennonite peacemaking, we briefly highlight the five groups in our study introduced in order of their size.

The **Mennonite Church** (MC) is composed largely of congregations, many of them east of the Mississippi, that reach back to Switzerland and South Germany. Earlier called the "Old Mennonite" Church, MCs number about 102,000 in North America with 10 percent living in Canada. The most rural of the five denominations, the Mennonite Church is currently undergoing rapid urbanization. The denomination is organized into regional conferences, most of which participate in the biennial Mennonite General Assembly.

The **General Conference Mennonite Church** (GC) is the second largest denomination with some 63,000 members. The majority live west of the Mississippi river and 47 percent reside in Canada. The General Conference Mennonite Church, formed in 1860, united Mennonites from South Germany, who had settled in Illinois and Iowa, with others who had broken away from the "Old" Mennonite Church in eastern Pennsylvania in 1847.

Mennonite Russian immigrants to the U.S. and Canada in the nineteenth and twentieth century also joined the GC Church. Today the majority of GC members are of Dutch-Russian background but a sizable number have Swiss roots. In recent years the MCs and GCs have explored a possible merger to expand their many cooperative activities.

The **Mennonite Brethren Church** (MB) of North America numbers about 44,000 members. Some 60 percent live in Canada. Members in the United States reside primarily west of the Mississippi River. Mennonites had migrated to Russia between 1788 and 1835 from settlements in Prussia. The MBs originated as a spiritual renewal movement in Russia in 1860, when they separated from the older Mennonite body (*Kirchliche* or establishment church).

The **Brethren in Christ Church** (BIC) reflects a synthesis of Anabaptism and Pietism that sprouted in eastern Pennsylvania in the 1770s. The Brethren in Christ number about 20,000 with some 15 percent living in Canada. Their primary concentrations are found in the eastern United States. Along with the other Mennonite groups the BICs participate in the service programs and peace activities of the Mennonite Central Committee.

The **Evangelical Mennonite Church** (EMC) with nearly 4,000 members is the smallest group in our study. Centered in the U.S. Midwest, they embody a Swiss cultural heritage once rooted in the Old Order Amish Church. Originally called Defenseless Mennonites, EMC members today hail from many different religious and ethnic backgrounds as a result of evangelistic efforts.[15]

A Dual Heritage

The Mennonite experience in America has been shaped by two cultural legacies: Dutch-Russian and Swiss-South German (Juhnke, 1988 and 1989). Most North American Mennonites flow from one of these cultural streams, which have shaped the composition and ethos of the different Mennonite bodies.

Swiss-South German Mennonites accent the dualism between church and world, separation from public life, the virtues of humility and simplicity, and the language of nonresistance. All things considered, Swiss-South German impulses are more sectarian—more withdrawing from the larger world—than those of the Dutch-Russian tradition (Juhnke, 1988 and 1989).

Dutch Mennonites, who fled into Prussia as refugees and later migrated to the Ukraine at the invitation of Catherine the Great, have molded the ethos of the Dutch-Russian heritage. Many migrated from Russia in the 1870s and 1920s to the United States and Canada, where they formed their own communities and sometimes mingled with Swiss-South German Mennonites.

Nineteenth-century Russian Mennonites had developed their own community life and attained considerable political experience by managing their own institutions. They had learned to accept responsibility for public affairs and gained a sense of worldly self-respect. As the Russian Mennonites migrated to North America in the late nineteenth and early twentieth centuries, they were more comfortable with political involvement in the larger society, less separatist in their social stance, and less apt to speak of humility and simplicity than their kindred Swiss-South German Mennonites. Although all Mennonite groups embraced the ways of peace, those with Dutch-Russian roots were less likely to use the explicit language of nonresistance.[16]

Nevertheless, the basic heritage of nonresistance in Juhnke's (1989:215-216) words "cut across boundaries of Swiss-South German and Dutch-Russian origins and across lines between early and late arrivers." Although many Dutch-Russian Mennonites filled the ranks of the Mennonite Church in the early decades of the twentieth century, all of the GC confessions of faith between 1895 and 1941 make explicit references to nonresistance (Loewen, 1985).

The rejection of forceful defense in the 1632 Dordrecht Confession had influenced the confessional statements of all Mennonite groups in North America. All Mennonite bodies, but not always all their members, rejected military service. There were, however, variations in the language and application of peacemaking.

The word nonresistance became tightly stitched into the Swiss-South German fabric alongside the strands of humility and separation from the world (Juhnke, 1989:35-36). North American Mennonites anchored in the Dutch-Russian tradition were equally committed to peacemaking, but less likely to use the explicit language of nonresistance. They tended to use positive, peacemaking language—"love," "the Christ-taught doctrine of Peace," and "the principle of peace."

C. H. Wedel and H. P. Krehbiel, turn-of-the-century GC leaders used the word nonresistance occasionally, but more typically they talked of "peace principles," "the Prince of Peace," "enemy love," and "amity." In Juhnke's words, the Dutch-Russians "were no less strongly peace-minded" but they "expressed the doctrine in different language."[17]

Mennonites with Dutch-Russian blood were also more likely to hold political office and participate in civic affairs than their Swiss-South German counterparts. Greater political activism and less orthodox use of nonresistant language among GC leaders was also encouraged somewhat by GC polity. The GC congregations enjoyed greater autonomy than MC congregations who were tethered quite tightly to regional conferences that wielded considerable authority over local congregations.[18]

The MB Church, born in Russia in 1860, used peacemaking language in its 1902 confession of faith remarkably reminiscent of the 1632 Dordrecht confession. A Committee on Nonresistance was appointed in 1919 and several MB district conferences appointed Committees on Defenselessness. Although earlier MB statements forbid participation in war and emphasized the "practice of peace and love," the explicit language of "nonresistance" became commonplace in MB peace declarations in the 1930s and 1940s.[19]

A 1954 statement designed to strengthen "our belief in nonresistance" listed seven reasons why the MB Church "believes in nonresistance" (Toews and Nickel, 1986:157).

The Brethren in Christ (BIC) denomination, reflecting the Swiss roots of their Anabaptist heritage, have typically used the language of nonresistance.[20]

Thus all of the major North American Mennonite bodies have historically rejected revenge and promoted peacemaking. The explicit language of nonresistance, however, became more deeply entrenched in the Swiss-South German heritage.

Early Statements and Expressions

Despite variations in the tone and mode of peacemaking, the pacifist impulse runs deep in the Mennonite soul. Apart from a high regard for the New Testament and an embrace of salvation in Jesus Christ, nonresistance has been one of the most widely and deeply held Mennonite beliefs over the centuries.

Nonresistance, symbolic code word for the pursuit of peace, nourished Mennonite self-understanding and defined the Mennonite version of the "nonresistant Gospel." Mennonite pacifism is of course premised on a personal faith in Jesus Christ as revealed in the New Testament. The Mennonite understanding of nonresistance was rooted in a communal understanding of the church and was inexorably tied to other theological understandings—understandings of God, ethics, suffering, and politics. Never a separate belief, it was an integral part of a larger theological gestalt.

Strands of Nonresistance

Mennonite historian C. Henry Smith (1938:27) contended that pacifism was the "distinguishing" Mennonite characteristic and "per-

haps the only excuse for the separate existence of the denomination."
North American Mennonites in the eighteenth and nineteenth centuries often spoke of the "nonresistant faith," "nonresistant Christianity," "the nonresistant Gospel," and at times "the Gospel of Peace."
They also spoke of Jesus as the "Prince of Peace," and described his
kingdom as a "peaceable Kingdom." Although they shared basic understandings of faith with other Christian believers, Mennonite minds
wove the strands of peace into the fabric of salvation itself.[21]

A Mennonite petition to the Pennsylvania House of Assembly in
1775, in Revolutionary War times, confessed that Mennonites, "by the
Doctrine of our Saviour Jesus Christ, are persuaded in their Consciences to love their Enemies, and not to resist Evil. . . ."[22]

Writing in 1804 Christian Burkholder (1857:243-44) said that
Christ had abolished revenge and defense by force, "because his
Kingdom is a Kingdom of Peace. Consequently we are not allowed to
'resist evil.' " Some years later, Abraham Godshalk (1838) wrote a
book on regeneration and contended that nonresistance was integral
to Christian conversion.[23] After describing Christ's death Godshalk
(1838:52) says, "The completed child of God . . . follows him in regeneration and does the will of God . . . doth not resist evil. . . . He loveth
his enemies."

At about the same time, Peter Burkholder (1837) of Virginia
penned a short, but eloquent essay on peace. Without mentioning the
word nonresistance, Burkholder lodges peace in the core of the gospel.

> God is a God of love and peace; and his Kingdom is a Kingdom of Peace;
> therefore all the partakers or subjects of his Kingdom must be children of
> peace; for without this requisite we are unfit either to possess or enjoy
> this Kingdom of peace or appear before its glorious King, the King of
> Peace.

Describing Christ's call to discipleship in Mark 8:34, Burkholder
writes,

> Now this self-denial *extends farther*, and *roots deeper*, than many consider,
> or are aware; for he that will deny himself must renounce his self-will, his
> self-love, carnal pleasure, high-mindedness, wrath, revenge and resis-
> tance by force; and be ready if required, to die for the name of Jesus
> Christ. . . ."[24]

Burkholder's lucid, eighteen-page expression of nineteenth-
century peace convictions refers to the "Peaceable Kingdom" and

"Kingdom of Peace" some two dozen times. He mentions "the God of Peace," the "Prince of Peace," and the " King of Peace," more than twenty times. On a dozen occasions, Christians are called "Children" and the "Children of Peace." For Burkholder, the pursuit of peace—even unto death—circumscribes the core of salvation; the very gospel itself.

In his booklet on warfare published amidst the War Between the States, John F. Funk (1863) confesses "we surely believe that according to the Gospel as taught and practiced by Jesus Christ, no man can . . . engage in legalized murder and robbery and still retain the love of God in his heart."

Beginning in 1864, MC leader Funk edited an influential paper, *The Herald of Truth*, which featured frequent articles on nonresistance. Through the last three decades of the nineteenth century, the front page of Funk's paper proclaimed, "How Beautiful are the feet of them that preach the Gospel of Peace." Its successor, *The Gospel Herald*, continued the proclamation on its masthead well into the twentieth century.

In the 1880s the Lancaster Conference in southeastern Pennsylvania "examined" applicants for baptism to discern if they were "at peace" and "willing to submit wholly . . . " to the "evangelical, nonresistant doctrine of the Gospel. . . ."[25] The Franconia Mennonite Conference, centered north of Philadelphia, customarily concluded its conference sessions by affirming "the simple and nonresistant faith of Christ" (Ruth 1984:512). The formal resolutions of the Indiana-Michigan Conference frequently mentioned the "nonresistant faith," "nonresistant Christianity," and occasionally the "Gospel of Peace" between 1864 and 1929.[26]

S. S. Haury, a GC Mennonite with South German roots and the first GC missionary to the Cheyenne and Arapaho Indians, advocated teaching nonresistance in Sunday schools in the 1890s. Haury (1894:8) contended that nonresistance—"the patient, bearing, and forbearing, the forgiving and self-sacrificing love"—is the "essence of Christianity," which Jesus "constantly practiced." A nonresistant life, Haury (1894:17) noted, "begins at the time of conversion when the sinner experiences all this in his own heart through the kindness of God and his Saviour."

Mennonite Church leader Daniel Kauffman (1898), in his first edition of *Bible Doctrine*, devotes a chapter to nonresistance. The first subtitle proclaims: "The Gospel of Christ, the Gospel of Peace." Kauffman (1898:205-206) argues that, "The doctrine of peace is . . . inseparably connected with the religion of Jesus. . . . The whole Gospel is a gospel of peace—peace with God, peace with the brotherhood, peace with all men."

Few rank-and-file Mennonites in the nineteenth century could match the eloquence of their leaders in verbalizing the inextricable tie between the gospel and the ways of peace. And, indeed, the legacy of nonresistance is littered with stories of wartime failure when some Mennonites heeded the call to arms, to the dismay of their elders.[27] Such wayward sons, usually in the minority, were often excommunicated, confirming the centrality of nonresistance to Mennonite understandings of the gospel.[28]

Despite their peaceful tenets, Mennonites sometimes squabbled with non-Mennonite neighbors and congregations which were occasionally torn asunder with strife and dissension. But amidst the periodic slippage from their lofty ideals, Mennonite understandings of peace were usually threaded into the very tapestry of the gospel itself.

A Deeply Rooted Peace

Peace convictions were not only central to Mennonite understandings of faith, they were the taproot of Mennonite life. An abundance of empirical evidence underscores the depth of pacifism in the Mennonite experience. Loewen's (1985:42-43) analysis of twenty-seven Mennonite confessions of faith between 1527 and 1975 revealed that the rejection of revenge was a "most central emphasis" in *all* of the confessions. Many of them devote a special section to nonresistance—highlighting biblical commands to love enemies, suspend revenge, overcome evil with goodness, embody the ways of love, abstain from military service, avoid litigation, and reject "carnal" warfare of all sorts. Christ is portrayed as the example of suffering love—the virtuous response to evil. The confessions reiterate the belief that Christian duty in the kingdom of God supersedes civic obligations to the state.

Loewen's (1985:35) study of Mennonite confessions unraveled a peace canon within the canon when Scriptures are cited. Mennonite use of Scripture clearly tilts toward the New Testament. And within the Gospels, Matthew's story predominates because of Mennonite deference to the Sermon on the Mount. Matthew 5 is quoted most extensively. Moreover, within chapter five the cluster of verses dealing with nonresistance and love of enemies (vv. 38-48) "receives the strongest emphasis by a margin of almost three to one," according to Loewen (1985:35). The unparalleled prominence of Jesus' nonresistant instructions (Matthew 5:38-48) in the Mennonite Confessions—

the canon within the canon—confirms the depth of the pacifist throb in the Mennonite heart.

The steady stream of peace literature produced by Mennonite individuals and groups in the first half of the twentieth century also evinces a robust peace commitment. The tide of peace literature rose as Mennonites became more literate and vigorous in their peacemaking efforts. Bert Friesen (1986) has identified some 530 public statements on peace and war written by various Mennonite and Brethren in Christ groups in Canada. The documents—which span the years between 1787 and 1982—articulate a biblical understanding of nonresistance, address government agencies, and describe alternatives to military service. The five hundred statements, proliferating of course during war times, exclude nearly seven hundred other pronouncements on church-state issues and relief and service concerns.

In a survey of district conference actions within the Mennonite Church and some Amish-Mennonite groups, Erb (1949) identified 162 resolutions on nonresistance between 1835 and 1945. Additional resolutions spoke to related issues—voting, office holding, jury duty, and liberty bonds. Erb's survey underscores the significance of peace concerns among local and regional conferences in the Mennonite Church prior to 1945.

Influential churchwide publications within the same denomination—*Herald of Truth*, and its successors *Gospel Witness*, and *Gospel Herald*—have promoted peace and nonresistance since the 1860s. In a survey of these periodicals from 1864 to 1907, Denlinger (1985) found 263 articles and editorials dealing with peace issues—excluding articles on political involvement.

Peachey (1980) collated some 231 peace and social concern statements produced between 1900 and 1978 by four of the groups encompassed in our study, as well as statements released by the Mennonite Central Committee.[29] The pronouncements articulate historic Mennonite peace convictions and address kindred issues—conscription, capital punishment, and nationalism, etc. About seventy of the statements articulate—often in detail—theological understandings of nonresistance and peacemaking.

TABLE 1.1
Peace Statements issued between 1900 and 1978
by Mennonite Groups

Group	Number of Statements
Mennonite Central Committee	93
General Conference Mennonite Church	42
Mennonite Brethren Church	35
Mennonite Church	32
Brethren in Christ Church	29

Source: Peachey (1980)

As Mennonite educational attainment rose the output of peace materials—pamphlets, booklets, articles, and books—soared. In their annotated bibliography covering a half-century (1930-1980) of Mennonite peace literature, Swartley and Dyck (1987) identified some 10,000 published items. The abundance of peace publications, conference resolutions, and denominational statements issued by North American Mennonites—astonishing in quantity—underscores the depth of the peace impulse in Mennonite hearts. Surely no other issue has captured Mennonite commitments with such enduring power over the generations.

The Broad Duties of Love

The legacy of nonresistance not only ran deep in the Mennonite soul; it also ran wide. Peace convictions were intertwined with a multitude of other beliefs and practices. Although Christians of many stripes commonly talked of personal peace with God, Mennonites emphasized the social dimensions of nonresistance. The "nonresistant way of life," a common phrase on Mennonite lips, underscored the broad social implications of peacemaking.

The nonresistant posture permeated Mennonite life and impacted *all* social relations—interpersonal and collective. "Nonresistance is not a mere policy," said MC leader Daniel Kauffman (1898:217).

> It is a living, Christian principle that shapes our lives, public and private. It makes the Christian peaceable in his home, in church, in society, in business circles. It restrains him from abusing his family, being overbearing in his dealings with his fellow-man, indulging in ill-natured criticisms of any kind, engaging in violent political discussions, murmuring against his government, and resisting by carnal means evil of any kind.

The first theological confession of Swiss Anabaptism was formulated in 1527 at Schleitheim. Among the seven articles of this "Brotherly Union" was a rejection of warfare.

Mennonite shepherds reminded their flocks that nonresistance extends far beyond the refusal to bear arms. In fact, S. S. Haury (1894:2, 17-18) said the "refusal to bear arms . . . is the least important part of the belief in nonresistance. . . ." Haury contended that nonresistance means practicing "all the duties of love in everyday life towards the brother, and in relationship to the neighbor and in our business."

Mennonite litanies recounting the implications of "practical nonresistance" include 1) loving and praying for enemies, 2) resisting no evil, 3) returning good for evil, 4) suffering wrong rather than inflicting violence upon others, 5) abstaining from revenge and vengeance, 6) avoiding disputes of all kinds, 7) refraining from using the law against others, 8) staying aloof from "machine politics," and 9) living peaceably with all people at all times. Admonitions to "nonresistant living" were always grounded on Scripture—especially Matthew 5 and Romans 12. The focus on "resist not evil" led to a categorical rejection of force and coercion.[30]

Although Mennonites spanked their offspring, sometimes beat their cows, and hunted game for sport, their rejection of force had sweeping implications for many social involvements. Especially among Swiss-heritage Mennonites, nonresistance meant a taboo on litigation because it entailed coercion. An 1847 letter by Mennonite leaders stated the contradiction boldly, noting that "law courts . . . are in totality contrary to the life, teaching and walk of our Lord Jesus. . . ."[31] Members in many congregations were liable for excommunication if they filed law suits. Consequently, very few Mennonites practiced law as a profession until the middle of the twentieth century.

Max Weber (1958:119) has noted that in contrast to the Christian admonition to "resist not evil," for the politician the reverse proposition holds, "thou *shalt* resist evil by force." Thus, for Mennonites nonresistance often meant avoiding political officeholding, which in Mennonite eyes was premised on the implicit threat of force. Congregations and conferences, especially those with Swiss roots, debated where to draw the line in holding public office. Which offices, if any, could be "consistently" held by nonresistant Christians? Major officeholding was generally taboo, but benign offices such as road commissioner, overseer of the poor, and school director were often acceptable.[32]

A few conferences prohibited voting, some discouraged it, but many considered it a personal matter. The stance toward voting fluctuated, of course, with the issues of the times, such as prohibition. Aspiring to leadership in political parties or participating in political campaigns surely violated the humble stance of nonresistance. Might serving as a bank director require a member to use the law in the case of necessary foreclosures? Serving on a jury and swearing the courtroom oath were off limits for "consistent" Christians. Serving on the police force was, of course, unthinkable for Mennonites.

In the twentieth century new issues troubled the nonresistant conscience. Some Mennonites worried that saluting the flag might imply a commitment to serve in the military.[33] Holding membership in a labor union that called coercive strikes also posed a violation of nonresistant principles to some Mennonite leaders. Other elders argued that nonresistance meant a categorical rejection of both capital punishment and abortion.

In the face of theft or robbery, nonresistant Mennonites sometimes felt that pressing legal charges mocked the scriptural injunction to overcome evil with good. And Mennonites with a tender conscience were reluctant to post "No Trespassing Signs" on their property which threatened wayward hunters with the force of law.[34] Articles in the *Gospel Herald* occasionally asked how nonresistant Mennonite hunters could conscientiously shoot game in hunting season.[35] Such talk stirred the ire of other Mennonites who stocked their closets with guns for the pleasures of hunting.

Pressing the broad implications of nonresistance, some writers argued that nonresistant drivers should always abide by speed limits to avoid highway injury. One youth speaker even argued that nonresistant drivers should not retaliate with high beam lights when oncoming drivers neglected their lower beams. In all of these ways, Mennonite commitments to nonresistance in the mid-twentieth century ran deep and very wide. The applications of nonresistance to daily life nurtured a political aloofness and separation from the larger culture, especially among Mennonites with a Swiss-South German legacy.

The Nonresistant Label

We have argued that peace convictions permeated the Mennonite experience in North America into the twentieth century. The legacy of nonresistance also defined Mennonite identity and interactions in the public realm. Indeed, a GC congregation in Kansas developed a brief confession of faith shortly after World War I because some outsiders had charged that, "nonresistance is the main and only principle of the Mennonite faith" (Loewen, 1985:152).

Mennonite literature and writings are replete with references to "nonresistant bodies," "nonresistant churches," "nonresistant peoples," and "nonresistant Christians." The adjective defined the character of Mennonite groups in the public sphere. In the German language they were *wehrlos*—a "defenseless" people.

In some cases the word "defenseless" was also used after the transition to English, although "nonresistant" quickly became the normative code word. Two Mennonite bodies, however, used the word defenseless in their formal names. The Defenseless Mennonite Church of North America (1864), often called "Defenseless Mennonites," changed its name to the Evangelical Mennonite Church in 1948. It is one of the five groups in our study. The Defenseless Mennonite Brethren in Christ in North America (1889) dropped defenseless from its name in 1937 to become the Evangelical Mennonite Brethren.

In Canada, several Mennonite groups formed a "nonresistant relief organization" in the context of World War I. This eventually paved the way for the Conference of Historic Peace Churches which was established in Canada in 1940.[36] Although most Mennonite groups did not include nonresistance in their formal names, they frequently referred to themselves and were tagged by outsiders as "nonresistant" people, churches, bodies, etc.

The nonresistant trademark distinguished Mennonites on several levels. It earmarked them for government officials as conscientious objectors who refused conscription in wartime, and who declined to swear oaths in the courtroom—folks who for the most part remained aloof from the political fray.

Within religious circles the nonresistant label set Mennonites apart from mainstream Protestants. The family of plain dressing groups— Dunkers (Church of the Brethren), Mennonites, Amish, and the Brethren in Christ—were frequently lumped together as "nonresistant bodies" in the late nineteenth and early twentieth century. Respected for their hard work and quiet ways, they were a different breed, outside the Protestant mainstream.

When peace movements mushroomed in the aftermath of World War I, the nonresistant label also distinguished Mennonites from other "pacifists"—a word that increasingly smelled of liberal and modernist odors to some Mennonites. Nonresistance, etched into Mennonite consciousness and tattooed on their public image, defined the essence of Mennonite identity.

Summary

Social analysts have frequently noted that pacifism thrives in sectarian soil—within religious groups that accent separation from the dominant culture.[37] Although not all sectarian groups advocate pacifism, such groups by definition perceive themselves in an adversarial relationship with the values and practices of the larger social world. Sectarians tend to withdraw or insulate themselves from the world, or they may seek to convert it to their own convictions. The bond between sectarianism and pacifism is a natural marriage because both impulses embody a minority consciousness, a protest stance toward the larger social system.

In addition to swimming against mainstream currents, sectarian groups minimize bureaucratic institutions and prescribe rigid expectations for the personal conduct of their members. Prior to World War II, Mennonites exemplified what Yinger (1970:266-273) calls an "established sect." Unlike short-lived sects, established ones find ways to perpetuate their beliefs over several generations. Established sects institutionalize their sectarian stance in powerful ways that persist despite economic and political prosperity. Their protest against the dominant culture holds over several generations as they remain more exclusive and less bureaucratized than accommodating religious groups.

But even established sects sometimes break out of their social cocoons. Although Mennonites had begun shedding some of their sectarian trappings in the first half of the twentieth century, in many regions of North America the shedding gained momentum after mid-century.

As we traced the legacy of nonresistance, we have discovered strands of peacemaking woven deeply into the Mennonite character. But what happens to the peaceful ways of sectarians when they swim into the cultural mainstream as Mennonites surely have done in the last half of the twentieth century? Do pacifist convictions weaken as sectarian groups walk up the denominational ladder and enter center stage in the larger society? As they find their social stride in the world and assume new civic responsibilities will Mennonite sectarians begin paying the price of citizenship? Will the duties of citizenship gradually dissolve peace convictions or transform them in new ways?

The erosion of pacifism is quite common when small religious groups trade off their minority status for social respectability and higher social status. Brock (1972 and 1991a) has carefully traced the evaporation of pacifist beliefs among European Mennonites. Dutch Mennonites abandoned nonresistance by the end of the eighteenth century. Although they delayed the demise of nonresistance longer than their Dutch cousins, German Mennonites began paying the price of citizenship in the nineteenth century.

In Switzerland, historic homeland of Anabaptism, as well as in France, nonresistance waned among the Mennonites who did not migrate to North America. In Brock's (1991a:152) words the culprits were, "economic factors . . . commercialization of their communities and increasing urbanization, as well as religious influences like that of evangelicalism. . . ." These same processes also worked to decay the pacifist resolve of Mennonites in Russia in the nineteenth century. Nonresistant convictions have been partially resuscitated in the twentieth century in some of the European Mennonite communities.

Perhaps even more ominous is the experience of a similar group in North America. The Church of the Brethren shared similar nonresistant convictions with Mennonites in the nineteenth century. But in the twentieth century the Brethren acculturated more rapidly and discovered that only 10 percent of their young men opted for conscientious objection in World War II.[38] A recent survey suggests that only a third of Brethren today would select alternative service if faced with a military draft (Bowman, 1987:9).

The historical evidence is clear: peace convictions are fragile. Stubbornly held by one generation, even to the point of death, they can quickly shatter with the winds of nationalism and social success in the next.

Having sketched the legacy of nonresistance among the Mennonites of North America we now explore their encounter with modernity in the twentieth century. As they wrestled with the powerful forces of modernization would they preserve their nonresistant ways or allow them to erode? Would Mennonites agree to pay the price of citizenship? Or might they discover other options—new ways of restructuring and transforming the legacy of nonresistance in the face of modernity? These questions propel our exploration of Mennonite peacemaking.

Ecumenical conversations with theologians from other religious traditions had a significant impact on the restructuring of historic nonresistance. Some Mennonite leaders attended the Christian Peace Conferences in Prague. This one held in 1964 included delegates and observers from more than 60 countries. Sitting at tables participants listened to presentations which were translated simultaneously.

CHAPTER TWO

Modern Challenges and Transformations

Mennonites for the most part were insulated from the winds of modernity blowing across North America in the late nineteenth and early twentieth centuries. To be sure, as Schlabach (1977) has shown, they felt some breezes of modernity already in the late 1800s, but their sectarian enclaves would not be dramatically uprooted until after World War II.[1] This chapter explores the Mennonite encounter with modernity and sketches a conceptual scheme for interpreting the transformation of Mennonite peacemaking in the twentieth century. First, however, a word on modernization.

The Winds of Modernity

Modernization, modernity, and modern are slippery concepts. Their conceptual beauty lies in their ability to integrate diverse elements of social life into a single interpretative framework. But their glory becomes their gloom when their conceptual elasticity stretches over virtually everything, evaporating their explanatory power. Modernization refers to massive changes, prodded by technology, that transform the social arrangements and collective consciousness of an entire society over time. The social conditions produced by modernization are commonly called modernity.

Technology stokes the fires of modernity. For Berger et al.

(1973:9) modernity consists of new social patterns which are produced by "technologically induced economic growth." In Levy's
(1986:3) paradigm, modernization is simply the ratio of inanimate to
animate sources of power. The development of machine power, technological production, the factory system, and a market economy have
all, in their own way, propelled the process of modernization.

Modernization, in short, consists of the application of technology
to virtually all dimensions of life—from birth control to embalmment,
from robotic production to genetic engineering. Societies of course
vary in the extent to which they have undergone these transformations, because modernization is always a matter of degree—a society is
never completely modern or nonmodern. Some aspects of nonmodern or traditional ways permeate even the most advanced societies.[2]

The process of modernization transforms two levels of social
reality—*structure* and *consciousness* (Berger et. al., 1973). Modernization revamps the social architecture, the structure of society, and it
also penetrates human consciousness and alters our ways of thinking.
The application of technology to all dimensions of life modifies structural patterns and social institutions. Factories and suburbs appear,
families shrink in size, and mobility fosters transitory social ties.
Changes in consciousness also emerge as humans develop new ways
of viewing and perceiving the world. Before charting the Mennonite
encounter with modernity we turn to several of its dimensions that
have particular relevance for Mennonite peacemaking.

Dimensions of Modernity

What are the social features that crease the face of modernity? The
indicators of modernity are nearly as many as its analysts. We focus on
three facets of modernity—*differentiation, rationalization,* and *individualization.* Widely agreed upon by social theorists as central to the modernizing process, these aspects of modernity are especially pertinent
to our investigation of Mennonite peacemaking. These dimensions do
not exhaust, by any means, the scope of modernity. But they do im-
pinge in special ways on the transformation of nonresistance in Mennonite life. Like other traits of modernity they are etched into both
structure and *consciousness*—into the architecture of social arrangements as well as the patterns of human thinking.

Modern life is highly *differentiated.* Whereas traditional societies co-
here around commonalities, modern societies are characterized by
differences. Common occupations and similar beliefs provide a social
adhesive for nonmodern communities. Basic social functions—birth,

play, education, work, worship, and death—revolve around the home in traditional, preindustrial societies. In the modern world these functions are scattered across specialized structures—birthing centers, fitness spas, daycare centers, grooming salons, church buildings, offices, and factories. Occupational specialization, urbanization, and mobility induce differences and discontinuities which in turn engender temporary social bonds, shaped primarily by economic and contractual concerns. The sweeping specialization in modern life produces a pervasive diversity—a plurality of distinctive groups and structures.

Beyond the proliferation of specialized structures, individuals frequently encounter diverse beliefs and clashing worldviews which are purveyed by mass media, public education, mobility, and global communication. Indeed teaching students to respect and celebrate diversity has become a major agenda of higher education in North America in the late twentieth century. The smorgasbord of diverse values scattered across the modern table erodes the certitude of traditional ways and nourishes relativity, ambiguity, and tolerance.

Rationalization also accompanies modernity. The social theorist Max Weber (1947) has argued that rationalization is *the* trait that sets modern societies apart from traditional ones. Weber did not have in mind everyday excuses for inappropriate behavior but rather the application of a calculating, rational mindset to human endeavors. Bureaucracies with their specialized roles and formal procedures are the structural embodiment of rationalization. The proliferation of formal organizations and the spread of government agencies, as well as the encroachment of regulatory controls at all levels of government, belie our endless attempts to create a "rational" social order.

In the realm of consciousness, rationalization separates ends from means and encourages calculation in both personal and corporate life. Attempts to control, plan, strategize, predict, and forecast fill the modern consciousness. On the personal level rationalization takes the form of birth control, time management, and career planning. Educators herald critical thinking and scientific experimentation, whereas in the business world, strategic planning and long-term forecasting reflect our ubiquitous attempts to control.

The unwavering embrace of science and education in modern culture signals the depth of our commitment to rationalization. By whatever ways and through all possible means, moderns seek to take charge of things and control their environments, tossing aside any residual traces of fatalism. The neglect of planning is, of course, the unthinkable, unpardonable sin of modernity.

Individualization is often cherished as the triumph of modern culture. Modernization unhooks individuals from the confining grip of custom and kin, and champions free-spirited individualism. In nonmodern societies individual behavior—regulated by religion, tribe, and village—must yield to collective goals. Personal identity is ascribed at birth by membership in clan, gender, and class, not by individual achievement. Specialization, mobility, and technology in the modern world unravel the structural ties that knot the individual into long term relationships with permanent groups.[3]

In tandem with this shift, modern ideology trumpets individual rights, privileges, and freedoms. It celebrates the individual as the supreme social reality and accents creativity and the "voice" of the individual in the arts. To doubt the unfettered rights of the individual, is, like the neglect of planning, a cardinal sin in the modern world. Assertiveness training, the ubiquitous résumé, a preoccupation with self-esteem, and the endless search for personal fulfillment underscore the supreme reign of individualism in modern life. In Gergen's (1991) words, the self has become saturated.

The blended impact of differentiation, rationalization, and individualization fills the modern air with options, alternatives, preferences, and decisions. Indeed, choice is branded into the very fabric of modernity, for the transition from traditional to modern ways is ultimately a shift from fate to choice, from destiny to decision (Berger, 1979). Individual choice, with its attendant burden of both anxiety and guilt which arise from endless decision making, is both the bliss and curse of modernity.

Structures, Brokers, and Agents

Before exploring the impact of modernization on Mennonite peacemaking, we take a brief excursion to consider the tie between ideas and their social context. Human beliefs do not mysteriously fall from the sky, nor can they be sustained in a social vacuum. Ideas and social structures are interlaced together in dynamic and reciprocal relationships. Ideas motivate humans to shape social structures which, in turn, remold the views of their human creators. The institutions which we create act back upon us—changing our behavior and revising our perspectives. The circular way in which consciousness and context feed each other means that modernization typically proceeds simultaneously at both levels.

Beliefs, however, are precarious. They are only plausible in certain social settings. Their continued credibility and believability requires a friendly social context. The ordination of women is scandalous in a patriarchal society. Slavery is of course abhorrent in modern societies that herald individual rights. The Mennonite belief in nonresistance is more believable and more likely to be sustained in some social settings than in others.

The social circumstances that lend credibility to a particular belief are what Peter Berger calls a *plausibility structure.*[4] Plausibility structures consist of the conversations, the networks of interaction, and the other social factors in a particular setting that render a belief believable. In other words, beliefs will likely wither over time unless they are rooted in the congenial soil of a supportive plausibility structure. To say it another way, it is hard to believe something when everyone else disagrees all of the time and when all the surrounding social factors militate against the belief.

Plausibility structures—social scaffolds that prop up ideas—can vary in density and scope. Thick plausibility structures exist when virtually everyone in a particular setting thinks and acts within the confines of institutional arrangements that eliminate competing ideas. A Hutterite colony, geographically segregated from the larger society, illustrates a fairly thick plausibility structure. Thin structures, with porous openings, permit competing views to circulate and challenge traditional ways.

Plausibility structures range in scope from interpersonal ties to total societies. The ongoing conversations of a marriage, for instance, provide a context that endows certain ideas with certitude for a particular married couple. On a larger scale, the political arrangements and civil codes in North American societies give the notion of individual freedom credibility in this particular social context.

There are of course multiple and overlapping plausibility structures that compete with each other in modern settings. Modernity pluralizes values and beliefs as well as their supporting plausibility structures. All things considered, the plausibility structures of modern life are more likely to be thin, porous, portable, and numerous than those in traditional societies. Consequently, beliefs in the modern world, often drained of certainty and stability, are absorbed with ambiguity and relativity.

Our study of peacemaking explores the fit between historic nonresistance and modern plausibility structures. What sort of social soil lends credibility to historic nonresistance? Under what social conditions will peace commitments thrive or whither? Our evidence suggests that nonresistance has experienced a dramatic reconstruction in the twentieth century as Mennonites have coped with the vicissitudes of modernity.

Beliefs are modified, of course, in the face of changing social conditions. This happens on the personal level as individuals digest novel information and collate new experiences. But what happens in a religious community when the credibility of a cherished belief threatens to evaporate? Esteemed leaders often play the role of *ideological brokers*. These brokers try to reconcile the legacy of historic beliefs with changing conditions.

Within the church, the brokers—typically theologians, scholars, and elders—must negotiate between traditional convictions and new social realities. Indeed, theologians make old Scriptures say new and meaningful things in the face of different circumstances. The brokers, in essence, tinker with the ties between beliefs and plausibility structures. They reshape doctrines to make them chime with credibility in the context of new conditions.

The ideological brokers often follow *change agents* who have already blazed new trails. In the transformation of nonresistance, Mennonite agents of change—persons and sometimes organizations— took the lead in stepping across traditional boundaries. Professors in the classroom, change-minded leaders, and activists on the street were redefining the meaning of nonresistance in practice. Responding to new conditions, seeking to be faithful to the Jesus of the New Testament, and hoping to restore the Anabaptist vision, the change agents embodied new expressions of nonresistance, with a more activist tone. With traditional nonresistance crumbling, much ideological work awaited the theologians who would need to reconstruct a new theology of Mennonite peacemaking.

The ideological brokers, following the forays of the activists, sought to reconstruct nonresistance in ways that would lend it credibility as Mennonites traveled through the throes of modernity. To discard it outright would have been to erase, as we have seen, the distinguishing mark of Mennonite identity.

Nevertheless, the historic formulations of passive nonresistance faced ridicule and sure demise in the crucible of modernity. Old Order Mennonite and Amish groups which insulated themselves from some of the more powerful influences of modernity were able to retain historic understandings of nonresistance with relative ease. However, the nonresistance of those Mennonites who were drifting into mainstream waters faced turbulent rapids.

For Berger (1967) the religious meanings that humans impose on social reality constitute a sacred canopy. As social conditions change the canopy must either shrink or expand to incorporate the new realities into the sacred order. The Mennonite sacred canopy had to be stretched—indeed reconstructed—to face the challenges of modernization in the twentieth century.[5]

The Mennonite brokers struggled with a formidable task—how to reconstruct pacifist beliefs in ways that paid deference to Anabaptist tradition and yet rang credible in modern Mennonite ears. A successful transformation would require the construction of an ideological bridge across the gulf between historical nonresistance and the new social conditions. The reconstruction occurred over several decades as Mennonite leaders sought to retrofit historic nonresistance in a plausible fashion for the new social circumstances they faced in the twentieth century.

Although the incipient stages of the transformation of nonresistance began prior to the turn of the century, the pivotal shift occurred after World War II. The rate of change varied among and within Mennonite denominations and proceeded at various paces in different regions of the country. The reconstruction impacted Mennonites with Swiss-South German roots most dramatically because their tradition carried the more classic formulations of nonresistance. Indeed the most strident resistance to revision came from conservative sectors within this tradition.

The transformation did not follow a neat, linear trail. Certain subgroups within the Mennonite family—pockets of conservatives, the Fellowship of Concerned Mennonites, and periodicals such as *The Sword and Trumpet* and *Guidelines for Today*—clenched older notions of nonresistance and resisted revision. The negotiated reconstruction was a dynamic process, played out with multiple actors in a matrix of ever-changing social conditions, with the final outcome always uncertain.

Dimensions of Restructuring

The restructuring of nonresistance filtered across *five* dimensions of Mennonite life: contextual, organizational, psychological, theological, and political (as outlined in Table 2.1). Although we treat the five dimensions in this particular order, they do not represent a causal sequence. It would be conceptually clean to argue that the forces of modernity have induced theological shifts which in turn have increased political participation among Mennonites. But such simplistic scenarios, however tempting, are rarely true reflections of the dialectical nature of social reality.

Indeed particular theological commitments may initially prompt a group to open its windows to the winds of modernity. But once open, the social breezes, in time, may restructure the very theological impulses that opened the windows in the first place. The dialectical interaction between ideas and social factors makes it difficult if not impossible to tease out the causal sequence of relationships. The five dimensions we explore are mere conceptual categories that in reality are interlaced together in dynamic and reciprocal patterns of causation.

In any event, many North American Mennonites in the twentieth century have moved across the spectrum from passive nonresistance to assertive peacemaking. The transformation has entailed fundamental shifts across the five dimensions to which we now turn.

Contextual Change

Social changes in the structure of American society impacted in significant ways on Mennonite groups that were receptive to overtures from the larger society. The modernization afoot in North America in the twentieth century brought a rise in urbanization, occupational specialization, educational achievement, geographical mobility, and global awareness. Although Mennonites resisted and delayed some of these changes for several decades, they eventually succumbed to many of them along with their neighbors.[6]

Turn of the century Mennonites were remarkably rural. As late as 1936 some 85 percent of the Mennonites in the U.S. were living in rural areas.[7] The bulk of them were farmers, often noted for their agricultural acumen. Despite the formation of several Mennonite colleges around the turn of the century, few rank-and-file members received higher education; many had only completed eighth grade. Mennonites for the most part lived on farms or in small, rural communities. Although they used rail transportation and eventually drove automobiles, Mennonites were usually anchored in stable social networks in the first half of the twentieth century.

The social cocoon that buffered them from the winds of modernity began to unravel rapidly in the forties and fifties. Some 40 percent of draft-eligible Mennonite men entered military service in World War II. Many of them returned to Mennonite congregations with new ideas. The involvement of many Mennonites in Civilian Public Service camps during World War II, in European relief work after the war, and in city hospitals where they performed Alternative Service in the fifties and sixties exposed them to new lifestyles and occupational opportunities which altered the character of Mennonite communities in a multitude of ways.

TABLE 2.1
The Impact of Modernization on Nonresistance
by Five Dimensions

Passive Nonresistance		*Activist Peacemaking*
I. CONTEXTUAL		
Rural	RESIDENCE	Urban
Similar	OCCUPATION	Diverse
Low	EDUCATION	High
Low	MOBILITY	High
Stable	SOCIAL TIES	Transitory
II. ORGANIZATIONAL		
Sectarian	STANCE	Denominational
Nonconformist	OUTSIDE WORLD	Integrationist
Strict	DISCIPLINE	Tolerant
Informal	MODE	Bureaucratic
III. PSYCHOLOGICAL		
Self-denial	SELF-UNDERSTANDING	Self-esteem
Meek	SELF-PRESENTATION	Assertive
Patience	VIRTUES	Control
Local	CONSCIOUSNESS	Global
IV. THEOLOGICAL		
Two kingdoms	MORAL REALMS	Ambiguous
Nonresistance	ETHICAL NORM	Love/justice
Communal	MORAL RESPONSIBILITY	Civic
Separatist	POSTURE	Cooperative
V. POLITICAL		
Subject	STANCE	Citizen
Reactive	GOVERNMENT INVOLVEMENT	Proactive
Forbidden	MILITARY SERVICE	Debated
Taboo	USE OF FORCE	Selective
Discouraged	POLITICAL ACTION	Acceptable

These experiences and others spurred an exodus from the farm, so that by 1972 only 11 percent of Canadian and American Mennonites were farming. Mennonites left their rural enclaves for suburban and urban life and entered a wide array of occupations. They typically bypassed blue collar work, moving directly from plow to profession. Vacating the farm and entering new professions required higher education which some 33 percent had obtained by 1972.[8]

Modern means of travel as well as the pursuit of higher education and professional jobs ruptured the bonds of stability in traditional Mennonite communities and splintered the plausibility structures that in earlier years had provided a supportive roost for nonresistance. The modernizing experience not only pulled Mennonites in from the fringes of society; it also propelled them upward in social status. No longer a persecuted minority, many Mennonites in the twentieth century were enjoying upward social mobility.

These demographic transitions thrust Mennonites into new roles and unfamiliar settings which placed historic nonresistance in jeopardy. Could Mennonites live in the modern world without filing lawsuits, joining labor unions, and flexing their political muscles? These and many other questions greeted them in new and pressing ways as they entered the market place of modernity. The exodus from the relative isolation of rural settings also raised new questions about political responsibility. Passive nonresistance might fit the social serenity of rural climes but would it survive the cutthroat politics of an urban world? And who should worry about the moral dirt that Mennonites found in the larger society?

Organizational Transitions

The changes awash in the larger society also brought internal changes to Mennonite groups and added new pressures for revising nonresistance. Throughout the twentieth century the Mennonite and Brethren in Christ bodies in our study underwent a gradual metamorphosis. They shed their sectarian character and began exhibiting more denominational traits—the rise of bureaucratic institutions, greater integration with the surrounding culture, and increased tolerance for the behavior of individual members.[9] The lifestyles of individual members became more heterogeneous and social relationships within congregations became more transitory with increasing mobility. In short, the tight plausibility structures of the past that provided a refuge for nonresistance were not only unraveling, they were also competing with new structures as Mennonites participated more actively in the larger world.

The sectarian stance of Mennonite groups—expressed in a cautious social distance from the outside world—has typically been called nonconformity. This doctrine, based on Paul's teachings in Romans 12:2, "be not conformed to this world," was a biblical legitimation of social separation from the dominant culture. Although the doctrine of nonconformity is found in the confessional statements of all the Mennonite bodies, it was promoted most vigorously among those with Swiss-South German cultural roots.[10]

Within the MC and BIC churches nonconformity meant not only separation from social activities—dancing, movies, fairs, television—it also prescribed forms of dress that drew sharp boundaries between the faithful remnant and the larger culture. A strong emphasis on dress nonconformity, practiced by some Mennonite groups in the first half of the twentieth century, became a means of protecting themselves from the winds of modernity and galvanizing their identity (Hostetler, 1987:245-271).

The twin "nons"—nonconformity and nonresistance—are found in tandem in many Mennonite writings and publications as the distinguishing tenets of Mennonitedom.[11] In confessions of faith, conference rulings, and other writings, the twins often appear side by side as the dual anchors of Mennonite identity. As Mennonite participation in the larger world increased, the plausibility of nonconformity eroded and the term gradually slipped from usage after 1950.

The rate of slippage of course varied from group to group. Nonresistance retained its credibility among nonconformed groups living in the context of rural enclaves, separated from mainstream culture. But with the demise of nonconformity among progressive Mennonites, nonresistance also began dropping from the Mennonite vocabulary. Some Mennonite elders argued that the two were a package—loss of nonconformity would surely signal the demise of nonresistance.

Such predictions have largely been verified by the historical forces at play within progressive Mennonite groups as well as within the Old Orders. Historic nonresistance has been held most firmly among Old Order Mennonite and Amish groups which remain entrenched in a nonconformity that keeps modernity at bay. The evidence suggests that the transformation of nonresistance was part of a larger organizational evolution—a shift from separatism to greater participation in public life.

The changing character of congregations and regional conferences also had implications for the bonding between individuals and Mennonite groups. Typical of sectarian orders, Mennonite bodies regulated some of the behavior of their members throughout the first half of the twentieth century. Baptismal vows represented a sharp break with the ways of the world and often called for obedience to conference or congregational disciplines that spelled out expected behaviors as well as taboos related to social activities and dress. Baptism signaled a serious commitment to the standards of the religious community. Those who strayed from faithfulness and refused to repent were often excommunicated.

Members were expected to embrace the virtues of nonresistance not only in time of war but in daily living as well. Whether it was joining the military, filing a law suit, entering the police force, or holding public office, those who violated the precepts of nonresistance were liable for excommunication.[12] The likelihood of excommunication, especially for litigation or officeholding, was higher among groups with a more sectarian, Swiss heritage. Excommunication for joining the armed forces continued in many MC congregations well after World War II and continues in some areas even today.

Denominations, shaped by the forces of modernity, emphasize tolerance rather than the strict regulation of individual behavior. Rigid behavioral expectations at baptism and a willingness to expel wayward members make it difficult to enter a sectarian group but relatively easy to get expelled. Denominations, by contrast, with vague baptismal vows and few behavioral guidelines, are fairly easy to join and virtually impossible to be expelled from.

As Mennonite bodies, swayed by the gusts of modernity, exhibited greater denominational features, they were more willing to tolerate a diversity of opinion on nonresistance. They were less likely to excommunicate those who joined labor unions, filed law suits, held major political offices, or even joined the military. Shaped by the fingers of modernity the Mennonite subculture became increasingly tolerant of individual choices, preferences, and options—even with regard to nonresistance.

In short, nonresistance in many congregations gradually faded as a requirement for membership and a cause for excommunication. Nevertheless, its ghost remained. Letters to the editor of the *Gospel Herald* in the summer of 1991 (following the Persian Gulf War) heatedly debated whether or not congregations should make peacemaking convictions a test of church membership.

With the control of individual members withering, the banner of peacemaking began to be carried in other ways. The modernization of Mennonite bodies brought a proliferation of new institutions for mission, education, service, mutual aid, and professional fellowship. As nonresistance dropped from the Mennonite vocabulary a newer, more assertive mode of peacemaking was promoted by many Mennonite institutions. Not only were Mennonite schools, publishing houses, and service agencies flying the flag of peace, new agencies were forming explicitly for peacemaking purposes—Mennonite Central Committee's Peace Section, Mennonite Conciliation Service, Christian Peacemaker Teams, World Peace Tax Fund, and the Victim Offender Reconciliation Program, to name a few.

Reflecting modern values, these agencies hoped to transform the heritage of passive nonresistance into new and relevant applications that stretched far beyond the parochial confines of historic Mennonitedom. The agencies that hoisted the banner of peacemaking in the last half of the twentieth century not only carried a different message, they also presented it in new ways. Without the authority of a bishop or the threat of excommunication, they now had to resort to persuasion, invitation, and the tactics of marketing and advertising.

Psychological Shifts

The transformation of nonresistance was part of a larger restructuring of Mennonite personality that accompanied the breakdown of group controls eroded by the process of modernization. Early Anabaptists often spoke of *gelassenheit*—a yieldedness and surrender to God's will in the face of persecution and martyrdom.[13] Michael Sattler writing in the 1520s said, "Christians are fully yielded and have placed their trust in their Father in heaven without any outward or worldly arms" (Yoder, 1973:23).

The passionate obedience and yieldedness of the martyrs, recorded in van Braght's (1985) massive *The Bloody Theatre or Martyrs Mirror of the Defenseless Christians* led to severe persecution. Marginalized and pushed to the social fringe by persecution, Swiss-South German Mennonite culture cultivated a modal personality that emphasized a quiet, nonassertive disposition. The meek personality traits, blended with spiritual virtues, emerged into a full-blown doctrine of humility by the mid-nineteenth century. Mennonites were known as *Die Stillen im Lande*, "the quiet in the land" and humility formed the foundation of their religious outlook.[14]

A cluster of theological and personality traits jelled to produce the nonresistant character of Mennonite life. Self-denial, humility, obedience, meekness, lowliness, and forbearance were the esteemed virtues of the Mennonite personality.[15] In face-to-face interaction these virtues

expressed themselves in a reluctance to use force in all social relationships and a rejection of revenge. The meek and lowly Jesus whose
nonresistant posture led to death on the cross was upheld as the model for Christian disciples. Schlabach (1988:99) reports that a bishop
describing the fruits of conversion in 1837 mentions the phrase "meek
and lowly" five times in nine lines of text.

Bishop John M. Brenneman (1873:36), writing a booklet on *Pride
and Humility* reprinted many times, described the Mennonite personality wrapped in humility.

> The humble man feels himself small, poor, bowed, cast down, and unwor-
> thy within himself and esteems others more highly than himself. He nev-
> er boasts or exalts himself or despises others . . . is usually of a quiet,
> meek and gentle disposition, knowing when to be silent and when to
> speak.

These spiritual virtues found natural expression in the Mennonite ret-
icence to exercise force. Nonresistance, wrote Daniel Kauffman
(1898:217), is "a deep underlying Christian principle that transforms
us into meek, peaceable, unassuming followers of the meek and lowly
man of Nazareth."

Kauffman's (1914) *Bible Doctrine*, written under the supervision of
a committee appointed by the Mennonite Church, was widely read by
MCs in the first half of the twentieth century. It devotes separate chapters to "Obedience," "Self-Denial," "Humility," "Nonconformity to the
World," and "Nonresistance." The chapter on self-denial asserts that,
"self-denial is the essence of the Christian religion and life"
(Kauffman, 1914:470).

The discussion of nonresistance presents Christ as "our example."

> "He suffered much, did not strike back, did not retaliate, rendered good
> for evil, and prayed for His enemies. By His patient suffering, His sweet
> disposition, and His self-denial, He set an example for all ages, for all na-
> tions, for all conditions of mankind." The writer explains that "nonresis-
> tance may lead to loss and suffering, yet it will bring a blessing from
> God . . . by practicing self-denial and patiently bearing the cross, the
> crown of life is promised as a sure reward" (Kauffman, 1914:535, 537).

The nonresistant personality of nineteenth-century Mennonites
collided with the rising tide of individualism, the charm of modernity.[16] To relinquish rights, to turn the other cheek, and to suffer in-
sult were unthinkable to modern minds. Nonresistance, to be blunt,
was a rather unmodern notion. Modern culture championed individu-

al achievement, personal fulfillment, self-esteem, and individual rights above virtually all other values. Moderns cringed at the talk of self-denial, meekness, and lowliness. Nonresistance smacked of self-degradation and a poor self-image; it sounded weak and sickly to modern ears. Moderns wanted to take charge of things, control outcomes, assert rights, and prevent injustice—not wilt in the face of threat.

As Mennonites absorbed the values of the modern world, self-denial slipped from their lips. They began to emphasize the unique "gifts" that God had given *each individual*. They opened the door to "healthy self-love" by noting that even the classic biblical text implied approval of self-love when it said, "Love thy neighbor as thy self." By the 1980s they were taking classes in assertiveness training—learning to assert their selves and express their feelings, to look out for their rights—albeit usually in diplomatic and "Christian" ways. Mennonites had surely not become the loud and boisterous in the city, but they were no longer the quiet in the land.

The meek and lowly personalities that nurtured nonresistant ways were gradually laid aside for modern understandings and assertive presentations of the self. Mennonite activists who engaged in nonviolent direct action called for voluntary personal suffering for the cause of social justice. Such non-conformist activists engaged in nonviolent protests that risked arrest and imprisonment. They transformed passive nonresistance into active resistance and quiet self-denial into voluntary suffering. This was a rather different expression of the self than that displayed by other Mennonites, who were asserting their claim to individual rights and self-expression in professional life.

The forces of modernity also stretched Mennonite consciousness. Although Mennonite migrations had cultivated some international awareness, nineteenth-century Mennonites sheltered in rural enclaves were, like most of their neighbors, rather local and parochial in outlook. Unlike their Old Order cousins, the more progressive Mennonite groups developed aggressive international mission and service programs in the twentieth century. They also, somewhat reluctantly but gradually, accepted modern mass media.

These developments created a greater sense of global consciousness regarding peace and justice issues. Mennonite schools and educational programs emphasized that God's kingdom transcended national boundaries. The growing global awareness in Mennonite consciousness raised a host of new issues about the plausibility of nonresistance in the face of international violence, oppression, and injustice.

A Theological Conversion

The reconstruction of historic nonresistance trailed a fundamental theological reorientation in Mennonite thinking. A two-kingdom theology that pitted the kingdom of God against the kingdoms of this world was foundational to Mennonite theology from its earliest expressions. The Schleitheim statement of Brotherly Union stated the ethical dualism in stark terms as early as 1527 by declaring that

> all those who have fellowship with the dead works of darkness have no part in the light. Thus all who follow the devil and the world, have no part with those who have been called out of the world unto God. . . . We have no fellowship with them [the wicked] and do not run with them in the confusion of their abominations. . . .

A section on separation from evil and wickedness rejects, "the diabolical weapons of violence—such as sword, armor and the like and all of their use to protect friends or against enemies—by virtue of the word of Christ: 'you shall not resist evil.' " Christians were "citizens of heaven," and "members of the household of God" (Yoder, 1973:23, 37-38). In a pastoral letter to a congregation in 1555 Menno Simons (1956:1045) reminded them that they "are the Lord's people, separated from the world, and hated unto death."

The clear-cut distinction between kingdoms was symbolized by adult baptism. Turning their back on worldly ways of violence, new members learned that nonresistance was the proper mode for dealing with each other as well as with external enemies. The use of the sword belonged to the worldly realm of wickedness. The moral and social chasm between church and world was widened by severe persecution in the early years of Anabaptism and reinforced by the social segregation of Mennonite communities as they took root in North America.

The doctrine of nonconformity—asserted vigorously in the late nineteenth and early twentieth centuries to thwart the pressures of modernity—provided a theological legitimation for the sharp church/world dualism. Although the two-kingdom dualism was articulated by all Mennonite and Brethren in Christ groups, it was, once again, more firmly held by those in the Swiss-South German tradition.

With their citizenship clearly fixed in heaven, Mennonites did not share the modern urge to usher the kingdom of God into the structures of society. It was, after all, God's kingdom, and they were satis-

Many Mennonites left their homes to serve in Civilian Public Service during WW II. This experience exposed them to new ideas and encouraged the transformation of historic nonresistance. Members of this CPS camp, in Colorado Springs, Colo., worked for the U.S. Soil Conservation Service.

fied to defer to God's designs. They hoped that their congregations gave visible expression to traces of the kingdom but they were content to patiently await its heavenly consummation. Although they were willing to do good and share a cup of cold water with those in need, Mennonites had little interest in taking charge of the world and trying to make it righteous.

As Mennonites moved into the mainstream of modern life in greater numbers in the mid-twentieth century their traditional theological categories began to collapse. The boundaries between church and world grew ambiguous as they entered professions and shouldered civic responsibilities. The nonresistance which rang with credibility in segregated rural communities sounded hollow in the midst of urban violence and oppression.

Could nonresistant Christians politely stand by as governments, evil social structures, and oppressive majorities trampled the disenfranchised and powerless? Were there really dual ethical standards— one for church and another for government? Did civil government truly have the moral license to do whatever it wished? Was it conscionable to merely stand by and pray as Hitler devastated nations and exterminated peoples?

The lines of moral responsibility also blurred as Mennonites moved into public life. Some began talking of the "lordship of Christ over all creation," and calling upon governments to exercise justice and equality whenever possible. Pleas for active love and calls for justice began to muffle the traditional appeals for nonresistance. Moral responsibility was shifting. The Mennonite entry into professional and public life, exposure to higher education, the civil rights movement, the Vietnam War, and many other public events broadened the scope of Mennonite moral responsibility.

The church and ethnic community were fading as the primary realm of moral responsibility. Mennonites were beginning to worry about the moral dirt in the larger civic order and to raise questions about social justice and the common good. As they began to grapple with these issues, often in conversation with other Christians who had worried about them over the centuries, the plausibility of passive nonresistance began to crumble. As the theological brokers searched for ways to relate the old Scriptures to the new questions with integrity and credibility, new words—love, shalom, justice, responsibility, peacemaking—found their way into the Mennonite vocabulary. Vintage nonresistance was undergoing a theological conversion which in time would have sweeping implications for Mennonite attitudes and participation in the political realm.

Political Transformations

The Mennonite stance toward the state shifted remarkably in the twentieth century in the process of modernization. Although they had stubbornly refused to take up arms on behalf of the government, the meek stance of nonresistance led to differential attitudes toward earthly rulers. Mennonites viewed themselves, in essence, as *subjects* in an earthly kingdom. The process of modernization turned them into *citizens* and sometimes strident ones. Mennonite writings and petitions to government in the eighteenth, nineteenth, and even early twentieth century portray grateful subjects humbly pleading for a privilege—not citizens demanding their rights from elected officials.

Bishop Peter Burkholder (1837:295-307) wrote that Mennonites, "are ready and willing, as loyal subjects, to submit to obey government in all things lawful, that do not oppose the doctrine of Christ and the dictates of consciences and are willing, duteously to pay tribute according to the doctrine of Christ." Ever mindful of the legacy of persecution, Burkholder in typical nineteenth-century fashion, invoked the traditional litany that Mennonites may, "lead a quiet, peaceful, and godly life."

A petition to President Lincoln which anguished over Mennonite involvement in the civil war also echoed the sentiments of subjects.

> We would humbly pray the president not to consider us too burdensome by presenting to him this, our weak and humble petition, thereby humbly praying and beseeching him to take into consideration our sore distress . . . be favorably inclined to us poor creatures of the dust. . . . We are now your humble servants. . . .[17]

By 1914 MC Bishop Jacob Brubacher was using the word citizen, but in a rather docile fashion. "If we are to 'resist not evil,' much less should we resist the powers that be. But meek submission to magistrates does not mean insubordination to the higher powers of heaven. . . . 'we ought to obey God rather than man,' " Brubacher asserted. But nevertheless, he concluded, "The Christian is the most submissive citizen on earth" (Kauffman, 1914:548). For turn-of-the-century Mennonites to instruct, advise, or criticize government officials would have felt downright arrogant—unbecoming to the disciples of the meek and lowly Jesus. Furthermore, the ephemeral kingdoms of government, rising and falling with human predilections, paled in comparison to the disciples' true citizenship in the heavenly kingdom.

The submissive stance toward government was most pronounced in the Swiss-South German tradition. Issuing a statement on war and conscription in 1915, the Mennonite Church instructed members to pray for their rulers and "have a meek, quiet, and submissive attitude toward our government. . . . Brethren drafted for military service should state their position on nonresistance meekly but unhesitantly" (Peachey, 1980:166).

Two years later in the midst of World War I, citing suffering and martyrdom in the past, MCs called again for passive submission.

> Even laws which seem unwise and unjust should be submitted to uncomplainingly and no thought should be entertained of doing anything but comply with all that they ask of us—unless they prescribe conditions contrary to the Gospel; in which case we should meekly but faithfully stand

true to the principles of the Gospel, even if the consequences entail suffering (Peachey, 1980:81).

The MB confession of faith in 1917 also rejected the idea of resisting government, "Whosoever, therefore, resisteth the power, resisteth the ordinance of God, and they that resist shall receive to themselves damnation" (Peachey, 1980:3).

The meek and submissive stance continued in MC statements into the 1950s. A major statement on nonresistance in 1951 concludes "we shall endeavor to continue to live a quiet and peaceable life in all godliness and honesty . . . and manifest a meek and submissive spirit, being obedient to the laws and regulations of the government in all things" (Peachey, 1980:173).

Meek subjection to civil authorities was the stance of classic nonresistance that flowed from the martyr tradition. But as Schlabach (1988:102) notes, irony threaded its way through the docile nonresistant posture. The Mennonite theology of humility "cultivated a deferential and self-effacing kind of personality. . . . Yet the humility doctrine also bolstered a stubborn, steely will to resist if government or society demanded anything contrary to Mennonite belief."

In the course of the twentieth century the quiet in the land found a new voice. They began speaking up as citizens and challenging government policies at home and abroad which they deemed unjust. Instead of reacting to government policies as docile subjects, Mennonites became animated in the political realm. They monitored policy and engaged in lobbying efforts when pending legislation violated their religious convictions.

Mennonite business, farm, and professional persons also began to participate in the lobby efforts of their professional organizations. Some, as we shall see, were elected to political office, and other forms of political participation were on the upswing as well. Litigation became commonplace and even military service, still frowned upon by religious leaders, was no longer cause for excommunication in many congregations. Clearly the nonresistant subjects of a former era were shedding their cloaks of meekness to shoulder the responsibilities of citizenship.

Summary

In this chapter we have provided a sweeping overview of the Mennonite encounter with modernity as it affected the belief and practice of nonresistance. Although nonresistance was fading, its legacy was not lost. Mennonites remained committed to peaceful ways. Nonresistance, however, was being radically transformed by the forces of modernity—differentiation, rationalization, and individuation—into active peacemaking and civic accommodation. The restructuring spread, as we have seen, across contextual, organizational, psychological, theological, and political dimensions (as outlined in Table 2.1). The transition emerged in several phases which we will explore in subsequent chapters.

Responding to new conditions and seeking to be faithful to their Christian calling a variety of Mennonite change agents led the transformation toward a more activistic mode of peacemaking. Following in the trail of the change agents, the theological brokers would find a way to turn the nonresistant tradition on its conceptual head to sanction even civil disobedience and nonviolent resistance. They would need to construct a theological rationale that would make it credible for the meek and mild to actively resist oppression and social injustice. The theological brokers would need to negotiate a credible theological formulation that tapped the legacy of nonresistance in believable ways in the modern context. The following chapters trace the emergence of change agents and the evolution of the ideological bargaining that eventually transformed nonresistance into activist peacemaking.

The Second World War was a major turning point that increased Mennonite involvements in Europe. The Mennonite Central Committee (MCC) opened a relief ministry in London. John Coffman, pictured here (2nd from L.), was one of the MCC workers in London.

CHAPTER THREE

Benchmarks and Turning Points

Chapter two traced the transformation of nonresistance *across* five dimensions of Mennonite life. We turn now to benchmarks in the evolution of Mennonite peacemaking in the twentieth century.[1] Which turning points made a difference as Mennonite peace convictions unfolded over the years? This chapter highlights pivotal moments in six decades (1890-1950). Subsequent chapters explore, in greater detail, the ferment of the 1950s and the strident spirit of the 1960s and 1970s.

The Metamorphosis of Mennonite Peacemaking

A careful reconstruction of the episodes and actors that transformed Mennonite peacemaking in the twentieth century lies beyond the scope of our study. We will simply highlight some benchmarks in the metamorphosis of Mennonite peacemaking that merit special attention. Although our discussion roughly follows a chronological sequence, the restructuring did not unfold in a simple linear fashion. The variegated nature of the Mennonite mosaic and the complexity of social change precludes the imposition of a neat linear transformation.

Our analysis pays special attention to linguistic changes, as reflected in key texts, that symbolize significant shifts in Mennonite consciousness throughout the twentieth century. Although our primary focus is on the internal transformation of Mennonite peacemaking, Mennonite developments have *always* had an ecumenical setting. Mennonites have been somewhat wary of formal ecumenical ties, but nonetheless they have been directly touched by developments in other religious traditions.

An Overview of a Century

Before exploring specific benchmarks in the saga of Mennonite peacemaking in the first half of the twentieth century, we pause for a panoramic view of the century. This overview flags the dominant themes that emerged in documents, statements, books, and pamphlets that were rolling off the Mennonite press between 1890 and 1990.

A scrutiny of the Mennonite statements dealing with war and peace in the twentieth century reveals eight themes that dominated particular historical moments. The various themes often represented the work of Mennonite brokers who were struggling with the forces of modernization both within the church and without. The eight themes identified in Table 3.1 reflect the shifting consciousness of Mennonite thinking in the metamorphosis from passive nonresistance to active peacemaking.[2]

Table 3.1
Dominant Themes in Mennonite Peacemaking, 1890-1990

Dominant Themes	Time Period
The Doctrine of Nonresistance	1890-1920
The Principles of Peace	1920-1940
Biblical Nonresistance	1940-1950
The Way of Love	1950-1960
Witness to the State	1960-1968
Nonviolent Resistance	1968-1976
Peace and Justice	1976-1983
Peacemaking	1983-1990

The restructuring of nonresistance proceeded at different paces among and within the various Mennonite groups. Some clusters of Mennonites resisted the change and the Old Order Amish and Mennonite groups were largely untouched by it. The eight themes, culminating in the peacemaking focus of the eighties, are elastic markers that flag the broad swells that rose and fell with the tides of history. The "principles of peace," a popular phrase between the world wars, reflected the optimism of the times. The "way of love" which emerged in the fifties marked an outward shift in Mennonite life and addressed growing concerns for racial injustice. Nonviolent resistance peaked with the civil rights movement and the war in Vietnam. Prodded by wars and other waves of history, key themes floated to the surface of Mennonite consciousness and dominated peace thinking for a time.

As various themes emerged, they marked the growing plurality of Mennonite peacemaking—representing new tributaries in the Mennonite experience. Once started, these tributaries often flowed alongside existing streams of thought. For instance, although the term "biblical nonresistance" rose in the forties and dwindled in the sixties, it continues to thrive today among conservative sectors of the Mennonite Church.

The "way of love," fashioned in the fifties, became an enduring phrase in subsequent decades. "Witness to the state," ascending in the sixties, remains a motivating force among some Mennonite groups today. As new themes emerged, older ones remained in currency generating a growing pluralism in Mennonite peacemaking.

The thematic labels that attracted attention for a time sometimes reflected the imagination of an intellectual elite more than the sentiments of rank and file Mennonites. Nevertheless, the various themes fed the plurality of tributaries that increasingly characterized the peace witness of the Mennonite family. This panoramic overview provides markers that guide our work as we explore the transformation of nonresistance in the twentieth century. We pick up the story at the turn of the century and briefly note some prominent benchmarks in the six decades spanning 1890 and 1950.

The Doctrine of Nonresistance

Nonresistance before 1890 was dominated by Swiss-South German influences, because Dutch-Russians began to shape the North American Mennonite experience only after 1890. As noted earlier, nineteenth-century Mennonites often spoke of the "nonresistant faith," and the "nonresistant gospel." Nonresistance for them characterized the very nature of the gospel itself. They had, in Schlabach's (1988:140) words, woven a seamless web, "around the principles of humility, non-vengeance, defenselessness, and church discipline . . . those who wove the web had included salvation by God's grace and Jesus' redemptive work, the new birth, and deep inner (not only external) piety."

Nonresistance prior to 1890 remained largely untouched by modernization. It was not highly rational or formalized. Few books and pamphlets were written on the subject.[3] The nonresistant outlook in many ways was simply taken for granted—wrapped into the texture of Mennonite life. Based on age-old interpretations handed across the generations, the nonresistant faith emphasized the personal qualities of meekness and humility, submission to government, avoidance of military service, rejection of force and revenge, and the traditional two kingdom dualism. Although some Mennonites could not articulate their nonresistant faith in elegant terms, it was nonetheless central to their identity. Their reluctance to use force had become a culturally ingrained impulse central to Mennonite understandings of the gospel.

The vibrations of industrialization, shaking North America more rapidly in the late nineteenth century, began to unravel the web of nonresistant faith. Social differentiation, rationalization, and individuation began reshaping the character of nonresistance. The quiet in the land were stirring in what Schlabach has called a "quickening."[4] Mennonites were becoming more active and assertive. Outward-looking leaders began promoting mission work and educational endeavors as well as building church institutions. As their pulse quickened they became more activist, eager to take charge of things beyond the confines of their local church communities. The activity brought increased contact with other Protestants in ways that began to reshape and formalize Mennonite theology and institutions.

Turn of the century theological statements showed streaks of modernity. They were becoming more rational, formal, and organized. Doctrine—a propositional presentation of the truth—became the operative code word, especially in the Mennonite Church. At the forefront of the doctrinal treatises was "the plan of salvation"—a sure sign of modern thinking enamored with planning and calculating.

Nonresistance, meanwhile, slipped from center stage in the new doctrinal constructions. Although the content of classic nonresistance remained intact, it now became merely one of many Mennonite "doctrines" and "principles." Daniel Kauffman's (1898 and 1914) widely read *Bible Doctrine* relegated nonresistance to a section of "Christian Principles," with the pejorative subtitle of "duties and restrictions." Nonresistance was no longer woven implicitly into the seam of Mennonite thought; it was becoming a specialized doctrine. Although the specialization and rationalization of modernity had forged a "doctrine of nonresistance" it nevertheless retained a prominent place in the hearts of Swiss-German Mennonites for several decades.

The Great War

Theological reflection on nonresistance was also shaped by the sudden jolt of the U.S. entry into World War I in 1917. The Great War caught American Mennonites by surprise. Their German heritage and reluctance to enter military service made them convenient targets for ridicule and mistreatment. Juhnke (1989:208-242) reports that wartime pressures, "delivered a major shock to Mennonite identity." Several dozen mob actions were launched in local communities against Mennonite "slackers."

Some church members entered combatant service but most refused to serve. Many were treated harshly in military camps because they refused to enter noncombatant service or even wear military uniforms. Dozens were imprisoned and court-martialed, and several hundred American Mennonites migrated to Canada.

Even passive nonresistance was a threat in wartime. Federal marshals with a search warrant seized 150 copies of a tract titled "Nonresistance" August 6, 1918, from the Mennonite Publishing Company in Scottdale, Pennsylvania. Distribution of the tract was considered a "felony" that caused "insubordination, disloyalty, muting and refusal of duty in the military and naval forces of the U.S . . . and obstructed the recruiting and enlistment service of the U.S. . . ." [5]

Ambiguous government policies, the unpreparedness of Mennonite leaders, and the hysteria of wartime patriotism made the war a wrenching experience in most Mennonite communities. Juhnke (1989:209) concludes that the war left most American Mennonites "with both a stronger sense of being separate and a new appreciation for America as a home for nonconformists."

The encounter with the war prompted U.S Mennonite leaders to formalize their nonresistant convictions by writing statements for their members and sending letters to U.S. presidents.[6] Both activities, as well as the presence of better trained leaders, lent formality to the Mennonite doctrine of nonresistance. In addition to frequent references to the "doctrine of nonresistance," new language was slipping into Mennonite vocabulary. MC statements in 1915, 1917, and 1919 spoke about "our testimony for peace," "our peace position," the "doctrine of peace," and the "principles of peace."

Nonresistance remained central, but the more frequent use of the word peace suggested a more activist, positive turn. To be sure, the MC statements were peppered with the older language of submission, suffering, meekness, and humility. But the frequent use of "our position" in GC and MC statements (seven times in the 1917 MC statement alone) conveyed a stronger sense of self-confidence and a more formally developed doctrine of nonresistance than the earlier nonresistance implicitly woven into the fabric of Mennonite life.

Constructing a "doctrine of nonresistance" and asserting "positions" betrayed traces of modern thinking. But in traditional fashion, the MC statement of 1917 entreated members to show "an attitude of submission and loyalty," and to pray that rulers would allow Mennonites to "lead a quiet and peaceable life." GC Mennonites issued fewer statements in the context of World War I, but their committee dealing with war questions declared that the church could not "speak for the individual conscience of the drafted men."[7] This conclusion was certainly shaped by modern understandings that the freedom of individual choice transcended responsibilities to the faith community and one's heritage.

The most modern language of the era, however, came from the Brethren in Christ. Troubled by the pangs of industrialization, they issued a statement in 1913 that used language forty years ahead of its time. It spoke of "injustice," "unjust wages," "industrial injustice," and advocated a surprisingly nonsectarian notion—"the body of Christ should bear a clear and unequivocal testimony on moral issues of public interest."

Although American Mennonite groups hoped to give a clear testimony to nonresistance by sending statements to the U.S. president, their language shows a remarkable shift in political posture. They surely remained submissive to civil authorities and were willing to suffer the consequences if forced to obey God rather than humans, but they were no longer pleading on their knees with hat in hand. Now in the context of World War I they were using the language of citizens, not subjects. In less humble tones than in former years, MC communications to the president "commended," "reaffirmed their position," "appealed," and "expressed appreciation." The GCs in turn also "commended" the president, "expressed heartfelt approval" and "appreciation," and told the Secretary of War of their "absolute opposition to war."[8]

Mennonites were standing more erect and speaking with greater confidence. They were gradually easing into the role of citizens who could evaluate elected officials and hold them accountable for public policies. Although the Great War left Mennonites with deep sectarian scars, they were nevertheless beginning to think and act in modern ways.

Between the Wars

The decades of the twenties and thirties witnessed a transformation in Mennonite consciousness and an outburst of peace activism—at least among leaders.[9] Shocked by the harsh realities of the war,

Mennonite elders realized that nonresistance could not be taken for granted among their own members or with civil authorities. Mennonite activism was also buoyed by the enthusiasm of a host of religious and secular peace organizations that aggressively promoted peace education in the decades following the war.

But there were other prods as well. The plausibility structures of the rural Mennonite communities were beginning to crumble. Mennonites were driving cars, listening to radios, and beginning to use tractors. And a few were moving to towns and working in factories. Although they remained overwhelmingly rural, they were beginning to feel the vibrations of industrialization that were cracking the walls of separation surrounding their communities. Moreover, more of their youth were attending college, and some were receiving graduate degrees. Not only was the outside world knocking at their door, a new generation of university trained leaders was eager to move beyond the confines of quiet nonresistance.

Emerging Principles of Peace

Although rank-and-file members were reluctant to discard historic nonresistance—especially in the older Swiss conferences in the east—forward-looking leaders wanted action, not meekness. Shaped by the impulses of modernity they wanted to take charge of things, generate goals, and create programs. They literally called for "aggressive peace work" (Miller, 1926a). The debates and controversies swirling through the twenties and thirties pivoted around modern issues and questions. It was, in Paul Toews' (1986:55) words, "the first modern discussion" of the Mennonite peace witness. The larger society and their relation to it was in flux, and Mennonite brokers needed to fashion new ways of thinking about nonresistance to prevent its credibility from draining away entirely.

A series of All-Mennonite Conventions between 1913 and 1930 provided Mennonites with numerous opportunities to rally around "our common doctrine of Peace." In his opening address to the convention in 1922, chairperson S. M. Musselman declared that Jesus "blessed the peacemakers." Did not Jesus "perhaps emphasize the *makers* of Peace?"[10] Making peace projected a modern posture—assertive, confident, activist—an about face from the docility of nonresistance. Orie O. Miller, secretary of a new MC Peace Committee, and later administrator of the Mennonite Central Committee, called for "Aggressive Peace Work" in an article by that title in 1926.

In the same year under the title, "Our Peace Message," Miller

(1926b:23) used new language with a remarkably modern ring.

> The teaching and spirit of Jesus clearly show that the effective force for the safeguarding of human rights, the harmonizing of differences and the overcoming of evil is the spirit of good will. Throughout his entire ministry, in all human relationships, Jesus was consistently animated by this principle of active and positive good will. . . ."

Miller's theological focus shifted away from how Jesus "resisted not evil" in the face of the cross to the positive activity of his life. This decisive theological shift would rise to the fore some forty years later to rescue nonresistance from oblivion in the face of the civil rights movement.

"Peace" was becoming the code word of the period. Positive and active, it alleviated the anxiety of Mennonite leaders tormented by the passivity of nonresistance. A 1936 MB statement said they "condemn war and advocate peace" and declared their "determination to practice peace and love." A 1939 MB "Handbook on Peace" offered scriptural reasons for a "program of peace" and talked of the "principles of peace."

In a letter to President Coolidge in 1924, GC leaders contended that "peace experts should wage peace," and they "lamented" plans for a national day of military mobilization. Moreover they called for a demonstration that the U.S. "is in harmony with the principles of peace and the Prince of Peace."

A 1935 GC statement noted that members had "striven to practice peace principles" and were using "opportunities whenever and wherever . . . to present and interpret our peace principles to others." Activist peace language was also slipping into MC consciousness as well. Their formal statement in 1937, "Peace, War and Military Service," talked of their "peaceful and nonresistant faith," "peace principles," "position on peace," and "convictions on peace." The focus on peace offered a common bond among Mennonites of various stripes and opened ecumenical conversations with other Christians. Such discourse gave Mennonites a new sense of confidence and civil acceptance.

Nonresistance, however, had not vanished from the Mennonite vocabulary. It was still on the lips of most Mennonites—especially those of the more conservative MCs. The "Doctrine of Nonresistance," found in Daniel Kauffman's *Bible Doctrine*, continued to be widely read as well as other booklets on nonresistance. Even GC students at Bethel College in 1939 used the word when they wrote to the chairman of the GC Peace Committee asking for more action because "our Mennonite doctrine of nonresistance is needed in this world."[11]

The shadow of the fundamentalist/modernist controversy raging throughout the twenties in Canada and the U.S. darkened the peaceful hopes of some (Epp, 1982:48-93). The national controversy played itself out in microcosm in the Mennonite groups in the '20s and '30s. Within the Mennonite church, the vociferous voices of fundamentalist-leaning leaders such as John Horsch, George Brunk, and John Moseman argued for a passive nonresistance that remained aloof from political entanglements.[12] "Christian people," in the words of George Brunk I (1929:6), should "mind their own business by teaching the doctrine of Nonresistance for Christians and stop meddling with the policies of nations."

The influence of dispensationalism and premillenialism sanctioned the warmaking conduct of governments "in this age" and legitimated Mennonite quietism. John A. Lapp notes that, "much of the controversy over nonresistance in *all* Mennonite groups was prompted by this *new* theology [premillenialism] which disrupted traditional communal political ethics."[13]

Premillenialists, such as John Moseman, were incensed with the growing references to peace. Moseman argued vehemently that attempts to prevent war and create international peace would only delay the arrival of the kingdom of God. Historian John Horsch and like-minded conservatives contended that peace activism was an erosion of historic nonresistance that would quickly lead to the swamps of modernist pacifism. Bishop George Brunk I in eastern Virginia suggested in 1933 that Orie O. Miller and Harold S. Bender had "communist connections."[14] In fact in the late 1930s the MC General Problems Committee charged their own Peace Problems Committee with excessive cooperation with "pacifist churches" and pleaded for the maintenance of "biblical nonresistance."[15] The transition toward activist peacemaking was tempered by the modernist/fundamentalist controversy as well as the reluctance of theologically conservative Mennonites to release their grip on traditional nonresistance.

But despite the resistance, a modern vocabulary was in the air—a vocabulary many Mennonites would champion a half-century later. In a major address to the GC Conference meeting in 1926, J. H. Langenwalter trumpeted an activist call—"every effort must be made to spread the idea of world peace as a practicable human effort; and to study the necessary conditions of peace" (cited in P. Toews, 1986:50).

A special conference on "War and Peace" at Goshen College in

1935 included discussions on "Our Peace Program," "Our Peace Testimony: Goals and Methods," and a "Peace Policy." The language reflected the growing rationalization of a modern consciousness. Although nonresistance would remain entrenched in the separatist plausibility structures of rural Mennonites for several more decades, its transformation was well underway among the Mennonite intelligentsia.

Sawatsky (1977:211-236) argues that two incipient understandings of Mennonite peacemaking vied for dominance during this period. A "politically reformist pacifism" with an activist bent was contending with a "chiliastic separatist nonresistance" articulated by those with fundamentalist sympathies. A synthesis of these competing versions of Mennonite nonresistance was eventually forged in the "biblical nonresistance" that emerged in the 1940s.

Vehicles of Peace

The shift in consciousness was accompanied by new vehicles to promote the vision. The Mennonite Central Committee, born in 1920 for relief activities, provided a new avenue for cooperative inter-Mennonite activities. It gave direction to outward-looking service and benevolent activities in the wake of World War I and soon developed into an important inter-Mennonite forum for peace-related ventures.[16]

Both the MCs and GCs appointed "Peace Committees" in the mid-1920s, while the MBs formed a "Committee on Nonresistance." These committees steered much of the activism related to peace education during this period. A Mennonite Peace Society formed in the early 1930s, based at Bluffton College, enjoyed support from GCs as well as a few MCs. The Society sent out summer "Peace Caravans" and sought to promote peace in a variety of ways.[17]

A Conference of Pacifist Churches, involving Friends, Mennonites, the Church of the Brethren, and others, met several times between 1922 and 1931. It received sharp criticism from conservative Mennonites who feared it would lead to liberal pacifism. A new gathering of peace church representatives (Friends, Mennonites, and the Church of the Brethren) called by H. P. Krehbiel in Newton, Kansas, gave birth in 1935 to a new fellowship—The Historic Peace Churches.[18] The name of the new fraternity judiciously abandoned the pacifist label.

But the more conservative MCs remained cautious—only five participated in the initial gathering. Indeed forty of the forty-seven Mennonites attending the first meeting of the Historic Peace Churches were GCs (Toews, 1986:53). Nevertheless, the new fraternity laid a foundation for cooperation between Mennonites, Brethren, and Quakers and provided a framework for their response to conscription in World War II.

Booklets and pamphlets distributed during the interwar period served as vehicles for peace education and afforded North American Mennonites an opportunity to construct theological understandings of nonresistance. But Mennonites still lacked a definitive treatment of their peace-related beliefs. On April 14, 1937, Harold S. Bender, chair of the MC Peace Problems Committee, asked the committee to commission a "Peace study book."[19] After considerable discussion the committee asked Guy Hershberger to write what Paul Toews (1986:56) has called "a conceptual triumph." Hershberger's *War, Peace, and Nonresistance*, eventually published in 1944, solidified another benchmark in the transformation of Mennonite peacemaking—biblical nonresistance.

Hershberger became the broker who negotiated the rift between historic nonresistance and activist pacifism in the context of wartime conditions. His conceptual triumph consolidated a wide array of Mennonite thinking and set the stage for a new phase in Mennonite peacemaking.

The Second World War

As the ominous clouds of World War II began to form in the '30s, nine out of ten Mennonites in North America were farming in rural enclaves, beyond the reach of urban influence. Most were still farming with horses, some were listening to radios, but television, of course, had not arrived. The Great Depression had slowed the acceleration of Mennonite mobility—rural roads were poorly developed and new cars were too expensive to buy. There was no thought of satellites encircling the earth or exploring far-off planets. And nuclear fission, of course, would only occur in 1941.

Mennonite leaders were unprepared for the upheavals that would rock their rural solitude when the war struck and forced them to face the world. A new diaspora was about to begin. Mennonite youth would encounter the draft and enter alternate service or the military. Leaders scurried about seeking alternatives to military service. American Mennonites walked the corridors of political power, brokering a program of Civilian Public Service (CPS) in lieu of military service. Meanwhile, behind the scenes, a reformulation of Mennonite peace convictions was also underway.

Biblical Nonresistance

In the early 1940s several publications set the stage for the rise of "biblical nonresistance." Guy Hershberger's (1940) *Can Christians Fight?* summarized the position in a small book for young people. Three years later in response to the "large volume" of fundamentalist publications arguing that Christian duty required participation in war, the Mennonite Central Committee issued *Must Christians Fight?*. Edited by Edward Yoder (1943), the seventy-page booklet addressed fifty-six questions—beginning with, "What is biblical nonresistance?" A year later, a pamphlet by John R. Mumaw, *Nonresistance and Pacifism,* (1944) drew a stark contrast between those two themes. But it was the publication of Hershberger's (1944) *War, Peace, and Nonresistance* that championed biblical nonresistance in the forties and fifties and became a benchmark in the legacy of Mennonite peacemaking.[20]

Harold Bender's (1944) seminal and influential paper, *The Anabaptist Vision,* and Hershberger's (1944) classic both appeared in the midst of the war.[21] In his "Anabaptist vision" Bender argued that nonresistance was one of three Anabaptist distinctives. Both Bender and Hershberger taught at Goshen College, where together with others, like theologian John C. Wenger and historian Melvin Gingerich, they were developing the "Goshen School" of Anabaptist studies and promoting "The Anabaptist Vision."[22]

Bender chaired the Peace Problems Committee of the Mennonite Church that had asked Hershberger to prepare a "student manual" with "a clear presentation of the Biblical teachings on war and peace" and "a sound analysis of the contrast between Biblical nonresistance and modern pacifism. . . ." (Bender, 1944:v). The little manual turned into the substantial *War, Peace, and Nonresistance,* and evolved into a classic with later editions in 1953 and 1969 and a 1991 reprint of the 1969 edition.[23]

The first edition (1944) reflected a somewhat sectarian outlook of two kingdoms, with the church set off from the larger world. This is not surprising, given that most Mennonites were rural, and that Hershberger, J. Winfield Fretz, and others promoted rural community life, which they felt offered hope for Mennonite survival in the modern world.

Despite his rural roots, Hershberger brokered a conceptual triumph that scholars would wrestle with in the following decades within and without the Mennonite community. Likely intending to bridge the gap between the activists and fundamentalists, Hershberger tilted toward the fundamentalists when he talked of the nonpolitical nature of nonresistance. However, his appeal to a single moral law throughout Scripture demolished dispensational categories. His call for social expressions of nonresistance buoyed the views of activists.

As Hershberger was writing *War, Peace, and Nonresistance,* the outcome of World War II was uncertain. Nearly 40 percent of drafted American Mennonites were in military service and the remainder were scattered around the country in CPS camps or working on farms with deferments. Hershberger (1944:320) recognized that industrialization and mobility had encouraged Mennonites to establish new social and business connections with outsiders, leading to a breakdown of "community brotherhood." The rural plausibility structures of Mennonite communities that had nurtured nonresistance were straining under the burden of modernity.

Growing industrialization, the harsh realities of war, new opportunities for political involvement, and a variety of voices—both pacifist and nonpacifist—were challenging traditional Mennonite views. The atrocities of the war were dashing the optimism of the "Peace Principles" era on the rocks of reality—confirming in many ways sectarian views of human depravity. The confluence of these factors provided a receptive audience for Hershberger's reassertion of historic nonresistance with its political aloofness. Hershberger's work articulated the sentiments of conservative sectarians in the Mennonite fold and soon overshadowed the optimism of Mennonite progressives. It was for some a backward step—yet a realistic one in the face of World War II.

Caught in the crossfire of at least six ideological fronts, Hershberger chose the term *biblical nonresistance* carefully. On the one side he rebutted non-Christian pacifists, such as Gandhi, who advocated nonviolent resistance. From another flank he faced the ridicule of liberal Christian nonpacifists, Reinhold Niebuhr and his disciples, who castigated Mennonites as social parasites. On the opposite side of the theological spectrum, strident fundamentalists argued that Christian duty required participation in military service.

A fourth group breathing hard over Hershberger's shoulder were Mennonite fundamentalists themselves, who grudgingly accepted nonresistance, but delayed its social relevance for a future millennium. *War, Peace, and Nonresistance* was also addressed to progressive Mennonites who were eager to plunge into political life and make the world a safer place for democracy. Finally, Hershberger also prodded those Mennonites, satisfied with the quiet ways of the past and with little interest in worrying about politics in a sinful world that they thought was headed for hell.

War, Peace, and Nonresistance was a conceptual triumph because it addressed all of these groups and articulated a vision grounded in biblical study and steeped in Swiss Mennonite perspectives. The "biblical" tag powerfully legitimated Hershberger's brand of pacifism, setting it apart from secular pacifism. In fact, Hershberger devoted an entire chapter to the differences between "biblical nonresistance" and nine other types of pacifism. Moreover the biblical label made Christian nonpacifists—both the liberals and especially the fundamentalists—squirm because it implied biblical negligence on their part. And for all stripes of Mennonites the cherished word "biblical" blessed Hershberger's argument—suggesting that he in good Mennonite fashion took the Scriptures seriously. Those who deplored his arguments could argue with the Bible.

The word *nonresistance* also branded Hershberger's views in special ways. It was, as we have seen, an emotive word for those in the Swiss tradition and could marshal Mennonite memories and resources like few others. Nonresistance was not polluted with the stains of modernist pacifism. It was not activist Christian pacifism and surely not political pacifism. Moreover, Christians and non-Christians alike who advocated nonviolent resistance quickly discovered that Hershberger's nonresistance was *not* resistant.

Hershberger's book began with the biblical record of peace in Old and New Testaments, followed by a history of peace and war in the early church, as well as a history of Mennonite peacemaking in Europe and America. Based on biblical and historical theology he then applied nonresistant principles to current issues—relief work, service, relations with the state, business, and race relations. It was a skillful blend of biblical and historical concerns addressed to the issues of his day.

In all of these ways, the conceptual triumph of biblical nonresistance consolidated Mennonite views and reappropriated them in the fluid matrix of the forties. Biblical nonresistance challenged theological liberals and fundamentalists alike, since both denied the practical relevance of the Sermon on the Mount for different reasons. Stunned by the harsh realities of the war, many Mennonites were ready to listen to a more sober vision that underlined an ethical dualism and argued for a heavenly citizenship. But still others, shocked by the scope of Hitler's atrocities, determined that people of goodwill must work harder than ever in the public realm to tame the triumph of evil.

The Essence of a Classic

What was the essence of *War, Peace, and Nonresistance*? Apart from rooting it in favorite biblical passages, Hershberger argued for *a single moral law*, threaded throughout the Scriptures, that upheld nonresistance. This new twist tormented Mennonite fundamentalists—some of whom remained troubled by it even into the nineties.

Unlike the fundamentalists who justified Old Testament warfare because it fell under a different "dispensation" in God's scheme, Hershberger (1944:x) argued that peace was inherent in God's "one fundamental moral law which has been and is valid for all time." To the same fundamentalists who relegated Sermon on the Mount ethics to a future dispensation, the subhead of one chapter taunted, "Nonresistance is for our time" (p. 53). Hershberger contended that a single moral law, transcending the Testaments, reflected God's will for all time.

The second feature that formed the crux of Hershberger's argument was his categorical rejection of force for Christian disciples. This stance, consistent with historic Mennonite thinking, underscored the two kingdom dualism because the state, in Hershberger's words, was "organized by the means of coercion" (p. 188). Although Hershberger's biblical nonresistance was "for our time" he accepted the two kingdom dualism, arguing that a Christian could "render society a greater service by remaining aloof and living a life of genuine nonresistance than by being politically active where sooner or later he must sacrifice or compromise this principle" (p. 198). "Compromise" was an unwelcome word for Hershberger, who called for obedience to the teachings of Jesus even if it brought "suffering"—a word he used nearly seventy times in *War, Peace, and Nonresistance*.[24] Hershberger contended that "the outlook of the New Testament is entirely unpolitical . . . unconcerned about the political questions of the day" (pp. 49, 188).

According to Hershberger, this view of the New Testament and the rejection of force led to a political "aloofness" and "detachment" (p. 197). Hedging just a bit, he said "it would seem difficult" for nonresistant Christians "to hold, with any degree of consistency, any responsible executive, legislative or judicial position in the modern state" (p. 193). His opposition to officeholding applied to "city and local government as well, except in minor situations rather far removed from the use of coercive methods" (p. 193).

Nonresistant Christians could, however, teach in state schools, serve on public school boards, and work in postal and public health services. They could serve as well in public programs in forestry, soil conservation, agriculture, scientific experimentation, and firefighting (pp. 194-195). But even in these activities the Christian needs to "be alert and ever on his guard . . ." not to perform functions "inconsistent with his nonresistant testimony" (p. 195). A few years later Hershberger (1950) conceded the need for some force in human life. He agreed that different persons draw the line at different places, and said, "I draw it somewhere between spanking and serving on the police force."

The rejection of coercive force placed Hershberger on a collision course with Gandhian forms of nonviolent resistance which were "very prominent" at the time (p. 215). Hershberger argued simply that "one cannot be resistant and nonresistant at the same time" (p. 191). The crucial difference between his view of biblical nonresistance and nonviolent coercion was "the question of social justice" (p. 215). Hershberger was fond of saying that the scriptural emphasis falls on *doing justice* rather than on *demanding justice*" (p. 216). Those who were faithful to the vision of biblical nonresistance would gladly aid the needy and distressed but not engage in provocative actions that demanded justice for others.

The pattern of word frequency displayed in Table 3.2 reveals the tilt of Hershberger's thought. Although he uses the word "justice" (41) nearly as often as "obedience" (47), it is always with a worried skepticism that justice concerns will lead to nonviolent resistance. The word "politics" does not appear in the index of the book and is only mentioned nine times in the text. "Submission" appears twice as often as "peacemaking" (19/8). The references "to pacifism" (102), "justice" (41), and "nonviolent resistance" (36) are typically negative and usually contrasted with biblical nonresistance.

Phrases that would rise to significance in the fifties were rarely mentioned—"the way of peace" (5), "peace witness" (3), "responsibility" (3), and "the lordship of Christ" (0). Although "biblical nonresistance" (36) appears less frequently than some other words it appears in the title of two chapters that vividly contrast it with other forms of pacifism.

Was *War, Peace, and Nonresistance* merely an ideological defense of a sectarianism, afloat in a faltering rural community? Hershberger's attitude toward political participation certainly smelled sectarian. Thus it was not surprising to hear Kermit Eby, Church of the Brethren professor at the University of Chicago, call *War, Peace, and Nonresistance* "a traditional four-square perspective on peace."[25] But despite his obvi-

TABLE 3.2
Word Frequency Use in *War, Peace, and Nonresistance** (1944)

Concepts		Frequency of use
Nonresistance		427
Nonresistant Christians	146	
Nonresistance (ant)	139	
Biblical nonresistance	36	
Nonresistant principles	32	
Nonresistant faith	30	
Nonresistant way	24	
Doctrine of nonresistance	20	
Peace (peaceful)		133
Love		109
Pacifism (pacifist)		102
Suffering		69
Obedience		47
Justice		41
Nonviolent resistance (coercion)		36
Force, use of		29
Coercion		28
Nonviolence		21
Submission (subjection)		19
Peacemaking (doing, creating)		9
Meek(ness)		9
Politics		9
Compromise		8
Humility		8
Nonconformity		6
Way of peace		5
Peace witness (testimony)		3
Responsibility		3
Lordship of Christ		0

*Note: Excludes historical chapters 1, 8, 9
Source: Hershberger (1944).
Compiled by Anne Weidner

ous sectarian sympathies, Hershberger only speaks of nonconformity a half-dozen times—primarily in a single paragraph which argues that nonresistance is "one application of the general principle of nonconformity to the evil of this world" (p. 333).

Despite his Amish-Mennonite upbringing, Hershberger had left the strict separation of Old Order groups behind. Indeed, Robert Kreider remembers that the more conservative sectors of the Mennonite Church didn't like Hershberger because "he was chipping away at their separatist ideas."[26] James Juhnke suggests that "Hershberger had a positive Jeffersonian view of American history. . . . In practice, Hershberger's dualism may have been softer than it appeared in *War, Peace, and Nonresistance.*[27]

Although Hershberger contended that "the primary duty of the Christian is to be a true disciple of Christ" rather than to pursue political missions, he argues nevertheless that nonresistant Christians have a "curative mission . . . to bring healing to society" (p. 301). Indeed *War, Peace, and Nonresistance* devoted a full chapter to "Nonresistance and Industrial Conflict" and another to "The Service of Nonresistance to Society." Already in 1944, Hershberger called for a "special effort" by nonresistant Christians to do justice in "the area of race relations," because prejudice "is a very subtle sin and leads most often to unjust practices . . ." (p. 330). He called for programs of ministry to the needy and for practicing nonresistance in business relations.

He clearly emphasized the primacy of duty within the Christian community, always rejected coercion, and was very selective about political participation. Yet he had not, in the strict sectarian sense, turned his back on the world. Mennonites who courted political participation were dismayed by Hershberger's dim view of politics, but "all the young bucks," in the words of a GC leader, "had to wrestle with him seriously and couldn't just wipe him off as we did with conservatives like John Horsch and J. L. Stauffer."[28]

In any event, biblical nonresistance came to dominate MC thinking in the forties and influenced GC views as well "due to a lack of articulated alternatives" (Sawatsky, 1977:250). Although competing versions of Mennonite peacemaking would flourish in the fifties and sixties, the Hershberger formulation was still alive in 1968 in the title of John C. Wenger's focal pamphlet, *Pacifism and Biblical Nonresistance.*

Paul Toews proposes that Hershberger, while still employing a two-kingdom doctrine, gives it a new twist.[29] Hershberger's appeal to a single moral law, notes Toews, radiates through both the church and the state and gives the church a new found relevance, even when its posture is quietistic. The two kingdoms look very different when the same fundamental moral law operates in both spheres. Then the church has pragmatic relevance.

Although Hershberger has a sectarian cast there is always, in Toews' words, "a dialectic in him between separatism and engagement, between church and world that is previously missing."

It is this dialectical tension in Hershberger that legitimates the activism of the postwar period. Hershberger's call for the church to embrace a "curative mission" leads to many forms of public witness and in Toews' judgment, "creates an opening for the shift from a passive nonresistance to a much more active engagement."

Thus there is an ironic twist to the legacy of *War, Peace, and Nonresistance*, which many considered sectarian in its political outlook. Hershberger's appeal to a single moral law that rankled the fundamentalists also quite innocently set the stage for later Mennonite scholars who would argue that one moral law, "God's righteousness," applied not only to the church but to civil government as well. This theological shift held the potential of obliterating in one stroke, surely to Hershberger's surprise, the historic two-kingdom dualism in Mennonite theology.

Summary

Modernization was spurred by the industrialization that throbbed with new vitality as factories expanded in the first decades of the twentieth century. Although Mennonites largely resisted modernization until after World War II, they were nevertheless ruffled by the breezes of change blowing already in the late nineteenth century. Indeed, the "old order" label used by both Amish and Mennonite groups came into usage as such groups sprouted in the late nineteenth century when they refused to accommodate to modernity (Hostetler, 1992). The old order groups, who were hedging by shunning modern ways, were best able to preserve nonresistance in its most pristine form. The more progressive, mainstream Mennonites encompassed in this book were more willing to sway with the winds of modernity.

The transformation of passive peasants into active peacemakers was a gradual metamorphosis stretching over a century (1890-1990). Our brief survey of benchmarks in the six decades between 1890 and 1950 reveals a rise and fall of optimism for worldwide peacemaking. The emergence of a "doctrine of nonresistance" reflected the specialization and rationalization of modernity already shaping Mennonite consciousness at the turn of the century. After a harsh confrontation with the state in World War I, many progressive Mennonite leaders caught the optimistic spirit of the twenties and hoped that an embrace of the principles of peace would usher in a new world order. However, Mennonite leaders with fundamentalist and millenarian views loudly objected to interpretations of nonresistance that fostered political activism.

With hopes for peace dashed by the horrors of World War II, "biblical nonresistance," articulated in *War, Peace, and Nonresistance*, was a middle road between the separatist nonresistance of the fundamentalists and the active nonresistance of the progressives. Indeed Hershberger's book not only dominated Mennonite peace thinking in the forties, it also became a major benchmark of the century. Although the transformation of Mennonite peacemaking was well under way in the first half of the twentieth century, its major restructuring came in the wake of World War II. The ferment of the fifties fanned a variety of issues that Mennonites would debate in the remainder of the century. To these debates we now turn.

The ferment of Mennonite peace theology was stirred by a series of four so called Puidoux conferences in Europe between 1955 and 1962. Several Mennonites participated in these conferences. Participants at the fourth conference held in the Netherlands in 1962 included (from left) John Howard Yoder, Gordon Kaufman, A. H. A. Bakker, H. Kossen, William Keeney.

CHAPTER FOUR

Ferment in the Fifties

The 1950s stirred new ferment in Mennonite thinking. The winds of modernization were already unraveling Mennonite plausibility structures as the new decade opened. Changes in North American society, growing theological challenges, and rising prosperity were revamping the Mennonite posture in the larger world. The forces of modernization were shaking rural Mennonite communities with greater intensity.

The end of World War II brought American Mennonites home from Civilian Public Service Camps and military service with new ideas and exposure to other ways of life. Hundreds of younger Mennonites had aided the cleanup of rubble in Europe. Indeed, by 1954 one observer estimated that some 1,500 Mennonites had "sailed the seven seas or flown the world's skyways," in postwar relief efforts.[1] Another Mennonite estimated that since 1943 Mennonites had served in relief work in forty-five different countries (Peachey, 1980:66).

Those who remained at home were also changing. A church leader in 1951 said, "The Mennonite Church is becoming highly trained in education, in business and in the professions. . . . We are world travelers now, with a world (and all too often a worldly) knowledge, as well as a world vision. Our prosperity borders on the phenomenal in many instances. . . ."[2] A new generation of Mennonite scholars, trained in prestigious universities in Europe and North America, was struggling to translate the heritage of nonresistance into the context of modern life within the shadows of the recent war.

A host of social and technological changes were sweeping Mennonites out of their rural isolation. They were listening to radios and reading popular magazines. A few were watching television. Jet travel, faster cars, improved roadways, and a wide array of new consumer products were nudging Mennonites into the modern fray. The consolidation of public high schools, well underway in the early fifties, exposed many Mennonite youth to the values of democracy and scientific thinking.[3]

Already in 1950 J. Winfield Fretz had declared, "Our nonresistant doctrine was vacuum packed, as it were, within the confines of the Mennonite cultural walls. The seal has been broken . . . we cannot retreat into the shell of isolated group experience."[4] The widespread changes that frayed the fabric of rural Mennonite communities produced a reactive attempt to promote rural community life. Led by Fretz, Guy F. Hershberger, and others, the Mennonite Community Association published its own magazine between 1947 and 1953 until it fell to the forces of urbanization. Old Order groups continued to resist the overtures of modernity, but many Mennonites welcomed the fresh air blowing into their rural enclaves.

Expanding the Vision

Beyond the press of urbanization and industrialization, the nonresistant tradition faced ideological threats from liberal Protestantism. Throughout the fifties the rising generation of Mennonite scholars wrestled with Reinhold Niebuhr's (1937:1391) challenge that Mennonites were irresponsible "parasites on the sins of others." They also cringed when mainstream social ethicists called nonresistance a "strategy of withdrawal."

The plausibility of biblical nonresistance was crumbling as younger scholars—conversant with modern ethical and theological thought—sought to fashion a new theology of peacemaking for Mennonites in the modern world. Mennonites were shifting their focus from their ethnic community to civic responsibilities in the larger society as they became more urban, educated, and mobile.

Winona Lake, 1950

The decade opened with a significant four-day conference at Winona Lake, Indiana, in November 1950. Called by MCC, eighty-five men and two women hailed from five Canadian provinces and eleven U.S. states. They represented the five churches in our study as well as nine smaller Mennonite groups. It was the first inter-Mennonite peace conference with delegates from virtually all the Mennonite bodies in North America. The gathering produced a statement with remarkably modern language and guided Mennonite peacemaking efforts for some forty years. Stimulated by the ecumenical Detroit conference on "The Church and War" held in May 1950, the Mennonites gathered seven months later "at a critical time in a generation marked by widespread and disastrous wars and shadowed by the threat of still more ruinous warfare."[5]

Older scholars and younger ones alike addressed the topics of "Nonresistance and the Social Order," "The Disciple of Christ and the State," "Our Peace Witness to Christendom," and many more.[6] Despising what some called "our minority inferiority complex" participants were outward looking, with a focus on the larger social order—especially the state. They struggled to define nonresistance and searched for "an expression . . . which better characterizes our position than the term, 'nonresistance.' " After debating whether nonresistance was a "fruit or root," of the gospel, the scholars concluded that it was, "integral to the gospel."

The conference statement, written by a committee chaired by Harold S. Bender and endorsed by the inter-Mennonite body, was also adopted by the Mennonite Church a year later in its general conference. The language of the statement is surprising. "Biblical nonresistance" is never mentioned and "nonresistance" appears only twice. "Peacemaking" appears once, but the positive, active word "love"—fast on the ascendancy—appears seventeen times! Other new vocabulary, "Lord" and "lordship of Christ," had eight references, "the social order" appears six times, and "witness" five as shown in Table 4.1.

Although speakers and participants discussed "responsibility" and "justice" frequently in the public sessions, "responsibility" appeared only once in the statement and "justice" never. The predominance of "love" was likely a compromise. More progressive persons chafed at the use of biblical nonresistance and "responsibility was a bad word for Bender," said one observer.[7] "Love," an active, positive, biblical word, was elastic enough to encompass and pacify all Mennonite perspectives. Love for many Mennonites took the form of nonresistance.

The accent on love represented more than a change in vocabulary. Reacting to Bennett's charge that theirs was "a strategy of withdrawal," Mennonites were struggling, in the words of the statement, with their "responsibility . . . to the *total social order* of which we are a part."[8] Even more astonishing was the new stance toward the state. No longer bowed down, hat in hand, they now spoke of the "lordship of Christ"

TABLE 4.1
Frequency of Word Use in the 1950 Winona Lake Statement

Concepts	Frequency
Love	17
Service	9
Lordship of Christ (Lord)	8
Discipleship	7
Social order (Society)	6
Peace	5
Witness	5
Nonresistance	2
Responsibility	1
Peacemaking	1
Justice	0

over governments and "our obligation to witness to the righteousness which God requires of all men, even in government. . . ."

The statement acknowledged that God set the state in its place of power, but recognized "the relative and conditional validity of any particular form of government . . . we must judge all things in the light of God's word and see that our responses to the relativities of the state are always conformed to the absolutes of Christian discipleship and love." Mennonites were not only refusing to take off their hats in deference to the state, they were also asking the state to take off its hat to the "lordship of Christ." This was new language which, along with love, would rise in prominence in the next decades as Mennonites sorted out a new understanding of the state.

In his concluding address to the Winona Lake conference, Harold S. Bender told participants that "the way of love is urgently needed in this world." Citing the challenge of Niebuhr and other critics, he said, "We are being challenged on all sides today. . . . How can we practice the ethics of love in a world of force . . . without withdrawing. . . ? How can we make nonresistance a positive force . . . in all our relationships?" Bender told participants, "We have largely left unfulfilled our obligation to witness . . . for the way of love and nonresistance."[9]

The "way of love" was becoming a fitting phrase for the fifties—fitting for a people emerging from rural byways, searching for a more positive stance. This newfound phrase was biblical, broad, and positive. Moreover, it provided a natural bridge for ecumenical conversations. Directed outward, it pointed beyond the confines of Mennonite communities.

Although the word "responsibility" appeared only once in the Winona Lake statement, it rose to the fore in the ferment of the fifties. At least three major conferences, called by MCs, GCs, and MCC, were organized around the theme of political responsibility in 1956 and 1957.[10] Several major articles and a dissertation appeared in 1957 and 1958 dealing with Mennonite responsibility in the larger social order.[11] Beginning in 1955 a group of young Mennonite scholars in Europe participated in ecumenical peace discussions in the "Puidoux Conferences" which focused on "the lordship of Christ."[12]

A dialogue about peace in ecumenical circles required coping with the issues of responsibility and justice. One of the Mennonite participants, Paul Peachey, wrote a series of five articles under the title of "Love, Justice, Peace" in the *Gospel Herald* in 1956. About the same time a series of articles in *Mennonite Life* urged Mennonites toward greater political participation.[13]

Embracing the Way of Love

Four major positions emerging across the Mennonite spectrum reflected the debate and growing pluralism of the fifties. The proponents of these positions, ranging from biblical nonresistance to active engagement, included Guy F. Hershberger and three younger Mennonite scholars, John H. Yoder, J. Lawrence Burkholder, and Gordon Kaufman.[14] The views of the four scholars reflected major streams of thought both within and beyond the Mennonite world.

The negative and passive-sounding ring of nonresistance troubled the younger scholars. Influenced by neo-orthodox theologians such as Niebuhr, they hoped to refurbish Mennonite understandings of nonresistance with positive, active language—"the way of love," "responsibility," "the lordship of Christ," "witness," "testimony," and "justice." Increasingly "the way of love," with its robust sound, appeared in tandem with, and sometimes replaced, nonresistance. Indeed, Harold S. Bender already in 1944 in his "Anabaptist Vision" had flagged "love and nonresistance," as distinguishing traits of Anabaptism. The "Way of Love" became the reigning phrase of the decade on Mennonite lips, but its use was not uniquely Mennonite.

Underscoring the importance of love brought a preoccupation with responsibility. What concrete forms might love take? As Mennonites evacuated secluded communities and came to grips with modern power structures, they grappled with how to live responsibly in the larger society—always, of course, with Niebuhr's charge of irresponsibility ringing in their ears.

Mennonites were known as conscientious and responsible folks. But like other sectarian groups, they worried little about the moral dirt in the larger world. The charge of irresponsibility, however, tormented their souls. Emerging from rural cocoons of social isolation, Mennonites became preoccupied with church-state relations and moral responsibility in public life. Acculturation into modern life, negotiations with U.S. authorities in the creation of Civilian Public Service, the rise of a Hitler, and a new generation of scholars, pushed church-state issues to center stage. This was a topic which Mennonites had thought and written little about so far in the twentieth century.[15]

As the "way of love" provided a rubric of consensus for a broad spectrum of Mennonite groups, a revised edition of Hershberger's *War, Peace, and Nonresistance* appeared in 1953. Several chapters were dropped and others shuffled, but the basic argument remained intact. Hershberger's earlier response to Niebuhr's charge of irresponsibility remained in a small section titled "Is the Nonresistant Christian a Parasite?"

Outside this section Hershberger rarely, if ever, addressed the question of responsibility—apparently not changing his mind. He did, however, make two other shifts. The New Testament chapter now included a section titled "Nonresistance an Integral Part of the Gospel"—a phrase he borrowed from the 1950 Winona Lake conference. Moreover, in this section he italicized the phrase *"the way of love and nonresistance"*—underscoring his own adoption of the more positive "way of love."

Other traces of change suggested a more outward-looking Hershberger seeking to relate nonresistance to the larger social order, though his basic stance remained unaltered. A new chapter titled, "A World Wide Peace Witness" contained three subtitles using the word "testimony" or "witness." The chapter on business relations, now tagged "The Social Implications of Biblical Nonresistance," contained a section on "An Awakened Social Conscience." A new conclusion to the book was titled "The Outreach of Christian Nonresistance." Although he had not hedged on the use of force or political participation, Hershberger was beginning to grapple with the complexities of the larger world.

Nevertheless, biblical nonresistance remained the orthodoxy of the "Goshen School" throughout the fifties. A younger group of scholars, however, soon began to stir the ferment and sometimes the ire of the Goshen patriarchs.

Shouldering Social Responsibility

Heeding the call of their elders and the needs of the world, the aftermath of the war led some "sons of Goshen" to relief work in Europe. A cluster of these, named the Concern Group, first met in Amsterdam in 1952 for a two-week retreat to reflect on their struggle with the modern world and their Anabaptist heritage. The seven were young Mennonite intellectuals living in Europe—attending graduate schools or working in the service of MCC and church mission agencies.[16]

Graduates of either Goshen or Eastern Mennonite College, all had pursued graduate degrees or secured doctorates. They began to challenge the Goshen establishment. Their quarrel was not so much with the Anabaptist ideals articulated by Bender and Hershberger, but with their reluctance to challenge Mennonites to radically follow the Anabaptist Vision. Many papers written by the Concern Group and others were published in the *Concern* pamphlets 1954-1971. Responding to the havoc of the war, ecumenical conversations, and the challenge of their heritage, these youthful intellectuals were dismayed by the reluctance of the established church to understand—let alone practice—the Anabaptist Vision.

Yoder's Agape Witness

At the first Concern meeting in 1952, Irvin Horst outlined the blurring of the Anabaptist Vision among Dutch Mennonites by assimilation into economic, cultural, and political realms. By implication the Mennonites in North America were also in jeopardy. Orley Swartzentruber argued that the home church was no longer spearheading the Anabaptist Vision. As general Christianity had become a "corpus christianum," so had Mennonites evolved into a "corpus mennonitarium." The strength of the Mennonite church, according to Swartzentruber, lay not in its theological acumen but in its sociological institutions. Mennonite leaders were reluctant to radicalize the basic structures of Mennonite communities. The Concern Group's lament about the disjuncture between "Anabaptist Vision and Mennonite Reality" was best expressed in a letter of John H. Yoder to Harold Bender in 1954.

What has happened to me is that in the process of growing up I have put together an interest in Anabaptism, which you gave me, an MCC experience to which you were instrumental in assigning me and a theological study to which you directed me, to come out with what is a more logical fruition of your own convictions than you yourself realize (cited in Toews, 1990b:112).

John Yoder's (1954) lead paper in the first *Concern* pamphlet was titled "The Anabaptist Dissent: The Logic of the Place of the Disciple in Society." His first sentence addressed "the church's responsibility in society" from a sectarian position. The "dissent of the sect" in Yoder's (1954:46) words was "its refusal to assume responsibility for the moral structure of non-Christian society." What divided sectarian ethicists from responsible ones was the presence of evil in the world. In Yoder's analysis, advocates of responsibility appealed so rigorously to the presence of sin that they ended up invalidating ethical principles that might achieve the good. The sectarian refuses to flatten God's goodness (Toews, 1990b:111; Yoder, 1954:61).

Yoder argued that a strategy of responsibility led "to ethical compromise which undermines the church's moral authority"—sweet music to Hershberger's ears. Yoder contrasts "sectarian" and "responsibility" ethicists. He concludes that the disciple is responsible to be obedient to the ethics of Jesus and the outcome of the larger social order is God's problem. A year later Yoder (1955) evaluated Niebuhr's critique of Christian pacifism and chided him for not sufficiently distinguishing the church from society. Christians, Yoder contended (1955:116), need to choose "the better instead of the good, obedience instead of necessity, love instead of compromise, brotherhood instead of veiled self-interest."

In 1955 John H. Yoder presented a paper on "The Lordship of Christ Over Church and State" at a study conference in Puidoux, Switzerland, which was later elaborated into *The Christian Witness to the State* (1964).[17] Yoder argues at length that Christ's lordship over the principalities and powers enables the church to "witness" to the state about the ethics of agape love. Yoder's new formulation

agrees with the traditional sectarian view in maintaining the norm of love as the only standard in the church, in maintaining the distinction between the presuppositions of faith and unfaith, in realistically expecting the standards and the achievements of the world to be less than love, and in considering love to be a relevant historical possibility distinct from self-immolation and from puritan benevolence (Yoder, 1964:71-72).

Yoder does not expect leaders of government to completely follow Christian ideals. Sin pulls them down from the high level of agape love. Civil officials are thus forced to operate at middle level ethical axioms because true revelation and the ideal will of God are unclear to them—or at least impossible to enact within the political structures of the state.

The church is the second realm in Yoder's scheme. Christians who follow God's agape love are supposedly able to attain a higher level of performance than the state. Human performance will always be less than the agape ideal, but the Anabaptists assumed that their behavior could at least approximate agape love. For Yoder there is only one standard—agape love—not separate norms for church and state. Anchored on the norm of agape, the Christian can then witness to civil authorities about God's high standard for all.

Yoder seems to assume that those in government work outside the realm of faith. What if Christians are elected to a government position? If Christian officials cannot operate on the principle of agape, must they resign? Or must Christians follow "middle axioms" below the agape standard, which presumably involves compromise? J. Lawrence Burkholder notes that Christians involved in business and professional realms often operate on middle level axioms when they are forced to fire an employee or make other decisions that may harm someone.

The traditional sectarian approach and Yoder's proposal both assume that Christians can approximate agape love. But this assumption perhaps downplays the reality of sin. Are Christians able to approach the perfection of agape love?

Yoder's "witness to the state" moves beyond Hershberger's apolitical posture. Yoder accepted Hershberger's sectarian stance that emphasized the primacy of the church community, and obedience to the norms of agape love. But introducing the "lordship of Christ" language and a single ethical norm—the ethics of agape—provided the basis for an active witness to the state. Emphasizing a christological basis for pacifism, Yoder's ethic obligated Christians to confront the world. In this sense his position struck a middle ground between withdrawal and responsibility.[18]

Burkholder's Social Responsibility

Thus far we have the makings of a sectarian-responsibility continuum, with Hershberger and Yoder tilting toward the sectarian pole. We now turn to J. Lawrence Burkholder and Gordon Kaufman, who lean toward the responsibility end of the spectrum. Although not entirely sectarian, Hershberger reflected traditional Mennonite values centered on faithful discipleship somewhat segmented from the world. John H. Yoder, endorsing the "lordship of Christ" and "agape ethics," called for witness to the larger society. But it was J. Lawrence Burkholder who took the major step toward social responsibility.

Burkholder, like members of the Concern Group in Europe, had served abroad. His service, however, took him to India, and then to China as a relief worker under the Mennonite Board of Missions and MCC. Exempt from the draft because of his ministerial status, Burkholder went to China (1945-49) voluntarily. Leaving his wife and small children behind, he joined the relief effort, "as a moral equivalent to war . . . I had to do something."[19] The words of a draft board member, spoken to him several years earlier, still rang in his ears: "If Hitler wins it's your fault."

In China Burkholder worked as the national director of Church World Service and carried massive responsibilities for distributing millions of dollars of relief goods and administering a large staff.

> I had to distribute thousands of cases of food in China. Any policy will help some people and hurt others. I had to divide goods to competing neighbors. I had to fire people and threaten to sue. I compromised a lot, but a lot of people were fed and clothed. As a copilot I had to push some people off an overloaded plane that was evacuating a Chinese city surrounded by communists. The pilot handed me his pistol to force the evacuation. This I could not do. So he held the gun at the heads of the Chinese while I literally pushed them out the door. We had to do it to save the others on the plane. . . .

Burkholder read few books in China but the harsh experience taught him "the difference between the ethics of personal relations and corporate responsibilities."[20] His administrative duties often placed him in authentic moral dilemmas. At times he found it necessary to use force against some so that others could be saved. Burkholder's Mennonite "innocence" and "good conscience" were quickly tarnished by "tragic necessity." These formative experiences profoundly shaped his theological reflection for years to come.

After his foreign service, Burkholder taught at Goshen College, then completed doctoral work at Princeton Theological Seminary. The confrontation with the moral dilemmas of power in public administration led Burkholder to reassess and critique traditional Mennonite ethics. His dissertation, *The Problem of Social Responsibility from the Perspective of the Mennonite Church*, was written in 1958 but not published until thirty-one years later in 1989. In the preface to the publication he writes,

> What impressed me most was the ambiguity of power. Without power nothing could be accomplished but when power was exercised, invariably some people were helped and others were either deprived or hurt. . . . Eventually I came to see life dialectically according to which multiple demands required one to choose between equally valid but contradictory obligations (Burkholder, 1989:iii-iv).

Burkholder (1989:iv) goes on to describe the response of Mennonite leaders to his ideas.

> I was disappointed upon finding that my experience of moral ambiguity met virtually no approving, let alone sympathetic responses from Mennonites in the 1950s—except from students. At that time Mennonite scholars were busy articulating a sectarian ethic for the Mennonite community. Social idealism seldom reached beyond church sponsored relief work. Furthermore, justice was given no place within the Mennonite glossary. Nonviolent resistance was considered "unbiblical." Hence I was reproved and the typed thesis, having been rejected for publication, turned brown in the dusty shelves of the libraries.

Guy Hershberger and Harold Bender, upon reading Burkholder's Th.D. dissertation which had received honors at Princeton, were dismayed by his acceptance of Niebuhr's concepts of power, ambiguity, and responsibility.[21] Although Burkholder doesn't remember Bender talking with him about the dissertation, "Hershberger," in Burkholder's words, "scolded me. At first he said my dissertation was 'brilliant' but after marking it up he said, 'we can't say this and this is too strong.' Later he had prayer for me."

Reflecting on his encounter with the Goshen patriarchs, Burkholder said, "Hershberger wanted to absolutize nonresistance as if we could always live by agape. I was committed to radical Christianity but I couldn't do it in the complexity of political situations. Jesus didn't administer anything, not even a family."

Reflecting on the ambiguities of nonresistant love, Burkholder said, "Harriet [his wife] and I agreed that we would be willing to give up our lives if necessary and that I would not protect her, but I cannot set up nonresistance as an all-embracing answer to all questions. . . . I do feel guilt for some of the hard decisions I made in ambiguous situations . . . unlike John H. Yoder, I feel responsible for history, for any way I can be effective in the world."

Burkholder returned to Goshen College to teach after his dissertation was finished, but "found nobody on my side, not a single faculty member sympathized with my view point." One colleague said, "you hit us at the center," signifying the centrality of nonresistance as a core belief. Burkholder's dissertation in his words was "kept under cover at Goshen. It was hush, hush for the sake of unity. I decided if I had to be quiet for a while I would."

When Burkholder asked Hershberger, "Must I leave the college and church," Hershberger didn't answer. Feeling distraught because of the cool reception to his views, Burkholder, in his words, "nearly left the church." He decided he had to leave Goshen College, "for psychological health reasons because I couldn't sleep at night." He accepted an invitation to teach at Harvard Divinity School in 1961, but after the change of guard at Goshen College he returned some ten years later as its president.

Meanwhile, the dissertation grew stale on the shelf. "I was shut up and the church wasn't ready. I was so sick of the dissertation that I never wanted to see it again. . . . I had sent it to the Mennonite Publishing House for publication but I never even received a response." One observer remembers Hershberger worrying that publication of it could split the church. So the dissertation lay dormant for thirty-one years until the Institute for Mennonite Studies published it in 1989.[22] Meanwhile the winds of modernity had changed the church—by the late 1980s it was ready to face questions of social responsibility.

How could one dissertation draw such a severe response? As the title suggests, Burkholder focused on *social responsibility*. In his pre-China years Burkholder had accepted traditional Mennonite beliefs and scriptural teaching on nonresistance. He had sought to follow Christ in radical discipleship, turning down lucrative positions to serve in China without his family. The moral complexities of his relief service in China pressed Burkholder to reexamine Mennonite ethics. At Princeton he discovered "categories" that in his words, "explained his ethical conflicts as an administrator—dilemma, power, ambiguity, compromise—and all those terrible things! Justice wasn't even considered a Christian term in the late '50s at Goshen."

Burkholder's use of "dilemma" implied that both social responsibility and Christian discipleship could be taken seriously and the notion of "dialectic" suggested that Christians could learn from both church and world. For sectarians who strictly separate the church from the world, such ethical give-and-take smacks of compromise. While John H. Yoder, like Hershberger, focused on biblical and theological norms, Burkholder used the insights of sociologists—Max Weber and Ernst Troeltsch—and the social realism of Reinhold Niebuhr to interpret his moral dilemmas shaped by concrete administrative experience.

"Those in the Concern movement," said Burkholder, "were ideologists, they had all the answers, they only wanted to carry out the Anabaptist Vision. John H. Yoder doesn't want to admit to quandary ethics. My views were shaped by the concrete ethical dilemmas faced by an administrator." Moreover, Burkholder notes, "Some scholars never got out of the ivory tower. They never stood on the picket line, worked in a factory, or administered large public programs."

Burkholder (1958:1) contends that "individual Christians and church bodies should maintain an interest in the affairs of the world and should relate themselves *responsibly* to the problems of the economic and political realms. . . ." His dissertation reviews Walter Rauschenbusch's contribution to social responsibility in the Social Gospel movement of the early twenties and Reinhold Niebuhr's formulations of responsibility in the thirties that rejected certain assumptions of liberalism. Burkholder wrote that

> no one can be *actively* responsible for all of society's problems. *Social responsibility does, however, imply a general attitude of identification with the world.* The social responsibility person believes that he is a participant in the human struggle for truth and justice as these values are manifested in the social and political realms. He identifies himself with the stream of secular history and feels obligated to the world. The problems of the world are at least in a general way his problems. . . . (Burkholder, 1958:12).

It was this stance—this deliberate identification with the world—that moved Burkholder beyond the sectarian fold. Thus the Christian as a responsible citizen becomes involved in the political process which pushes one into complex ethical dilemmas. As the Mennonites of Burkholder's generation were leaving farms for businesses and professions, they were becoming involved in society and learning of world needs. They were struggling with new moral dilemmas. The elders at Goshen, however, were dragging their feet.

As Mennonites became increasingly urban, educated, and immersed in society, conflicting duties multiplied. Burkholder (1958:33) argued that love demands responsible participation in society, for here the Christian meets the neighbor. Avoiding responsibility is "passing by on the other side." On the other hand, Christian purity demands separation from the world, an "in but not of" position.

Burkholder acknowledges that moral dilemmas often require

"compromise," an unfortunate term that implied a moral stain on the sectarian purity of Bender and Hershberger. Self-giving love is possible only in part, if sinful disobedience is taken seriously. Here the dialectic of give-and-take, for Burkholder, becomes real because humans live in the tension between concrete realities and the ideals of God.

The severe response of the Goshen scholars to Burkholder's notions of discipleship and responsibility was itself a sectarian political response—an attempt to weed out those who spurned the standards of purity. In Burkholder's words he was challenging "the innocence of the church." His frequent use of "compromise" suggested serious moral backsliding. John H. Yoder, by contrast, integrated his terminology more carefully with traditional language. By the 1980s a more urban Mennonite constituency, shaped by the complexities of modernity, was more receptive to Burkholder's notions of power, ambiguity, and compromise.

Kaufman's Cultural Engagement

In the same year (1958) that Burkholder's dissertation appeared, Gordon Kaufman published an article titled "Nonresistance and Responsibility." It directly addressed John H. Yoder's "Anabaptist Dissent," published four years earlier. Kaufman's essay and later theological writings place him beyond Burkholder in the sectarian-responsibility continuum.

Hershberger, Yoder, and Burkholder were rooted in the Mennonite Church and shaped by the "Goshen school." With Gordon Kaufman the scene turns to Bethel College at Newton, Kansas. Both Kaufman and Burkholder taught at the Harvard Divinity School, but Kaufman came out of the General Conference Mennonite tradition. The General Conference had been founded partly for the purpose of pursuing education and missions—both designed for greater outreach and involvement in the larger society. Kaufman's parents had followed the call to foreign missions in China.

After returning from China, E. G. Kaufman, Gordon's father, finished his Ph.D. at the University of Chicago, began teaching at Bethel College, and soon became its president. Gordon Kaufman spent his youth on the Bethel campus, entered alternative service during World War II, and then took an M.A. in sociology at Northwestern University. Later he completed theological studies at Yale where he studied with Richard Niebuhr, brother to Reinhold. Gordon Kaufman emerged out of the "Russian Mennonite trajectory" of culturally engaged pacifism, flowing from the line of C. H. Wedel, David Goerz, H.

Mennonite involvements with Christian service organizations around the world encouraged engagement with the larger culture. Mennonites participated along with other historic peace churches in EIRENE (Greek for peace): International Christian Service for Peace. Mennonite Peter J. Dyck (2nd from L.), MCC Director in Europe, meets with other members of EIRENE.

P. Krehbiel, P. H. Richert, and E. G. Kaufman in the Newton, Kansas, area (L. Friesen, 1991:16-22).[23]

Lauren Friesen (1991:22-23) calls Kaufman's pacifism "cultural engagement" because he links peace witness with cultural advancement and nonresistance with responsibility to society. In this view, active love, rather than separation from the world, is the true expression of nonresistance. Love vaults Christians into the world, where they try to act redemptively. "To withdraw from the world is to fail to love, because Christian love always takes responsibility for the sinful situation" (Friesen, 1991:22). John R. Burkholder (1991a:5-9) labels Kaufman's peacemaking "Nonviolent Statesmanship" with unconditional neighbor-love as the primary principle. Such statesmanship may at times "call for public political action that violates personal conviction."

Kaufman's (1958:6-7) views hinge on active love. Withdrawal from the social order is, for him, a theological embarrassment that "negates" the very nature of love. For Kaufman (1958:8), love "goes to the very heart of the most sinful situations that it can find, and it gives of itself without any reservation whatsoever." Love, in other words, by its very nature seeks responsibility and "badly compromises itself" if it withdraws.

For Kaufman, Christian responsibility has three dimensions. First is the missionary task of preaching the gospel. Second, Christians should seek to love and understand their neighbors (society) with integrity. Christians cannot impose a Christian ethic on a society that does not claim one. Third, Christians should encourage neighbors and nations to act consistently with the nation's ideals, even if the national behavior violates Christian norms. To "truly act out of love, we must enter into the situation, helping our society come to the best decision of which it is capable . . . and then support it as best we can," even if we don't agree with it (Kaufman, 1958:19-20).

Later, in a chapter in his book *Nonresistance Responsibility*, Kaufman (1979:101-102) says,

> All of the issues appear to me to be aspects of one crucial problem, the relation of the church and/or the individual Christian to the world in which they find themselves. Though perhaps not all would go so far as to say that the church's very existence is for the world—in the sense that the church is here as the continuing wedge of God's act to save the world—all parties would agree I think, that a major portion of the church's business here on earth is with the world. Christians are called upon to witness to God's saving act in Christ, to love and serve others as God has loved them. The church, therefore, cannot sit in some sort of splendid isolation and purity and remain Christ's church. She must enter into the world of rebellion.

Kaufman's (1979:102) critics are inclined to withdraw from the world. He asserts, however, that "an ethic of radical nonresistant discipleship . . . necessarily leads us *into* the world rather than away from it."

In fact, Kaufman (1958:8-9) pushes the logic of love farther and calls for an assertive engagement of the Christian in the world.

> The Anabaptist-Mennonite tradition has always tried to interpret love in the radical sense of the New Testament, but in its tendency to withdraw from participation in the power struggles of the world it has badly compromised itself. . . .
> The crucial question, then, is not whether as Christians we have some sort of responsibility for the social and political orders in which we live,

but rather, what is the nature of that responsibility, and how must it express itself.

Kaufman (1958:25) argues that radical obedience to love might lead to the paradox of a Christian urging government representatives to vote for a conscription bill because it is the proper policy for the nation as a whole while the same disciple refuses to register under "the same bill in order to bear his witness to his deepest Christian convictions."

While Hershberger worried that Mennonites were endangered by compromise if they engaged in the world, Kaufman suggests the reverse. Mennonites compromise themselves, and the radical demands of the way of love, if they withdraw from the world. Kaufman asks how Christians should work responsibly in the world, not whether they should. According to him, Mennonites compromised the gospel and their heritage by promoting separation. Some of his critics, however, contend that he never specifies exactly how to work in the world. Thus Hershberger and Kaufman stake out polar positions on the sectarian-responsibility continuum.

Lauren Friesen (1991:22-23) proposes that

> C. H. Wedel's theology of cultural engagement reaches maturity in Kaufman's views, where . . . a rationale has been articulated for dialogue and suasion between the church and culture. . . . In Kaufman's view, Christian love, nonresistant love, calls nation and neighbor to be authentic in their claim that they seek justice and peace. On the basis of this love, Christians can join others in the political or cultural arena in a common quest for truth. "Radical nonresistant discipleship . . . leads us into the world rather than away from it" (Kaufman 1979:102).

Friesen (1991:25) contends that Mennonitism in the "Russian trajectory" shied away from "nonresistance" or turned it into a reason for responsible participation in the political realm because of their experience in administering Russian Mennonite communities.

Brokers in Dialogue

We now explore selective exchanges between some of the key theological brokers across the spectrum. These episodes of dialogue between the brokers illustrate the emergent issues of the times. The stimulating interchange of ideas helps to clarify the various positions that were stirring the intellectual ferment of the late fifties and early sixties.

Compromise: Hershberger to Burkholder

The year 1958 was a remarkable, vintage year for Mennonite theology. Not only did Burkholder's dissertation and Kaufman's essay on "Nonresistance and Responsibility" appear, Hershberger (1958) also produced a new book, *The Way of the Cross in Human Relations*. The ferment of the fifties influenced Hershberger in ways that became evident in his new book. He directly addresses the Niebuhrian challenge of responsibility and indirectly Burkholder, whom he knew was writing about responsibility in his dissertation. Indeed, when Hershberger was writing the book, Burkholder told him "there is not one way of the cross but many conflicting crosses in ambiguous situations."

Hershberger indeed was changing. Love—the way of the cross—became his central concept. It sounded more outgoing and positive than nonresistance. And he was talking about responsibility, justice, and the lordship of Christ—but still from a traditional perspective. Several chapters in *The Way of the Cross in Human Relations* (1958) deal with the social gospel, Christian action, and political responsibility, as well as industrial and race relations. Hershberger was, in essence, responding to the moral issues surrounding social responsibility.

Writing about Reinhold Niebuhr's approach and the influences of neo-orthodoxy, Hershberger says that

> neo-orthodoxy in general has chosen the sinful social order as its frame of reference for social action rather than the New Testament ethic itself. . . . The best the Christian can do is to choose between the lesser of two evils or more evils. After saying many fine things about the Sermon on the Mount they usually conclude that in this world some other course is necessary, despite the fact that Jesus said: "You therefore, must be perfect, as your heavenly Father is perfect," and that Paul said: "Do not be overcome by evil, but overcome evil with good" (Hershberger, 1958:102-105).

Niebuhr assumed that involvement in the social order made it necessary to compromise. Hershberger counters that Christ provides a higher ethic of reconciliation. He worries that Niebuhr's ethical thinking accents the relativity of societal standards and downplays biblical and Christian norms.

Hershberger accepts John H. Yoder's (1955) critique of Niebuhr's view of pacifism. Yoder argued that choosing the lesser evil involves two fallacies. First, war is less harmful than tyranny. Second, responsibility between agents is not distinguished (it is the tyrant's fault, not the Christian's).

Accepting Yoder's critique, Hershberger (1958:115-118) argues that Niebuhr's answer to the human predicament is not the New Testament answer. The biblical ethic is based on the cross and resurrection, the church as the body of Christ, the need for individual regeneration, and the doctrine of the Holy Spirit—biblical resources which counter secular mores. For Hershberger, Niebuhr's ethics derive too much from the human predicament. Interestingly, Hershberger (1958:108, 114) cites two letters from J. Lawrence Burkholder (30 December 1953 and 16 January 1954) to bolster his arguments against Niebuhr.

> J. Lawrence Burkholder has pointed out the significant fact that in rejecting the absolute ethic of the New Testament in favor of a doctrine of relativity, the Christian Action group has virtually established a new absolute in its concept of social responsibility, a concept that if not given New Testament limits seems to demand the use of whatever means the evil social order itself approves for its own defense and perpetuation.

Although Hershberger was ready to address real social issues in new ways, his basic orientation remained unchanged. Nonresistance and faithfulness to the Bible remained the last words. He argued that justice was a "fruit of love and obedience," that "the Christian community was a colony of heaven," and as before he insisted that the Christian "responsibility is that of calling sinful men to repentance . . . the Christian does not exercise vengeance in order *to obtain justice*. He suffers, even lays down his life if need be, in order that he might *do justice* and bring reconciliation among men" (Hershberger, 1958:20). In short, Hershberger was still unwilling to compromise by using force to obtain justice.

Nonviolence: Burkholder to Hershberger

Nearly twenty years later Burkholder critiqued Hershberger in a short essay "Nonresistance, Nonviolent Resistance and Power" which appeared in *Kingdom, Cross, and Community* in 1976 to honor Hershberger. Burkholder primarily addresses the Hershberger of the forties. Although Hershberger's basic position remained unchanged, he was by now taking the world more seriously. In the later fifties and sixties he was influenced by Martin Luther King, Jr.'s nonviolent resistance without fully endorsing it. Burkholder, of course, had the benefit of reflecting on the civil rights movement and the Vietnam War.

J. Lawrence Burkholder (1976:132) chided Hershberger's tendency to understand "nonresistance as the determinative if not exclusive principle of peace." Burkholder contended that Hershberger insists that nonresistance . . . means that one does not resist in any way an enemy or those in power, even for the sake of justice.

He makes it abundantly clear that one does not resist for the sake of "getting justice" for oneself or others. Rather one "does justice" for others.

Nonresistance is really a way of life which is called "the way of the cross." . . . Cross-bearing takes the form of nonparticipation in the struggles of society—particularly struggles in the political arena. Nonresistance and cross-bearing become the search for neutrality.

Hershberger rejected nonviolent resistance like Gandhi's *satyagraha* because it used coercion to force the British to relinquish power. Thus Burkholder (1976:134) claims that Hershberger's hard distinction between nonresistance and nonviolent resistance

cuts the theoretical ground out from those who would participate directly in social action. The reason is simple enough—nonviolent resistance is resistance; resistance is a form of force; force is inadmissible in any form. . . . By exalting the absence of conflict rather than the peaceful resolution of conflict, it [nonresistance] encourages passivity.

Burkholder (1976:34) argues for both nonresistance and nonviolent resistance to enlarge the Christian's scope of activity in society. He agrees that Christ died a nonresistant death as a suffering servant showing the magnitude of love. However, he says,

We must distinguish between the nonresistance of the cross and what led to the cross. What led to the cross was an aggressive confrontation with the Jewish authorities in which Jesus criticized the status quo and presented himself as the legitimate ruler of Israel.

His entry into Jerusalem was provocative, and the cleansing of the temple was a most audacious, coercive act. Turning over the tables of the money-changers is, to be sure, not an instance of injurious violence, but it can hardly be said to be the expression of pure nonresistance (Burkholder, 1976:134).

Burkholder's Jesus was irritating the rulers, healing on the Sabbath, and criticizing the Pharisees—reflecting various forms of love. He was crucified as an insurrectionist because his confrontations with authorities had stirred so many to hatred.

Burkholder (1976:135) agrees that Jesus rejected destructive power and gave his life to nonviolence but argues that "Jesus resisted the authorities by use of various ways and by various means. *This leads then to the main point of this essay: namely, that the issue is not between nonviolence and nonresistance, but between violence and various forms of nonviolence.*"

Burkholder suggests that if Martin Luther King, Jr., had not resisted injustice he would probably be alive today. "The people who bear the cross today are those who try to change things. Ironically those who withdraw from world conflict as 'the way of the cross' seldom die on a cross" (Burkholder, 1976:136). Mennonites who witnessed the Russian revolution in the early 1900s might argue with him but, nevertheless, his point is credible. Burkholder (1976:136) thinks the church needs to learn "how to use power in a Christian way." It is a question that is "far more difficult than the question of how to be nonresistant. It means that we must learn how to relate love to the struggle for justice—a problem which was seldom faced positively by previous generations of Mennonites."

In Burkholder's mind, "Guy Hershberger and Harold Bender never wrestled with the questions of power." Summarizing his basic difference with Hershberger, Burkholder (1976:137) said, "Mennonites must move in theory from an absolutist ethic to an ethic that engages honestly the relativity of a complex reality."

Hershberger was not amused with Burkholder's critical essay. To Hershberger it was "an extremely warped interpretation that makes *War, Peace, and Nonresistance* a straw man to knock down." Hershberger felt Burkholder gave "the worst possible interpretation" to nonresistance and was trying to "develop a theoretical ethic to baptize the church's failure to live up to New Testament ethics."[24]

The differences between Hershberger and Burkholder focused around "compromise" and "nonviolent resistance." Hershberger contended for the pure "colony of Heaven" and feared that greater involvement in society would bring moral compromise. Burkholder thought Hershberger's nonresistance was too passive and endorsed nonviolent action for the sake of justice.

Responsibility: Kaufman to Yoder

Gordon Kaufman's (1958) original essay, "Nonresistance and Responsibility," was a direct response to John H. Yoder's (1954, 1955) assessment of Reinhold Niebuhr's pacifism. Kaufman (1958:5) hears Yoder insisting anew that serious disciples motivated by nonresistant love cannot participate in the power struggles of a non-Christian world. This implies, for Kaufman, that Christian ethics leads disciples away from "the deepest problem of society."

While Yoder "witnesses" to the state from the insights of agape ethics and hopes the state will improve its behavior, Kaufman argues that love never retreats from evil, but "advances into it totally without regard for itself." The more sinful the situation, the more imperative that love enter it. Kaufman writes that

> love is in fact not a "that" at all which can exist in and by itself; love exists only as a relationship in which one person gives or sacrifices everything in himself, not for those who deserve such sacrifice nor for those who love him, but just for those who would destroy him. . . . Love goes to the very heart of the most sinful situations that it can find, and there it gives of itself without any reservation whatsoever.

Kaufman (1979:81) agrees with Yoder (1955:113) that Christians hold some responsibility for the social order, a responsibility derived from Christian love. Kaufman, however, is uncomfortable with Yoder's discharge of social responsibility merely via "witness." Kaufman believes the radical requirements of love demand intervention into the most evil situations where love gives of itself without reservation. And while Yoder argues for witness, Kaufman respects the integrity of other persons and nations to decide what they consider in their best interest and then calls on Christians to support those decisions even if they violate pacifist convictions.

Furthermore, Kaufman (1979:81) disagrees with Yoder's (1955:114) contention that "right action can be identical for all" because it is so abstract as to be meaningless. Kaufman contends that "love always takes account of the concrete needs of the other toward which the action is directed and the situation or context of action." Kaufman's critique of Yoder underscores the need for the church, out of obedience to radical love, to enter into the heart of evil in the world. Kaufman (1961) elaborates the importance of the social context for such interventions in his book, *The Context of Decision*.

Relativism: Yoder to Kaufman

The debate between Yoder and Kaufman revolves around the church's responsibility in the world. Yoder's (1963:133-138) extensive review of Kaufman's book *The Context of Decision* sends several bouquets, saying it is "philosophically promising."

> Gordon Kaufman's Menno Simons lectures of 1959 could be analyzed as a novelty on the level of sociology. Seldom in North America have thinkers stemming genuinely from sociological Mennonitism taken a place within the broader Protestant intellectual world without some sort of break with their cultural rootage, and still less often, if ever, have they sought explicitly as does Kaufman in this volume to relate the ancestral and the wider worlds in fruitful conversation. . . . This approach is more

original than the lay reader is likely to recognize through the simplicity of the exposition. The present reviewer finds this approach helpful.

Yoder (1963:134) likes Kaufman's approach because he makes Jesus normative "in a way the brothers Niebuhr do not" and, true to Anabaptism, he focuses on the cross and its meaning. Yoder (1963:134) agrees that any serious Mennonite disciple would want to go to the heart of an evil situation, but he faults Kaufman for not providing advice on what to do upon arriving there.

For Yoder, Kaufman's radical love is too abstract because it doesn't prescribe appropriate action in a helpless situation. Yoder (1963:134) worries that Kaufman's abstract love will become unhitched from the norms of Jesus: "If redemptiveness means concern for the sinful and the needy, it means going where the sinner is; Kaufman therefore castigates, with good reason, Mennonites' search for ideal places to live and for ways of living which will pose them few moral problems."

While Yoder (1963:134) agrees with Kaufman's Christ-centered approach, he has difficulties following the outcome of such action, especially because Kaufman does not specify what to do in particular contexts.

> It seems to be implied (p. 94ff.), yet without samples and without demonstrations of the reasons, that self renunciation means also the sacrifice of one's moral commitments and the acceptance for oneself of ethical obligations which in themselves are in some sense "sinful." We know what this would mean from the pen of Hans Morgenthau or Reinhold Niebuhr; from Kaufman's it is only confusing. To go to the heart of any sinful situation, no serious Mennonite thinker would seek to avoid; but what should we do there? To give no situation up as hopeless is the gospel's demand; but how to decide what to do in the apparently hopeless situation is not thereby made clearer. In short, Kaufman leaves us wondering whether he criticizes Mennonites for betraying their own vision or for holding to it too faithfully.

Yoder is intrigued by Kaufman's attempt to provide more social context for Christian decision making, but he wants more specificity.

Yoder (1963:135) applauds Kaufman's call to providing a greater social context for the Christian church.

> Between his chapters on humanness in general and on the individual's making his own decision Kaufman inserts a treatment of "church and world". . . . The gospel is not a mere message; it is a continuum of loving relationship extending in a chain—imperfect, to be sure, but historically real—from Christ to those who today become recipients and givers of

love. The church is not an end in itself; it exists for the sake of the world. It is in fact nothing but transformed world. . . .

This rediscovery of the church both as an historical reality and as a pointer to the place of the agent's faith or non-faith as a factor in ethics, to say nothing of the missionary dimension, was sorely needed in American post-Niebuhrian ethics and brings Kaufman nearer not only to his own heritage but also to current European and ecumenical conversations. Again we greet Kaufman's originality and ask only whether he has fully exploited it. . . .

Yoder (1963:137-138) first challenges Kaufman not to react too much to his Mennonite heritage and fear of sectarianism, but to seek more uniformity. He says diversity is a mixed blessing which allows more tolerance but also brings too much relativity and potential confusion.

Second, Yoder (1963:135) contends that Kaufman neglects the role of the church in the context and process of deciding what to do in the sinful situation. Kaufman leaves the individual Christian making the decisions in the world "all by himself."

Third, Yoder thinks Kaufman's "world" is less rebellious than the biblical view of the world. Yoder in sectarian fashion sees the world more negatively—less likely to be "progressively transformed into the church" as Kaufman suggests. Moreover, Yoder (1963:138) says that Kaufman's cure for the "disease of sectarianism . . . is no cure for it confounds several kinds of diversity . . . that result from unfaithfulness, false doctrine and concrete disobedience."

Summary

The ferment of the fifties stretched the boundaries of Mennonite peacemaking in many directions. As plausibility structures were shifting, the theological brokers were busy creating new understandings of peacemaking that leaned on the past but which also addressed the new social realities of Mennonite life. Under the canopy of "the way of love" four major positions emerged ranging from sectarian caution to cultural engagement as typified by Hershberger, Yoder, Burkholder, and Kaufman.

Although all four of the theological brokers accepted "love" as their primary category for Christian ethics, it propelled them in four different directions. The embrace of love as a key moral directive was a turn from the passive nonresistance of the past. Love carried more credibility for Mennonites now entangled in new and often conflicting plausibility structures. The specialization incipient in modernity was nurturing a pluralism in Mennonite peacemaking.

Many features of "the way of love" garnered it credibility as Mennonites joined the modern world. First, it rang with biblical fidelity. Second, its advocates were rooted in the biblical heritage of Anabaptism. Third, it was positive and active—fitting for modern folks interested in addressing contemporary social issues.

Fourth, the concept of love linked Mennonite concerns for peacemaking into conversations with mainstream Protestants—the Niebuhrs and their disciples. Mennonites were no longer farmers clinging to simpleminded nonresistance. They were now conversing with the theological heavyweights—with the Niebuhrs and theologians representing the World Council of Churches in the Puidoux Conferences and in other ecumenical conversations.

Fifth, love in typical modern fashion was abstract. It provided a common language for a modicum of consensus, yet it was elastic enough to stretch over the proliferating pluralism of the Mennonite community.

Indeed, love permitted the four Mennonite ethicists to move to diverse spots across the separatist—engagement continuum. Advocating the way of love and nonresistance, Hershberger argued for an uncompromising New Testament ethic that was faithful to the way of the cross but wary of political participation. Yoder, heralding the ethics of agape love, called for witness to the social order while maintaining a somewhat sectarian stance in the "disciple community."

But it was also love that led Burkholder to social responsibility for the larger social order with all its ambiguities, compromises, and dilemmas. Moreover, it was radical love that pulled Kaufman to the very heart of the sinful situation, even when support of the outcome differed with his personal beliefs. In all of its diverse expressions, love provided a plausible ideological fit for the growing complexity of Mennonite peacemaking.

The civil rights movement pushed Mennonites toward more active forms of peacemaking. Martin Luther King, Jr. gave a lecture at Goshen College, Indiana, on March 10, 1960. Goshen professors Willard Smith (L), and Guy F. Hershberger (C) are pictured here with King.

CHAPTER FIVE

The Strident Sixties and Seventies

The sixties were years of conflict, revolution, and protest from which even rural Mennonites could no longer extricate themselves. In *Stride Toward Freedom* Martin Luther King, Jr., (1958) charted his nonviolent resistance to racial injustice. The famous Montgomery, Alabama, bus boycott of 1956 launched King's campaign which abruptly ended with his assassination in 1968.

In Canada, the death of Premier Duplessis in 1959 triggered Quebec's quiet revolution which escalated into the October crisis. This eventually led to the separatist movement of Rene Levesque and culminated in the 1980 independence referendum.

John F. Kennedy, the first Catholic and youngest U.S. President, was assassinated in 1963. The murders of King and Robert Kennedy followed in 1968. These racial, revolutionary, and national tragedies of the turbulent sixties were only the prelude, however, to America's Waterloo—Vietnam.

Strident Social Settings

This kaleidoscope of social conflict atop escalating modernization changed values, structures, and visions forever. Mennonites were no longer immune to change. Civil unrest had arrived at their doorstep in those heady times. The baby boom bulge also brought more mouths to feed, schools to build, and jobs to fill. Opportunities blended with aspirations and visions for drastic societal changes. The older Mennonite wineskins were no longer able to contain the ferment.

King's Stride Toward Freedom

On December 1, 1955, Rosa Parks, a seamstress, boarded a downtown Montgomery bus and sat in the first available seat (King, 1958:1). Tired from long hours on her feet, she refused to move to the back of the bus to make room for whites as Negroes (as they were then called) were expected to do. Her arrest triggered the famous Montgomery bus boycott. Black people in Montgomery were mobilized. Some 7,000 leaflets were distributed in the segregated black community asking members to boycott the buses. Monday morning buses, typically packed to capacity, now ran empty. The black revolution had begun.

Martin Luther King, Jr., with a recent Ph.D. from Boston University, had taken the pastorate of the Dexter Avenue Baptist Church in Montgomery, Alabama, in the fall of 1954. He soon led the Southern Christian Leadership Conference, which spearheaded the civil rights movement. In *Stride Toward Freedom* King outlines his "pilgrimage to nonviolence" via Gandhi's call to nonviolent suffering and Jesus' agape love. In King's (1958:84-85) words,

> Agape is not a weak, passive love. It is love in action. Agape is love seeking to preserve and create community. . . . Agape is a willingness to sacrifice in the interest of mutuality. Agape . . . doesn't stop at the first mile, but it goes the second mile to restore community. It is a willingness to forgive, not seven times, but seventy times seven to restore community. . . .

Mennonites could understand the words "agape," "community," and "love" spoken by this black Baptist preacher. Soon Mennonites Elmer Neufeld, from Chicago's so-called black belt, and Guy Hershberger, representing the MC Peace Problems Committee, visited the deep South. They contacted King and the Southern Christian Leadership Conference. Leo Driedger, Executive Secretary of the GC Peace and Social Concerns Committee, appeared on a panel with Martin Luther King, Jr., in Louisiana to discuss the black voter registration drive in the South.[1] Nonresistant Mennonites found King's movement to be nonviolent and Christian but were wary of his impatience, as expressed in *Why We Can't Wait* (1964).

The rising tide of civil rights—gaining momentum after the bus boycott of 1956—posed new questions for nonresistant Mennonites. Could they quietly stand by and merely pray in the face of racial discrimination? Should nonresistant Christians *resist* civil laws that permitted and perpetuated racial discrimination? While Reinhold Niebuhr seemed too action-oriented for many Mennonites, Dietrich

Bonhoeffer's "costly discipleship" struck a responsive chord.

King seemed willing to follow Bonhoffer's course. In 1968 as the GC Peace and Social Concerns Committee met in New York, they were interrupted by the news of King's assassination. That night as U.S. cities burned, members of the committee joined the crowds milling on Times Square under the watchful eyes of scores of police on almost every corner.[2]

Racial Immersion in Chicago

A cluster of Mennonites had felt the agonies of racial injustice before King's stride to freedom. In 1945 the GCs had located their Mennonite Biblical Seminary (MBS) in the heart of Chicago. Situated in the Woodlawn area near the University of Chicago, MBS affiliated with Bethany Biblical Seminary (Church of the Brethren) until 1958 when MBS moved to Elkhart, Indiana.[3] The Woodlawn community in these thirteen years changed from a white neighborhood to virtually all black. The Woodlawn Mennonite Church on the seminary campus was racially integrated, with both white and black pastors.

White seminary students, preparing for pastoral ministry at MBS, had firsthand experience with blacks—often for the first time. Schools, playground activities, and other community events were racially integrated. The GC Mission Board located its "Mission House" across the street so missionaries on furlough could study, worship, and work in a black context.

The seminary served as a halfway house for rural Mennonites who were entering the big city for the first time. MBS hosted conferences, seminars, evening classes, and informal meetings for the diverse Mennonite community in the heart of Chicago's so-called black belt. This immersion in urbanization prepared the way, especially for GC Mennonites, for greater involvement in the strident sixties—including social responsibility toward other races and the poverty of the inner city.

Located near the University of Chicago, the seminary community attracted Mennonites who attended the university, served in alternative service, or worked in the city. E. G. Kaufman and J. Winfield Fretz were among the first Mennonites to receive Ph.Ds from the University. A host of Chicago university students would eventually become church leaders—Stanley Bohn, Leo Driedger, C. J. Dyck, Vincent Harding, Howard Kauffman, Robert Kreider, Elmer Neufeld, John Oyer, Calvin Redekop, Don Smucker, Alden Voth, and others.

Many leaders and pastors took apprenticeships in Chicago and later fanned out into local congregations, schools, and institutions, carry-

ing new sensitivities about racism with them.⁴ Delton and Marian
Franz, pastoral leaders in the Woodlawn congregation, later went to
Washington, D.C., where Delton directed the MCC Washington Office and Marian headed the campaign for a Peace Tax Fund. Black
Mennonite pastor Vincent Harding, also from the Woodlawn congregation, began challenging Mennonite students and leaders to link
their nonresistant tradition with the civil rights movement. Indeed,
one observer speculates that "Vince did more to convert many Mennonites to active nonviolent peacemaking (a la King) than any of the
theologians or official pronouncements of the church!"

Vietnam as Waterloo

Alongside racial turbulence, the divisive war in Vietnam also prodded Mennonites toward active peacemaking. When the French were
defeated at Dien Bien Phu in 1954, the Americans sought to save the
southern half of Vietnam from communist rule. But by 1968, 525,000
American soldiers could not stop the Tet offensive.

The Americans had mobilized their military machine but Saigon
fell in 1975 at a staggering cost of 1.7 million dead, 3 million wounded,
and 13 million refugees. In Levant's (1988:2263) words "The U.S.
dropped 7 million tons of bombs, 75 million liters of herbicide, lost
10,000 helicopters and warplanes . . . 56,000 U.S. soldiers . . . with
303,000 wounded . . . at a cost of $140 billion . . . indirect costs esti-
mated at $900 billion." It was the United States' first military defeat.

Vietnam was an unpopular war. Carnage and torture streamed
across TV screens in North American living rooms day after day. Na-
palm incendiary bombs smashed villages and mutilated the bodies of
innocent Vietnamese. The herbicide Agent Orange defoliated massive
forests to expose the enemy. David and Goliath were at it again and
Goliath lost. The American military draft continued into the seventies,
forcing Mennonite youth to make choices about peace. Many opted
for alternative service, but some refused registration and/or induction. John A. Lapp (1970a:23) says that by 1969 some 10,186 Mennonite conscientious objectors had completed alternative service assignments and 7,641 were currently in such assignments.

Frank Epp (1970:7) estimated that 60,000 Americans fleeing the
draft entered Canada in the sixties, and still more came in the seventies. Epp, editor of *The Canadian Mennonite*, flew to Vietnam and returned home to speak about its horrors in many churches. In those
years numerous U.S. draft dodgers stayed in Canadian Mennonite
homes for weeks or months. Some returned home but many became

Canadian citizens (Epp, 1970). In *I Would Like to Dodge the Draft Dodgers, But* Epp (1970) documents some of these experiences. Later he chaired the MCC Peace Section.

The heart-rending conflict between youth fleeing an unjust war and their patriotic parents is poignantly illustrated in this mother's letter to her deserter son.

> Dear Greg:
> What can I say to a son who has become a deserter and traitor . . . a sucker for the easy way out . . . to live with the scum of the U.S. . . . . I don't think you are capable of real love for anyone . . . it would be more merciful if you had killed all of us. . . . No, you didn't hurt us—you killed us. . . . As far as we are concerned you are DEAD. . . ." (Epp, 1970:95).

These were the agonies and legacies of the Vietnam war—an undeclared war, thousands of miles from home, in which millions were shamed.

Quebecois Nationalism in Canada

In Canada, Premier Duplessis' death in 1959 ushered in a new age of urbanization and industrialization in Quebec. Major struggles for power occurred between old and new elites and between Francophones and Anglophones over language, culture, economics, and politics (Linteau, 1988:1810). Mennonites in western Canada should have understood well the pangs of urban transition experienced by the rural French in Quebec, but few did because the Mennonites knew little French, having opted for the English of their neighbors.

In 1976, Rene Levesque's Parti Quebecois (PQ) came into power in Quebec, with the intent to separate from Canada. Bill 101 made French the sole official language of Quebec. A 1980 referendum on sovereignty, however, was defeated with 60 percent voting against separation from Canada (Archibald, 1988:1625).[5] By 1985 the PQ had lost power to the Liberals.

The constitutional crisis, however, continued unabated into the nineties. Like other Canadians, Mennonites followed the political struggle as various regions sought to gain an upper hand in this fragile federation. Canadian ethnic groups celebrating their "cultural mosaic" and its diversity are less prone to assimilation than their U.S. counterparts.

Canadians differ from U.S. citizens in other ways as well. With nationalized health care, transportation systems like Air Canada and Canadian National Railways, and socialized insurance in some provinces, Canadians are vastly affected by government programs. In contrast to their American cousins, Canadian Mennonites, in a middle-power country with limited military might, view the state more as benefactor than as military giant.

The Mennonite Response

In tandem with the turbulence of the sixties, the internal character of the modern state was also changing. Still bearing swords, even nuclear ones, modern Caesars were supporting a new array of benevolent activities. In the aftermath of the Depression, North American governments rapidly expanded their social welfare functions. Canadian and U.S. democracies were not merely friendly, they were doing good and offering Mennonites opportunities to do good as well through the channels of civil service.

Moreover, Mennonite institutions—colleges and mental health centers—were beginning to feed at the trough of federal aid. In cooperation with the U.S. government Mennonites operated alternate service programs from 1952 to 1975 which involved some 15,000 Mennonite and Brethren in Christ men.[6] Conscientious objectors served in the "I-W program" in lieu of military service. Many worked in hospitals and other public agencies while others entered voluntary service programs. All of these activities increased Mennonite involvements with the state.

International tensions also stirred new interest in Mennonite understandings of the state. The Korean conflict, the Cold War rhetoric, the nuclear arms race, and the brewing war in Vietnam prodded Mennonites to rethink their relationship to the state. The convergence of these domestic and international events made the sixties and seventies a turbulent time for Mennonite peacemaking. Living in democratic societies that espoused freedom of religion, welcomed religious minorities, and respected conscientious objectors was eroding the historic cleavage between church and state in Mennonite minds. The plausibility structures of a benign democracy made it difficult to sustain a strict separatism. These changing social conditions forged new, dramatic revisions of nonresistance.

Responsibility and the State

Debate about the church's responsibility in the larger social order had animated Mennonite theologians in the late fifties. The spotlight in the early sixties however shifted to a specific sector of responsibility—the state.[7] The code word "responsibility" was replaced with "witness" and Mennonites could discharge some of their social responsibilities by "witnessing to the state." No longer "irresponsible sectarians," they now began to call the state to the high standards of God's righteousness for the benefit of all. A paper by Elmer Neufeld bridged the transition from social responsibility to witness to the state. Neufeld shifted the focus to the state and paved the way for the growing accent on "witness."

The Mennonite Central Committee—especially its Peace Section—was rapidly becoming the voice for inter-Mennonite peace concerns. Neufeld's paper, presented at a 1957 MCC conference on "Christian Responsibility to the State," outlined the new Mennonite posture toward the state.[8] An observer at the conference noted that Neufeld's approach, "united all of us including the most conservative and most liberal. There was an element that touched most of us."[9] However, when Neufeld's paper was published in the MQR in 1958, the voice of an urban Mennonite sounded worrisome to rural Goshen ears. Harold Bender's (1958:82, 110) editorial warned that his conclusions may sound "quite radical."

Neufeld (1958:143) affirmed the classic two kingdom dichotomy but then asserted, "we have used a legitimate and important teaching (separation from the world) to escape responsibilities that are clearly ours within the gospel of Christ." Neufeld had served with the National Service Board for Religious Objectors in Washington, D.C. His encounter with political and military personnel as well as Christian lobbyists in the nation's capital formed his "radical" views.

Neufeld (1958:142) lamented that

> we freely testified in defense of our own religious liberties but had little to say about the liberties of others. Still ringing in my ears are the words of a now-deceased army colonel: "You Mennonites are fine folk to get along with. We like you. It would be nice if there were more people like you. But . . . you do nothing about sin, about social wrong, about corruption in government, about international tensions, etc."

Neufeld's involvement in Washington, his dialogue with academics at the University of Chicago, and his experience living in the "Mission House" in Chicago's black community had ruptured the plausibility of passive nonresistance.

Neufeld's (1958:144-150) article began with a theological analysis, reflected on Richard Niebuhr's (1951) *Christ and Culture*, and then proposed fifteen principles to guide Mennonites in political situations (summarized in Table 5.1). He grounded his argument in the biblical tradition of Hershberger and Bender but clearly endorsed greater political responsibility.

TABLE 5.1
Neufeld's Principles for Christian Responsibility in the Political Order

---

1. View with caution human attempts to limit social responsibility.
2. Study the Scriptures for criteria to guide political involvements.
3. The kingdom of Christ should not be identified with social or political programs.
4. Christians should not resort to non-Christian moral standards for guidance in the political arena.
5. Nonresistant Christians cannot perform the functions of government that resort to military force.
6. Since separation from culture is impossible, faithfulness to God, not separation, should guide involvements.
7. Christians can participate in vast areas of government that involve welfare activities.
8. Allegiance to Christ may involve social and political responsibilities.
9. Political involvement should be motivated by a ministry of reconciliation—not personal enhancement.
10. The ministry of reconciliation includes evangelism and preaching, as well as compassion for those in physical, social, and emotional need.
11. Christians should be concerned for the personal reconciliation of individuals in government alongside political objectives.
12. Social situations and times vary and political participation must be adapted to the times.
13. The Christian who participates in the political realm should expect tensions and compromises and should participate with a sense of contingency.
14. Political involvement has limitations, so Christians especially should look for nonpolitical ways to be politically relevant.
15. Christians who participate in the political arena should expect differences of opinion, uncertainty, and ambiguity.

Adapted from Elmer Neufeld (1958:141-162).

Hoping to avert being bogged down in sectarian solitude on the one hand, and in the quicksand of Niebuhr's "compromises" and "ambiguities" on the other, Neufeld embraced greater political responsibility—based on the gospel call for evangelism and outreach—which in turn led to a "witness to the state." Neufeld's proactive stance, grounded in the gospel, called for reconciling initiatives even in the political arena.

Witness to the Powerful

In a short span of eight years (1961-68) Mennonites devoted an astonishing level of attention to church-state relations. A 1961 GC conference, held in the Chicago YMCA hotel, resulted in a 1963 publication titled "Christian Responsibility in Society." The MCs likewise issued a major statement on "The Christian Witness to the State" in 1961. In the same year, the MCC Peace Section sponsored its first "Washington Seminar" on church-state relations for its constituent groups. And Bethel College students also appeared in Washington in 1961 to protest nuclear weapons and the arms buildup.

A year later the MCC Peace Section declared that "Christian Witness to the State is a new frontier that we are entering cautiously" (Epp and Epp, 1984:10). John H. Yoder's *The Christian Witness to the State* appeared in 1964, the same year that MCC's Peace Section organized a study of church-state relations involving 150 persons across the U.S. and Canada. Participants met in twelve discussion groups that gathered more than eighty times under the growing shadow of the Vietnam conflict. The conversations culminated in a Church-State Relations Conference sponsored by MCC in October 1965.

For several days in May 1965, Mennonite leaders joined other religious delegates in Washington, D.C., to witness against the war in Vietnam. Two months later the GC general conference issued a resolution on Vietnam containing three specific proposals to the U. S. government. The MC general conference, in August 1965, fired off a telegram to President Lyndon Johnson. Mindful of their "mandate . . . to witness . . . to the righteousness which God requires of all men and nations," the telegram registered "deep concern" about the morality of the U.S. policy in Vietnam. A year later in 1966 an MCC gathering issued nine guidelines for "witnessing to government."[10]

The focus on the state continued as MC leaders met in 1967 with John H. Yoder to discuss church-state issues and grieve "about the dreadful silence that we exercise in relation to the evils of our society."

A few months later, in September of 1967, the MC general conference asked a special church-state subcommittee, deliberately reflecting widely divergent constituent views, to grapple with the emerging church-state issues. Committee members wrestled with the issues in four different meetings for "eight full days," then reported their agreement to disagree in a public meeting in Archbold, Ohio, in the spring of 1970.[11]

The crescendo of interest in witnessing to the state culminated in 1968 with the establishment of a "Washington Office." Under the aegis of MCC the new office hoped to observe, equip constituent groups, and "seek to understand how . . . biblical teachings on nonresistance and love may aid the government in better establishing justice . . . and minimizing the effects of evil."

The word "witness" does not appear in the rationale for the "listening post" but surely was a motivating factor in establishing the first Mennonite office in the corridors of power—an effort director Delton Franz would some twenty years later call a Mennonite "lobby."[12] A similar office was opened in the Canadian capital of Ottawa in 1975. Some 55 percent of Mennonites and Brethren in Christ favored such "listening posts" in 1972 and by 1989 their support had climbed to 72 percent.

Three key statements issued by Mennonite groups in the sixties— "The Christian Witness to the State" (MC 1961), "Church-State Relations" (MCC 1965), and "Faithfulness to Christ in Situations of International Conflict" (MCC 1966)—reveal a major paradigm shift in Mennonite peacemaking. The theological brokers had restructured nonresistance in credible ways in the context of new plausibility structures—urban and educated Mennonites, benevolent welfare democracies, the civil rights movement, and the brewing conflict in Vietnam.

The prominence of the word *witness* bridged the gulf between conservative Mennonites and those pressing for action. A cherished word, witness was mined from the vocabulary of Mennonite mission efforts which were highly regarded across the church. Its new use in church-state relations legitimated the efforts of the activists with some conservatives and also reminded the activists that they were not merely playing political games but were indeed religious envoys.

The traditionalists, in essence, permitted the church to intensify political activism if it could be pushed under the canopy of witness. The activists agreed to call their activity "witnessing" in order to receive theological legitimation. And surely most of the voices calling for witness did so out of genuine faithfulness to the Christian gospel.

In any event, the use of witness was an ingenious way of restructuring traditional Mennonite convictions to legitimate political activism in the context of rapid changes both in the church and the larger society. Mennonites remained unwilling to fight on behalf of the state but under the rubric of witness they could now, in the words of the conservatives, "tell the government what to do."[13]

The MC Peace Problems Committee had appointed a subcommittee in 1959 to reexamine its peace theology, "because we seem to be moving into new territory. . . . We must move ahead . . . not sliding or drifting by a current over which we have no control."[14] The subcommittee prepared a thirty-two page report which proposed using the lordship of Christ as a viable concept to push their witness forward. After debating the report for a day the full committee declared that it "opened a new area of witness for nonresistant Christians; and that the new territory should be surveyed and occupied."[15] The MCs occupied the new conceptual territory by drafting a major statement which their General Conference approved with little opposition in 1961.[16]

The 1961 MC statement, "The Christian Witness to the State," diverged from the traditional two-kingdom view. The brokers had erected a new theological canopy—the lordship of Christ—that stretched above *both* church and state. The state served as "the minister of God for good" but also as an "agent of the principalities and powers of darkness . . . in rebellion against the lordship of Christ."

Called rebellious five times, the state was now viewed as "an agent of the forces arrayed against the Lord of history." The 1961 statement, in modern fashion, also recognized the ambiguous character of the state. The most evil state "is in some sense a minister of God for good," and even the best state is "in some sense an agent of the rebellious powers."

The prophetic witness envisioned by MCs in 1961 called the rebellious powers to "follow the righteousness which God requires of all men." No longer kneeling hat in hand and pleading for special privileges, the statement called Mennonites "continually" to challenge statesmen "to seek the highest meanings of such values and concepts as justice, equality, freedom, and peace."

And how should the church discharge its prophetic witness under the lordship of Christ? Any means were acceptable if they were "consistent with New Testament teaching and the historic Anabaptist Mennonite Vision"—an ambiguous phrase that both muffled conservative skeptics and opened the door for activists.

One Moral Standard

A church-state conference convened by MCC in 1965 issued a lengthy statement that *never* mentions nonresistance but clearly rejects coercion. The text is filled, however, with references to "the lordship of Christ," "the righteousness of God," "prophetic witness," "God's sovereignty," and "the kingdom of God." Christians express their love for their country when they "challenge national leaders to seek . . . justice, equality, freedom, and peace . . . [and] constantly witness to the righteousness which God requires of all men."

Conference participants also welcomed the welfare functions of the state which stretched beyond the "shadow of the sword." They condoned participation in this new "middle ground of cooperation," but warned that it remained an "unredeemed battleground, a world of conflict and temptation."

The conference concluded that Christians should not split their lives into sacred and secular spheres, but "recognize Christ's lordship and glorify him in *all* of their activities." The lordship of Christ provided a *single* standard of morality (the righteousness of God) to which all persons, nations, and governments were called. In addition, it opened the door to the corridors of political power by blurring the lines between sacred and secular.

Growing hostilities in Vietnam produced another MCC conference in December 1966. Some eighty participants struggled with "Faithfulness to Christ in situations of international conflict." A findings report, peppered with "witness to government," included nine specific "guidelines for witnessing to government." The text frequently mentions "all relationships," "all men," "all Christians," and "the righteousness and justice of God to which all men will be held accountable."

Instead of implying a single ethical standard the December statement boldly declared it. "Our emphasis on *one morality* reflects our conviction that the Christ who is the one way of salvation is at the same time the norm under whose judgment *all men* stand. Although the world and the state fall below this norm, *all* nevertheless stand under its judgment."[17] Nonresistance was missing from the text.

A month later, in January 1967, the MCC Peace Section noted that the findings committee had little time to prepare its December statement. So in January a new "Message on Nonresistance" was released to constituent peace committees. "Nonresistance" suddenly appeared five times in the January message and the reference to "one morality" disappeared. The message concluded that "any witness to the secular order should be *modest and selective.*"[18] The dramatic difference between the December statement and the January "Message on Nonresistance" reflected a gap between visionary leaders writing the first statement and the more conservative local peace committees who received the January "message."

Acknowledging doctrinal disagreements, the January message noted that "the diversity of our interpretations of the meaning of nonresistance" undercuts the moral authority of Peace Section to speak with clarity. Nevertheless, the message affirmed that nonresistant Christians have a "special responsibility" to make a "distinctive witness" to governments regarding war and peace. The message ended with a tepid plea, "If this understanding is shared by Mennonite and Brethren in Christ Churches, we request . . . prayer . . . finances, patience . . . and guidance toward a more adequate definition of our mandate." Leaders were playing both to urbanites who demanded more action and to rural constituencies who were content to pray.

The single moral standard of God's righteousness to which Mennonites were now giving witness broadened the scope of their peace concerns. For example, both MCs and GCs issued a statement in 1965 opposing capital punishment. MCC followed with a similar statement in 1978. Statements on abortion, race relations, and international development also evidenced the widening scope of peace concerns.[19]

The Lordship of Christ Canopy

The prominent accent on "witness to the state" in the sixties hinged on a major theological transformation—perhaps the most significant of the century for church-state relations. The prominence of the "lordship of Christ" produced a paradigm shift that revolutionized Mennonite thinking about the state.[20] Prior to the fifties, Mennonites who accepted a traditional two-kingdom view looked across a cultural moat separating their peaceful kingdom from the sword-bearing kingdoms of this world. At times on their knees, they looked up to the monarchs of this world and pleaded for special privileges. The erection of the lordship canopy in Mennonite consciousness brought a dramatic change in position and perspective as shown in Figure 5.1.

The kingdoms of this world suddenly dropped in esteem. They were now viewed sometimes as agents of rebellious principalities and powers—disobedient to the high standards of God's righteousness which God required of *all* under the lordship of Christ. No longer looking across the moat of separation, Mennonites were now looking *down* to the rebellious agents of darkness, and giving a "prophetic witness." They called the rebellious powers to live *up* to the holiness and righteousness of God, to the Lord of history to whom "all men were accountable." Mennonites, in brief, had demythologized the state.

The theological construction of the new canopy—the lordship of Christ—was a paradigm shift of major proportions. It revised Mennonite understandings of the state, led to a restructuring of nonresistance, and shaped the mode of Mennonite peacemaking for the rest of the century. The lordship of Christ language was ingenious. It tapped the reservoir of Anabaptist heritage and reappropriated it in plausible ways in the modern setting. Moreover, it provided a theological rationale, rooted in Anabaptist thought, that would serve as a sacred canopy to legitimate activist forms of peacemaking which in time would change the character of nonresistance.

Proponents of the lordship of Christ argued that the new concept had "not blurred the line between the two kingdoms." Indeed, they hoped it "sharpened the line and added meaning and strength to the concept of Lordship."[21] The theological reconstruction permitted Mennonites to have their theological cake and eat it too! The new concept maintained a sectarian line between those who accepted and rejected the "lordship of Christ." But by stretching the lordship canopy over *both* church and state, the church could now urge the state to be more just, "with the confidence" that its urgings were "an expression of God's claim on the state." Mennonites who had worried about their social responsibilities in the fifties could now discharge them by witnessing to God's righteousness.

The canopy was staked in central Anabaptist affirmations, including the centrality of Christ, the New Testament Scriptures, the primacy of the church, and the ultimate pledge that "we ought to obey God rather than man." But the canopy was also pegged in the modern world. It was abstract and elastic—a single-ethic canopy—no longer staked on simplistic ideas of separation. The new canopy captured a broad middle ground of support by reaffirming the primacy of the church without advocating classic Mennonite separatism.

Moreover, the lordship of Christ and the righteousness of God fit the plausibility structures of a participatory democracy. Acculturated Mennonites could participate in the political order as modern citizens under the rubric of the lordship of Christ. The lordship of Christ provided an ideological legitimation for Mennonites who were *already* involved in social and political realms far beyond the confines of rural Mennonite communities. By engaging in prophetic witness, disciples could call elected officials to accountability—to the high standards of

---

FIGURE 5.1
Conceptual differences between the "two-kingdom"
view and the lordship of Christ canopy

---

a. The two kingdoms with dual moral standards

Within the Perfection of Christ   Beyond the Perfection of Christ

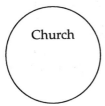
Church

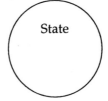
State

b. The lordship of Christ with a single moral standard

Lordship of Christ

(the righteousness of God)

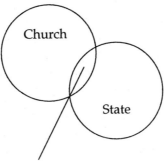
Church

State

Middle ground of cooperation

God's righteousness. Indeed, this was "the great responsibility" of the church, in the words of the 1961 MC statement.

No longer the quiet in the land, Mennonites could now under the shadow of the lordship of Christ noisily implore the nation to repeal the laws of racial discrimination and to stop the bombing in Vietnam.

And Mennonites could even work within political channels, holding public office and helping to achieve God's righteousness within the political system since *all* systems were under the shadow of the lordship canopy. Although the state was under the lordship of Christ, it certainly did not mean that Mennonites were willing to do anything in the name of the state. When appeals and political participation failed to nudge the rebellious powers toward God's righteousness, prophetic witness might take the form of active resistance—a reality that loomed large in the late sixties.

An added benefit of the paradigm shift was ecumenical solidarity. The major groups within the Mennonite fold were comfortable with the currency of "the lordship of Christ," a theme that offered amiable access to the larger ecumenical community as well. In all these ways the brokers had constructed a conceptual triumph by staking the new canopy in both Anabaptist and modern turf.

The Rise of Activism

Prodded by the civil rights movement, the counterculture revolution, and the war in Vietnam, Mennonite witness to the state sometimes took strident forms in the late sixties and early seventies. These included greater political activism, nonviolent action, and civil disobedience. The turbulence of the times swept across Mennonite churches as well. A spirit of revolution and dissent filled the air. The ideas of social responsibility and the lordship of Christ, earlier percolating in scholarly circles, now became embodied in Mennonite activism.

The tumult of the times brought growing political activism—voting, civil service, and officeholding. Some Mennonites, of course, had been politically active throughout the twentieth century, but the cauldron of the sixties and seventies boosted political activism. The quiet in the land believed that Jesus called them to walk the lowly paths of humility and long-suffering love. They taught separation from the world, obedience and respect to government, a meek and mild manner. They categorically rejected the use of force in human relations. Thus the political realm was largely uncharted terrain.

Political Activism

Mennonites, especially in Canada, were rapidly moving into civil service roles—a shift Frank Epp (1968:180) endorsed in *Mennonite Life* when he argued that civil service was *not* "a break with the Mennonite position on nonresistance." Such involvement, Epp contended, did not depart from the European Anabaptist tradition although it was "perhaps of a different degree and/or at a different level."

In the U.S., voting among conservative Mennonites was spurred by the fear of a Catholic sitting in the White House when John F. Kennedy ran in 1960. In Kansas, Mennonite James Juhnke ran unsuccessfully for Congress in 1970 on the Democratic ticket as a "peace" candidate who called for "rapid and complete" withdrawal from Vietnam.[22]

Greater participation in regional and national politics flowed with the tide of accommodation. The growing acceptance of television brought political issues into Mennonite living rooms. Heightened political activity did not directly violate the precepts of nonresistance, but it did place Mennonites in a wider berth of roles that sometimes entailed the use of force and coercive power. The growing involvement of Mennonites in political activities will be charted more extensively in chapter 8 which deals with political participation.

Other Mennonites became involved in more strident activities—signing petitions, promoting letter-writing campaigns, sending telegrams and delegations to elected representatives, and participating in public demonstrations. As early as 1959, GC Mennonites in Kansas joined in a letter-writing campaign to President Eisenhower protesting plans to install an ICBM missile base some ten miles north of Bethel College (Bush, 1990:226).

Although the nuclear arms buildup and the civil rights movement in the sixties prodded some Mennonites to act, the Vietnam War stirred many others into action. Official statements issued by church bodies in the late sixties and early seventies, crafted now under the umbrella of the lordship of Christ, echoed with critical tones and explicit directives for public policy.

Some Mennonites challenged immoral and oppressive government policies—laws that endorsed racial discrimination and the war in Indochina. Mennonites who engaged in such public activities were typically acting, as citizens in a democratic state, on behalf of the victims of discriminatory laws and military policies. Such activists were not merely protecting vested Mennonite interests but were seeking to use their influence as citizens to make their country and the world a better place through political action.

Nonviolent Action

For other Mennonites, telegrams, petitions, and delegations were not enough. Both the civil rights movement and the Vietnam War prompted provocative public action. As early as 1957 Paul Peachey (1957), writing in the *Gospel Herald*, gently blessed direct action as a form of witness against racial discrimination. Two years later Edgar

Metzler (1959) challenged traditional compliance with military conscription by calling on Mennonites to refuse registration with Selective Service.

In the spring of 1959 John R. Burkholder joined a public vigil at Fort Detrick, Maryland, to protest the preparation and production of germ warfare. By January Burkholder (1960), in a paper entitled "Radical Pacifism Challenges the Mennonite Church," was urging the church to "give serious consideration to radical protest, direct action if you will, as a necessary part of its evangelistic and prophetic peace testimony."[23]

Eventually small numbers of Mennonites turned to public demonstrations, symbolic direct action, marching with civil rights advocates, eating in segregated restaurants, burning draft cards, hanging Uncle Sam in effigy, washing the American flag, pouring blood on draft files, and trespassing on nuclear weapons facilities. Although relatively few Mennonites engaged in such confrontations, the brashness of the few irritated some elders because public provocation—especially civil disobedience—went far beyond the proprieties of traditional nonresistance.

Although most Mennonites remained out of the tumult, those on the radical flank fanned controversy across the churches and forced a crisis upon historic nonresistance. Indeed, the tremors of the sixties threatened to push the timid of the land into assertive peacemaking or what their conservative critics called "militant nonresistance" (Shank, 1970:7). Calls for forceful direct action, participation in boycotts, sit-ins, and marches—which broke local laws and agitated authorities—were quite different from passing virtuous resolutions at church conferences on pleasant summer days in the company of friends. This was a defining moment in the reconstruction of nonresistance, as meek and peaceful elders listened to their offspring argue that faithfulness to Christ and the Anabaptist heritage compelled them to defy civil authorities.

Few Mennonites lived in large cities, few in Southern states, and fewer still were black. Thus for many Mennonites racial tensions were skirmishes in faraway places. The glaring injustice of racial discrimination, however, fermented Mennonite activism and further eroded the plausibility of passive nonresistance.

In a stirring message, black Mennonite pastor Vincent Harding challenged participants at the Mennonite World Conference at Amsterdam in 1967 to care about civil rights. Mennonites were willing to plead and petition civil authorities on behalf of their own conscientious convictions, but would they protest, march, and even break laws on behalf of others who were suffering obvious discrimination?[24] Would nonresistance provide a convenient detour, a ready excuse, from moral responsibility?

Earlier some Mennonite leaders, students, and pastors headed south where they had joined in protest marches. Several were arrested and jailed for a brief time—including J. Lawrence Burkholder and Vincent Harding. Few Mennonites, however, were mobilized to protest. Most remained content to pass statements condemning racism and to read the lively debate in denominational papers about the implications of nonresistance for the civil rights movement.

In the *Gospel Herald* alone, some 114 articles on race relations appeared between 1957 and 1969, peaking with twenty-four in 1965 (Kremer, 1974). Martin Luther King's effective use of nonviolent action and Vincent Harding's persistent voice pressed Mennonites to ask if the use of nonviolent force for the sake of social justice was compatible with the gospel of peace. King's visit to Goshen College in 1960 forced some Mennonites to face the issue squarely.[25]

Even Guy Hershberger, in his 1968 preface to the third edition of *War, Peace, and Nonresistance*, confessed that his treatment of pacifism would have been quite different had he been exposed to King earlier. As early as 1960 Hershberger (1960:578) had called King "a Christian pacifist who sincerely seeks to follow Christ." Hershberger argued for "kindly persuasion" and "long-suffering love," and even opened the door to civil disobedience when he said nonresistance should not be "confused with obedience to all laws." The civil rights movement, although directly involving few Mennonites, cracked the credibility of nonresistance and led some to consider—even endorse—civil disobedience on behalf of *others* who were the victims of unjust laws.

Noncooperation with the Draft

If the civil rights movement impinged only tangentially on Mennonites, the Vietnam War touched them personally. Sons were drafted and Mennonite tax dollars, filling U.S. coffers, helped to fuel the war. Mennonites became incensed about the war for several reasons. Some one hundred Mennonite mission and service representatives working in Vietnam since 1954 fed a steady stream of firsthand critiques of the war to the Mennonite community via church agencies and denominational papers.

Budding activists Gene Stoltzfus and Doug Hostetter were some of dozens who witnessed the carnage firsthand and quickly grasped the concrete implications of "foreign policy." Many Mennonites, out of sincere commitments to nonresistance and the way of peace, felt compelled to speak out as American imperialism devastated a country and its people. And for once they were on the right side of history—pacifism was popular.

These factors pushed some Mennonite leaders to act. In 1970 "dozens of Mennonites filled the halls of Congress" to protest the U.S. bombing of Cambodia. A delegation of seven Mennonite and Brethren in Christ leaders representing the MCC Peace Section delivered a "Declaration of Conscience" to congressional representatives in June of 1972. They harshly criticized U.S. involvement in Vietnam, called on Congress to terminate all funding for military activities in Indochina, and asked for reparations for war victims. The declaration concluded, "Repent! Turn about, make a fresh start."

The direct encroachment of the war into Mennonite lives also pushed some members to noncooperation. They refused to register for the draft and to pay war taxes. Noncooperation in the sixties and seventies represented unnecessary, almost mischievous, civil disobedience in the eyes of many Mennonites. Youthful draft resisters had a ready option of serving in alternative service and bypassing military service. Indeed church leaders worried that provocative refusals to enter alternative service might jeopardize the entire program for the rest of the church.

The youthful resisters contended that alternative service had become part of the system of conscription. They could only render a prophetic witness by refusing to register with Selective Service—denying in essence its authority and existence. Embroiled in the counter-culture movements and Vietnam protests, some young Mennos refused to register with Selective Service. Others burned their draft cards to protest their own as well as the U.S. involvement in the Vietnam War.

Would their elders consider such protests in harmony with the spirit of peaceful nonresistance? Or were youthful protesters desecrating the way of peace? The noncooperation movement captured the center stage of MC attention at the general conference at Turner, Oregon in August 1969.[26] Several long-haired "resisters" in blue jeans brought a statement outlining their refusal to cooperate with Selective Service. They pleaded, "We do not attempt to willfully rebel against the state, but recognize that our first loyalty and obedience is to God" (Peachey, 1980:84). After tense negotiations between resisters and conference officials, delegates were asked to "recognize the validity of noncooperation as a legitimate witness and pledge the offices of our brotherhood" to support the resisters.

The delegates faced a quandary. To support long-haired resisters would virtually turn the tradition of nonresistance on its head. Yet Anabaptism was itself a radical protest movement from the beginning. Nevertheless, the word "noncooperation" was more palatable than "resistance" and "witness" signaled a more bonafide motivation than "protest." So after much agony the conference at Turner recognized "noncooperation as a legitimate witness."

Several months later in November 1969 the MCC Peace Section followed suit with a bold statement declaring that, "conscription . . . violates the essential freedom of each person. This evil should be abolished along with the military system which supports it." The statement recognized noncooperation, "as a valid expression of nonconformity and peacemaking." Surprisingly, "nonresistance" was missing from the lengthy text, which contained frequent appeals to "discipleship" and "witness." Noncooperation fit more comfortably within the tradition of nonconformity, discipleship, and witness than with the legacy of nonresistance.

By 1971 the GC general conference declared noncooperation "a valid witness"—if based on loyalty to Jesus—and pledged the resources of the church to support noncooperators. Draft resisters met more resistance among MBs. Two district conferences refused to recognize noncooperation as a valid alternative in 1969. The U.S. MB conference, meeting in 1971, concluded that it could not support noncooperation.[27] Peace statements issued by the Brethren in Christ in 1970 and 1972 were silent on noncooperation.

The vast majority of Mennonites drafted in the sixties and seventies cooperated with Selective Service and entered either a voluntary service program administered by the church or worked in approved jobs for pay in public agencies in lieu of military service. Approximately fifty men illegally refused to cooperate with Selective Service and were arrested, imprisoned, or fled to Canada. Although few in number, noncooperators significantly touched the life of the church as it struggled to redefine nonresistance in the face of the war.

War Tax Resistance

As Mennonite youth struggled with the draft, some of their elders were tormented by paying tax dollars to feed the war. They worried that while praying for peace they were actually paying for war. Most rank-and-file Mennonites contended that the Scriptures clearly called for the payment of taxes. War tax resisters and their sympathizers, however, argued that Jesus never clarified exactly what belonged to

Mennonite pastor Vincent Harding (L) was an eloquent speaker who urged Mennonites to become involved in civil rights and social justice. Here David Augsburger (R) interviews him for *The Mennonite Hour* radio program in 1963.

Caesar and what to God. Moreover, as citizens in a democracy they felt conscientiously liable when their taxes were used for wanton destruction.

Like the noncooperators, tax resisters were a minority, but a vocal one. As early as 1959 the GC general conference agreed to study the war-tax problem. Donald D. Kaufman's study book, *What Belongs to Caesar?* appeared in 1969. Two years later the GC general conference agreed to "stand by those who feel called to resist payment" of war taxes. Additional GC resolutions supporting war-tax resistance appeared in 1974, 1977, 1980, and 1983.

A special GC conference, called to explore war tax options in 1979, mandated their General Board to use all possible means to achieve a legal exemption for war tax objectors. In 1983 the GC conference meeting in Bethlehem, Pennsylvania, adopted, by a substantial majority, a position of civil disobedience in refusing to withhold income tax from employees who objected to war taxes. The MC followed with supportive resolutions in 1979, 1981, 1985, and 1987.

With legal options sparse, numerous Mennonites over the years have lobbied U.S. congressional representatives for passage of a Peace Tax Fund designed to allow conscientious objectors to funnel their tax dollars into peaceful projects.[28]

Summary

To be sure, Mennonite draft and tax resisters were a minority in the strident sixties and seventies. The overwhelming majority of Mennonites cooperated with selective service and paid their taxes without protest. Nevertheless the endorsement of resister positions by major Mennonite bodies and Mennonite involvement in nonviolent direct action charted a new phase in Mennonite peacemaking. Nonviolent action represented an about-face in the legacy of nonresistance—not because it perpetrated violence but because it embraced the use of strategic action and nonviolent force to accomplish political goals. It gave a modern twist to the saga of nonresistance.

Unlike passive nonresistance that yielded the outcome of even terrifying situations into God's hands, activist Mennonites of the sixties and seventies were taking charge of things and engaging in strategic acts of force—albeit nonviolent ones—to achieve specific goals, even honorable ones. In this sense direct action reflected the spirit of the modern age. The conservative *Sword and Trumpet* called the ideological U-turn "militant nonresistance . . . an embarrassing compromise of the good" (Shank, 1970:7).

As Mennonites turned toward more activist forms of peacemaking, some participated in public marches and demonstrations. A number of Mennonites joined some 40,000 other protesters in this march to end the Vietnam War in Washington, D.C., in November 1965.

CHAPTER SIX

New Patterns of Peacemaking

The transformation of nonresistance in the twentieth century culminated with a peacemaking focus in the eighties and nineties. Justice had already entered the Mennonite vocabulary in the late seventies and early eighties. Peacemaking, however, reigned supreme as the word of choice among Mennonites who wanted a plausible peace theology in the context of modern life. Occasional references to peacemaking had occurred prior to the sixties, but the word gradually slipped into usage in the late sixties and flowered in the eighties.

In 1968 a series of Peacemaker Workshops in Mennonite congregations across the U.S. and Canada grappled with civil rights, Vietnam, revolution, and other issues that had forced a crisis in historic nonresistance. Study documents from the workshops were published in 1969 in *Peacemakers in a Broken World*, edited by John A. Lapp. "The Way of Peace," a 1971 GC statement, also contained references to "peacemaking," indicating the word's growing popularity. Moreover, the peacemaking label enabled easier ecumenical dialogue as the nuclear arms buildup spiraled in the early eighties. It was not until the late eighties, however, that "peacemaking" became the centerpiece of Mennonite peace talk.[1]

The restructuring of nonresistance did not occur simply because the ghost of modernity waved a mysterious wand. Identifiable forces led to the changes. This chapter explores some of the agents and institutional vehicles that led the evolution, samples the theological work that legitimated the change, and briefly describes some new peacemaking programs that emerged in the eighties. Although the transformation peaked in the 1970s and 1980s, the change, of course, had stretched over several generations.

Agents of Transformation

The transformation can be roughly traced through three sometimes parallel phases (as shown in Figure 6.1). First, the broad, macro forces of modernity—social, political, and theological—reshaping the larger society were pressing upon Mennonites as well.

Second, a variety of mediating structures—change agents and ideological brokers—bridged the gap between the external changes and grass roots Mennonites by shaping new interpretations of nonresistance. These agents of transformation filtered the changes, experimented with new expressions of nonresistance, and reinterpreted the biblical and Anabaptist heritage in novel ways.

Third, the emergent expressions of nonresistance were institutionalized into new programs of peacemaking.

These three phases often overlapped each other, and the same persons were sometimes involved in all of them—leading the action, authoring statements, and initiating programs.

Increased education, urbanization, industrialization, and mobility had led some Mennonites to pursue higher education and to study the history of their own heritage. Expanding technology and international communications enabled Mennonites to develop mission and service programs around the world. Urban exposure and service abroad, combined with higher levels of education, made Mennonites more aware of world need and social oppression and exposed them to government power structures in a variety of cultural settings.

At the same time, Mennonites were learning about the Anabaptist Vision of their sixteenth-century forebears, many of whom died for their convictions at the hand of the state. The Anabaptist vision articulated by Harold Bender in 1944 was taking root in the fifties and sixties. In addition, modernizing Mennonites were more open to ecumenical conversations and influences. In tandem with these developments, Mennonites felt the social tremors of the sixties that shook the larger society.

The coalescence of these forces in the 1960s had reciprocal, mutually reinforcing effects. Mennonites with higher education, overseas experience, ecumenical ties, and new visions of their Anabaptist heritage were confronted with the swirling crises of the sixties and seventies. The mix of these forces cracked the credibility of passive nonre-

FIGURE 6.1
Influences Shaping the Emergence of Active Peacemaking, 1950-1990

Macro Forces	Mediating Structures	Outcomes
Societal Urbanization Education Mobility Individuation	Agents of Change Activists Educators Leaders Pastors	Individual Attitudes Behavior
Political Civil Rights ('50s - '60s) Vietnam War ('60s - '70s) Nuclear Arms ('70s - '80s) Women's Rights ('70s - '80s) Central America ('80s)	Vehicles of Change MCC Peace Section Washington/Ottawa Office Colleges Congregations New Call to Peacemaking	Institutional Programs Christian Peacemaker Teams Victim Offender Reconciliation Program Mennonite Conciliation Services Local Peace Centers Criminal Justice Ministries Women's Concerns
Denominational MCC Service Overseas Missionary Experience I-W and Voluntary Service	Ideological Brokers Theologians Academicians Writers	Ideological Books and Pamphlets Statements
Theological Anabaptist Vision Ecumenical Conversations Liberation Theology		

sistance and blazed new pathways of active peacemaking.

The conglomeration of forces redefining Mennonite peacemaking in the sixties, seventies, and eighties thus included urbanization, higher education, theological training, growing mobility, rising socioeconomic status, Anabaptist studies, overseas missionary service, international relief and service work, the civil rights movement, and of course the Vietnam War. These multilayered and interwoven experiences pushed Mennonites ever forward on the path of active peacemaking.

In response to these changes a variety of innovators—individuals and some institutions—veered off the traditional trails of nonresistance and charted new modes of peacemaking. The ideological brokers who followed the change agents provided a theological rationale for what in many cases was already happening. In turn the new theological formulations often spawned new forms of peace witness which sometimes became institutionalized. The change agents—individuals and institutions—served as mediating structures to span the gap between the macro forces of modernity and the attitudes and behaviors of rank-and-file Mennonites as shown in Figure 6.1. These intermediaries facilitated and directed the restructuring of Mennonite peacemaking.

Activists

Mennonites were not merely pawns on the chessboard of modernity. Individuals interpreted the forces at play and responded to the changes. They made decisions. Some clung to traditional nonresistance. Others sought new ways to be faithful to the gospel of Jesus Christ in the crucible of new conditions. The vanguard of change was led by a variety of change agents who stepped over the old moral boundaries which had long preserved passive nonresistance.

The innovators—activists, educators, leaders, and pastors—in both Canada and the U.S. responded to the challenge of the hour by speaking and acting, often in courageous ways which sometimes irritated those who preferred the quiet paths of nonresistance. Although the engaging stance of the activists at first blush appeared as the opposite of passive nonresistance, the activists—like nonresistant martyrs of the past—were willing to endure voluntary suffering for the cause of peace.

Many of the activists were viewed by mainstream Mennonites as leftist-leaning, anti-American, and unpatriotic. Dozens of activists engaged in nonviolent direct action and other forms of public witness and protest throughout the sixties, seventies, and eighties. The string of prominent nonviolent activists would surely include Steven Clemens, Peter Ediger, Doug Hostetter, Dorothy Friesen, Hedy Sawadsky, Mary Sprunger-Froese, Peter Sprunger-Froese, Gene Stoltzfus, Ann Zook, Al Zook, and Becky Yoder, among many others.

For Canadian Hedy Sawadsky the path to nonviolent direct action was triggered by a two-year experience as an MCC relief worker in Jordan and Israel in the late sixties. A well-educated Palestinian woman said, "Hedy, what you're doing here is fine, but it's Band-Aid work. You came after the war, after the damage was done. Why don't you go home and work for peace and get at the root causes of evil and war?" The MCC programs were doing good things and ministering well through effective personnel, but the question of Band-Aid work tormented Sawadsky.[2]

After returning to the U.S. in 1970, Anabaptist studies and conversations with other Christian pacifists pushed Sawadsky into war tax resistance and other forms of nonviolent direct action. With other Mennonite activists, she joined in public witness events at local post offices, the Pentagon in Washington, and the nuclear weapons plant at Rocky Flats, Colorado. In the mid-eighties she spent about five years in public witness activities and vigils at the Pantex plant in Amarillo, Texas, the final assembly site for nuclear weapons. Sawadsky's commitment to nonviolent direct action was rooted in a Christocentric base, shaped by international experiences, and inspired by the courage of sixteenth-century Anabaptists as well as contemporary followers of Christ.

The turning point for activist Doug Hostetter was serving in Vietnam (1966-1969) with Vietnam Christian Service. Transported by a U.S. military helicopter one day, he was seated on boxes of machine gun ammunition with gunners on both sides at open doors. The gunners were soon exchanging heavy fire with the enemy on the ground. Such Vietnam experiences taught Hostetter "the importance and difficulty of worshiping a God who is above religious, national, and ethnic boundaries. Serving God requires vigilance to ensure that our work is not used to serve the national or ideological ends of warring parties."[3]

For activist Dorothy Friesen, a pivotal point was a stint in the Philippines in 1976-1979 as co-director of the MCC program. Friesen says,

> My work in the Philippines provided an economic and political education which I could never have received at an American university. The faith of the people at the grass roots deepened my own spirituality. . . . Nothing

was ever the same after that Philippine experience. There was no way to go back to business as usual in the belly of the beast.[4]

Upon returning to the U.S., Friesen (along with other former MCC workers) organized Synapses, a peace, justice, and action network based in Chicago. In an essay that envisions the shape of "The Mennonite Peace Witness Tomorrow," Friesen (1990:298) argues that "Preparation for the challenge of peacemaking in a new arena will include deeper spiritual formation, biblical discernment, social analysis, and, above all, commitment to direct engagement with the powers that be."

A seminary course on the Old Testament taught by Millard Lind pushed Mary Sprunger-Froese toward nonviolent action and civil disobedience.[5] Lind proposed that "worship is a political act—a declaration of allegiance." With that biblical insight, nonviolent direct action became a means of declaring her allegiance to the kingdom of God in the face of the nuclear threat. Mary stepped across the line of passive nonresistance in 1979 at a mass demonstration at the Rocky Flats nuclear weapons plant in Colorado. She was arrested. Returning the following Sunday she was arrested again and jailed for five days.

In 1981 Mary Sprunger-Froese and Steven Clemens were two Mennonites among six trespassers arrested at the Pantex Plant in Amarillo, Texas—the final site for the assembly of nuclear weapons. Jailed for some six months, the Indiana natives served half of the time in a county jail and the other half in a federal prison.

Between 1979 and 1989 Mary Sprunger-Froese was arrested some ten times and imprisoned four times for a variety of nonviolent actions aimed at protesting the nuclear arms race, as well as militarism in American society and the so-called Star Wars program.

Her Canadian born husband, Peter Sprunger-Froese, has also carried the torch of nonviolent resistance against the militarization of American society. He was arrested some two dozen times and imprisoned on fourteen occasions for nonviolent direct action between 1979 and 1992. Peter likely carries the distinction of being the most frequently arrested Mennonite.

Products of Mennonite colleges and seminary study, Peter and Mary's convictions were shaped by biblical study, their parents' commitment to living the Christian life, their Anabaptist heritage, a GC missionary couple in Colombia, conversation with religious activists in the Catholic tradition, and the nonviolent teachings of Gandhi and Martin Luther King, Jr. The Sprunger-Froeses represented a small group of Mennonite activists—post civil rights and Vietnam War— who pressed for a public peacemaking witness in the face of the nuclear arms race. Many of their actions, often centered in Colorado Springs and Denver, Colorado, involved other religious activists, many of whom had Catholic ties.

Nonregistrants were also agents of change. The U.S. draft registration, in effect since 1948, ceased in April 1975 with the end of the Vietnam War. Dozens of Mennonite youth had refused registration or induction during the war. A new round of protest rose when President Carter began registration in response to the Soviet Union's invasion of Afghanistan in 1980.[6] Nonregistrants were denied federal aid for education and job training programs. Eighteen American draft resisters were publicly prosecuted, including Brethren resister Enten Eller and three Mennonites—Mark Schmucker, Kendal Warkentine, and Chuck Epp.

Schmucker's jury trial ended in a sentence of three years probation, two years of community service, and a four thousand dollar fine. His conviction was later overturned on the basis of selective prosecution. Warkentine, trying to model nonresistance toward the government, stood mute at his arraignment. Judge Sam Crow entered a plea of guilty for him and delivered a sentence of two years of unsupervised probation. Charges against Epp were eventually dropped by the government.

Although these three cases received national press coverage, the number of Mennonite resisters was much higher. More than sixty attended a gathering of nonregistrants in 1982. The numbers varied from year to year. Many undoubtedly remained quiet about their actions! A Mennonite *Noncooperators Newsletter* was launched in 1980.

Educators

Many of the activists were encouraged by educators in church colleges who sought to infuse biblical and Anabaptist convictions with new relevance for a new generation. The academicians, wary of arrest and worried about antagonizing administrators and constituencies, were nonetheless critical agents in the transformation of nonresistance. The long roster would surely include the likes of Elmer Neufeld and Robert Kreider (Bluffton College), Bill Keeney and Duane Friesen (Bethel College), Ray Gingerich and Titus Bender (Eastern Mennonite College), Frank Epp and Walter Klaassen (Conrad Grebel College), John R. Burkholder and Atlee Beechy (Goshen College), and of course John H. Yoder, as well as Willard Swartley (Associated Mennonite Biblical Seminaries).

The pilgrimage of John R. Burkholder exemplifies the multitude of influences converging in the classroom that inspired a generation of Goshen College students toward active peacemaking.[7] Already in the late fifties, Burkholder, based in Philadelphia and working part time for the Fellowship of Reconciliation, was "marching, vigiling, and courting arrest" in a variety of public demonstrations. These activities linked him into the growing peace movement of the fifties and sixties which included such persons as A. J. Muste, John Swomley, Bert Bigelow, and George Willoughby. During graduate studies at Harvard, Burkholder debated Reinhold Niebuhr on the radio and developed ongoing contacts with the likes of the Berrigan brothers.

Burkholder then began a twenty-year teaching stint at Goshen College in 1963. He soon inherited Guy Hershberger's classic course on "War, Peace, and Nonresistance" and exposed a generation of Goshen students to new expressions of peacemaking. Burkholder and colleague Atlee Beechy launched the Peace Studies program at Goshen College in the late seventies. Along with thirty others, including six Mennonites, he was arrested in Representative John Hiler's office in South Bend, Indiana, in a protest of U.S. support for the Nicaraguan contras (fighters against the Sandinista government) in the mid-eighties. In his role as educator, Burkholder, as well as many teachers at other colleges, inspired scores of students to enter peacemaking vocations.

Some of the educators played an active role in leading church organizations toward more active peacemaking. Bill Keeney (of non-Mennonite background) attended Bluffton college, joined the General Conference Mennonite Church, and then served with MCC in Europe.[8] Later, he taught at both Bluffton and Bethel, and served as chair of the MCC Peace Section for ten years (1963-1973). He was instrumental in drafting documents that led to the establishment of MCC's Washington office in 1968. Keeney drafted the proposal to establish a Mennonite Conciliation Service in the early 1980s.

In addition to teaching peace studies at Mennonite colleges, Keeney was active in the growing network of colleges across the nation that were developing peace study programs in the 1970s. He served as executive director of the Consortium on Peace, Research, and Development (COPRED) for six years (1978-1984). Keeney symbolizes the change agent who was able to straddle the worlds of academia, church, and public action.

Another group of innovators, tilted more directly toward the church, included pastors and institutional leaders who led and encouraged new expressions of peacemaking. Edgar Metzler, active with the MC peace and social concerns committee for many years, was in the words of one observer a "shaker and mover." Metzler, a major architect of "The Christian Witness to the State" adopted by the Mennonite Church in 1961, served as executive secretary of MCC's Peace Section for four years (1962-1966).

John A. Lapp teacher, churchman, and administrator who also served as executive secretary of MCC's peace section for three years (1969-72) typifies an activist leader. He nudged the transformation of Mennonite peacemaking forward through committee work, public lectures, and organizational support. His edited collection of *Peacemakers in a Broken World* (1969) symbolized the growing shift among MCs to conceive of nonresistance in positive and outgoing expressions that reached beyond the confines of Mennonite ethnicity.

For some fifteen years Frank Epp edited the *Canadian Mennonite*, the national Mennonite weekly which molded social opinion. A founding member of MCC Canada, he served with MCC for more than twenty years. He frequently was embroiled in conflicts related to peace and justice. His editorials, coverage of marches, reprinting of sermons and speeches, plus his own trip to Vietnam reported in the *Canadian Mennonite*, stirred the cauldron of peace and social concerns in Canada.

Later Epp worked in Ottawa, the national capitol, monitoring government policies. He was also active with the MCC Peace Section, which he eventually chaired. Epp co-authored *The Palestinians* (1976) and *The Israelis* (1980), two books which may have cost him election to the Federal government when he ran in Waterloo County, Ontario, in the early eighties. Jewish voters despised his sympathy for the plight of Palestinians, which had emerged out of his research in Israel and the West Bank.

Less visible than some of the theological leaders in the paradigm shift, change agents working at the grass roots translated new understandings of nonresistance into the political realities of the sixties and seventies. Innovators pushed the transformation forward in pulpits, classrooms, committees, conferences, and newspapers—constructing a new peace theology and paving the way for an accent on justice in the eighties. Edgar Metzler summed up the feelings of many activists, "I felt more 'Anabaptist' sitting in a jail cell outside the Nevada nuclear test site with Dan Berrigan and Jim Wallace than I ever did sitting around a committee table at MCC."[9]

These brief sketches of change agents are but a few of the scores of innovators which could be documented and highlighted. Agents of change—deeply involved in churches as pastors, teachers, editors, and organizers—carried the banner of peacemaking on the streets, in the pulpits, and in the classrooms. Born in rural communities, many of these change agents joined the fray in a creative moment in Mennonite history, as the church struggled with the converging forces of modernization. Can the momentum be sustained as Mennonite suburbanites become increasingly lured by individualism, materialism, and secularism? Will vigorous commitment prevail as peacemaking is domesticated in a variety of institutional programs?

Vehicles of Change

Beyond the individuals who fostered change, institutional vehicles also carried the vision forward. Peace committees in the various denominations, colleges, publishing efforts, mission boards, and MCC service assignments served as vehicles of transformation in Mennonite peacemaking.[10] The alternatives to military service—Civilian Public Service in the forties and the I-W and voluntary service programs in later decades—scattered hundreds of young people into new settings. Here their parochial and sometimes naive notions of nonresistance were challenged. These institutional vehicles pushed Mennonites in the direction of active peacemaking. The liaison with the New Call to Peacemaking, linking Mennonites, Quakers, and the Church of the Brethren in common efforts, provided another organizational channel for peacemaking activities.

Undoubtedly the most important institutional vehicle for change in the fifty-year period from 1942 to 1992 was MCC's interMennonite Peace Section.[11] Formed in 1942, Peace Section served as a clearinghouse, facilitator, and initiator of a vast array of peace concerns. Operating under a separate board that paralleled the larger MCC board, Peace Section enjoyed, in John Stoner's words, "a prophetic independence."[12] It could say things that needed to be said and do things that needed to be done, all the while maintaining distance from MCC and denominational programs.

Peace Section was often on the cutting edge, dealing with controversial issues—draft resistance, nonregistration, war tax resistance, and women's concerns to name a few. This prophetic voice would likely have been silenced had it been directly harnessed to a denomination or the MCC board itself. As a prophetic vehicle, Peace Section could monitor, facilitate, and encourage more activist forms of peacemaking which otherwise would have been stifled by the more conservative denominational structures.

In 1970 John A. Lapp (1970b:291) summarized the threefold focus of MCC's peace mission: (1) nurturing peace convictions, (2) staying out of military service, and (3) expanding peacemaking in conflict situations and promoting peace concerns among other Christians. Some twenty years later Atlee Beechy, reflecting on Peace Section's fifty-year history said,

> It played very important roles in developing peace awareness and as a prophetic witness and interpreter to Mennonite groups. The peace witness of the various Mennonite groups would be substantially weaker without the nudging and encouragement of Peace Section.[13]

The Washington office, established by Peace Section in 1968 (the year of King's assassination) was to be the "ears and arms, but not the mouth" of the church, according to Bill Keeney, one of its founders.[14] In addition to monitoring developments in Washington, its director, Delton Franz, accepted over one hundred speaking assignments and feedback sessions in congregations, conferences, colleges, and seminaries between 1970 and 1980. Through speaking engagements and newsletters, the offices in Washington and Ottawa have provided an important channel of communication between Mennonite leaders and government representatives in both the U.S. and Canada.

A scan of the Peace Section minutes and its newsletter shows the host of issues that have flowed through its door over the years. They include alternatives to conscription, draft counseling, peace education, peace literature, draft resistance, nonregistration, war tax resistance, the U.S. peace tax fund. Other concerns include ecumenical dialogue, women's concerns, government relations, and public policy analysis performed by the offices in Washington and Ottawa.

Peace Section supports annual meetings of an Intercollegiate Peace Fellowship for college students. In the seventies and eighties, Peace Section organized a series of peace theology colloquiums. Many of its concerns were fringe issues for grass roots Mennonites, but Peace Section's interest and support of them pushed the peacemaking agenda forward.

Through staff persons such as Brethren in Christ pastor John K. Stoner, executive secretary from 1976 to 1988, the Peace Section called the church to new modes of faithfulness under the growing specter of nuclear war. For Stoner and other Peace Section members, the threat of nuclear war was of central concern to Christian faithfulness. Under Stoner's guidance a large poster publicized Richard McSorley's terse condemnation, "It's a sin to build a nuclear weapon."

Another widely circulated poster paraphrased M. R. Zigler's admonition, "Let the Christians of the world agree that they will not kill each other." In a pastoral but prophetic manner, Stoner supported public demonstrations and acts of civil disobedience that confronted the menace of nuclear arms.

Stoner observed that an "unprincipled civil disobedience of breaking the speed limit is common among Christians while principled resistance to immoral laws is rare." To the many Mennonites uncomfortable with prophetic initiatives of the Peace Section and its challenge of the unconditional claim of the state to wage nuclear war, Stoner suggested that they remember an old proverb, "When the barn is on fire, those who are watching should not complain too loudly about the method of those carrying the water."[15] Many Mennonites, however, were watching. Supporting the nuclear arms build-up of the Reagan years, some 72 percent of the U.S. Mennonites who voted in 1988 cast their vote for George Bush.

In Stoner's mind the shift toward activism in Mennonite peacemaking was "a return to something closer to the original shape of Anabaptist life. Quietistic nonresistance was a move away from the original vision. Compelling evidence shows that the early Anabaptists were often in trouble with the power structures."[16] For Stoner and others, convictions for active peacemaking that at times confronted the authorities were not only propelled by the gospel and the political conditions of the moment, they were also fostered by the radical character of the sixteenth-century Anabaptist vision which Harold Bender had resurrected in 1944.

Perhaps even more significant than its initiatives, education, and policy analysis were the social networks that coalesced around MCC's Peace Section. It not only symbolized the activist edge of Mennonite peacemaking but also provided a network for hundreds of Mennonites who found support and solidarity for convictions which would have likely been silenced or marginalized in their home congregations. In the words of John Stoner, Peace Section "prodded the lukewarm, encouraged the weary, and supported the energetic in peace witness and action."[17]

Reviewing the fifty-year history of Peace Section, John A. Lapp (1992:2) reflected,

> Peace is not merely a theology and a vision. Peace is for the human situation. Peace is incarnated in people and becomes alive in interpersonal and communal situations . . . a vast network of individuals served on the

peace committee, filled staff positions, and went on special assignments to communicate the special insights of the Mennonite peace tradition.

The convictions for activist peacemaking shared by this vast network of persons were nurtured and nudged into action via the institutional vehicle of Peace Section.[18]

Ecumenical Influences

In addition to the agents of change, ecumenical conversations molded the emerging Mennonite theology and practice of peacemaking. Although Mennonites have often been wary of formal ecumenical ties, their new understandings of peacemaking were surely shaped by ecumenical influences. John A. Lapp observes that, "Mennonite developments *always* have an ecumenical setting."[19] Indeed, most Mennonites understand their peacemaking convictions not as a unique Mennonite franchise but as flowing from the long historic stream of Christian pacifism.

Already in colonial America, Quakers were affecting Mennonite thinking (MacMaster, 1985). The Quakers who were the subject of Guy, F. Hershberger's doctoral dissertation influenced his views through their writings and through his personal acquaintance with some of their leaders. The Quakers and the Church of the Brethren were partners along with the Mennonites in the formation of the Historic Peace Churches in 1935—a venture preceded by periodic Conferences of Pacifist Churches. The loose partnership between the three groups was revitalized in 1976 when the Mennonites, Brethren, and Friends joined together in a "New Call to Peacemaking," which held three national conferences in 1978, 1980, and 1982.[20]

The ecumenical influences on Mennonite peacemaking, often arising out of dialogue with exponents of the just war tradition in the larger circles of Christendom, sharpened, clarified, and influenced Mennonite thinking. In turn, however, the absolute pacifism exposed by Mennonites and other historic peace church representatives prodded the perspectives of those in the mainstream as well. In charting forty years of ecumenical dialogue John H. Yoder (Gwyn, et al., 1991:93-105) has identified some three dozen meetings, conferences, and ongoing committees which involved significant dialogue between representatives of the historic peace churches and a variety of theologians and leaders of other Christian traditions.[21] Many of these consultations were related to committees and assemblies of the World Council of Churches. Frank Epp, John H. Yoder, and John R. Burkholder have been among prominent Mennonite envoys in ecumenical dialogue.

The important Mennonite "Winona Lake Conference" of 1950 grew out of Mennonite involvement in the Detroit Conference on the "Church and War" in 1950 attended by Donovan E. Smucker and Harold S. Bender. As noted before, the four so-called "Puidoux Conferences" in Europe (1955-1962) had a significant influence in feeding the concept of the lordship of Christ into Mennonite understandings of church-state relations. Mennonite thinking and practice was clearly shaped by the rise of nonviolent resistance embodied in the campaigns of Martin Luther King, Jr. Resistance to the Vietnam War in the late sixties and to the nuclear arms race in the seventies and eighties linked Mennonites arm-in-arm with Christian pacifists from a variety of other denominations.

The pacifist vein in Catholic spirituality was especially influential among Mennonite activists in the seventies and eighties. With the daunting specter of nuclear war rising with Reagan's election in 1980, Mennonites were frequently invited to dialogue with mainline Protestants and evangelicals because the credibility of the just war logic was cracking under the weight of the nuclear burden. Indeed, some religious communions came forward with new peace statements in the eighties. Although not endorsing absolute pacifism, they tempered their enthusiasm for just war thinking in the face of the nuclear threat.

John R. Burkholder (1988:19) summed up the dramatic shift in the ecumenical perception of Mennonites some forty years after World War II.

> The peace churches are no longer looked at as irrelevant, insignificant, or even heretical. The major Protestant denominations today recognize the validity of the absolute pacifist position. . . . Most mainline churches have strong statements on the necessity of action for peace and disarmament.

Theological Formulations

Although the activists often blazed new trails of peacemaking, the ideological brokers following on their heels negotiated new theological understandings to bridge the gap between their biblical Anabaptist heritage and the ever-changing social climate. The theological brokers in essence needed to reinterpret the old Scriptures in new ways to address the current realities. Theological brokers such as John H. Yoder were often engaged in ecumenical discussions which, of course, influenced and tempered their formulations. The new theological statements played a dialectical role in relation to the activists. The statements not only created plausible theological justifications for what was already happening, they also stimulated new initiatives by the activists.

The Politics of Jesus

The rise of nonviolent action in some Mennonite circles found its legitimacy in new theological formulations. To turn the heritage of passive nonresistance on its head without breaking faith with the Mennonite legacy or Scripture presented a major challenge for the theological brokers. How could they legitimate assertive peacemaking and even civil disobedience? The brokers were up to the task. They discovered a new Jesus—one who engaged in direct political action.

Theologians took the abstract concept of the lordship of Christ and concretized it into the politics of Jesus. Jesus was a political king, they argued, who hung on a cross because his nonviolent actions infuriated the authorities. This new understanding provided a plausible Jesus— one who fit the strident spirit of the late sixties and early seventies.

Responding to Edgar Metzler's call for nonregistration to the military draft in 1959, Harold Bender (1960) argued that "Nonresistant Christians cannot justify disobedience of the law merely because they have good ends in view." Trying to stifle any mischievous disobedience, Bender contended that one could only disobey a law if it required or forbade something clearly taught by Scripture. This eliminated, in one sweep, draft and tax resistance as well as direct or symbolic action aimed at social change.

In January of 1960 John R. Burkholder (1960:14) had called for "radical protest" and "direct action" in a paper addressed to fellow theologians. Two years later, Walter Klaassen (1962), writing in *Mennonite Life*, opened the door to active peacemaking by contending that Jesus practiced "nonviolent resistance." Moreover, Klaassen proposed that in the face of violence Christians should be "far from nonresistant." They should "resist it, not by violence, but through the service of reconciliation."

By 1962 Bender had died and Mennonite leaders in the heat of the civil rights movement and the Vietnam conflict were struggling with the passivity of nonresistance. Stanley Bohn's (1967) "Toward a New Understanding of Nonresistance" emerged out of the civil rights movement. For Bohn, the credibility of nonresistance, "turn the other cheek . . . stay out of fights . . . don't cause anybody any trouble," evaporated in the face of racial oppression. In the midst of racial evil, "one must choose sides . . . nonresistance does not mean being an umpire . . . it means being a reconciler." This new view of nonresistance, argued Bohn, "is based on the incarnation"—a view other Mennonites were rather quickly endorsing. J. Lawrence Burkholder (1969), writing in the *Canadian Mennonite*, also put his blessing on nonviolent resistance.

Speaking to the Intercollegiate Mennonite Peace Conference in 1968, C. Norman Kraus charged that neutral nonresistance was often an excuse for noninvolvement. Arguing that Jesus was crucified precisely because he was not neutral—because he threatened political and religious establishments—Kraus called for a theology of involvement. Speaking in Canada in 1969, Kraus argued that nonresistance was a cultural product, produced by "the quiet in the land," and was "neither New Testament nor Anabaptist. . . ."

Kraus then argued that Jesus was "political," not in the traditional sense of engineering political reform, but in acting out the righteousness of God which had "an immediate and startling impact upon the political, social and religious order." Jesus was a "noncooperator" and a "demonstrator" who refused to cooperate with Jewish authorities and demonstrated on behalf of the poor when he flipped over tables in the temple. Kraus' call for action circulated among MCs in a series of four articles on revolution in the *Gospel Herald* in 1970.

Nonresistance for Kraus (1969:5) was "not withdrawal from responsibility . . . it is suffering persecution for the sake of God's justice." Jesus was crucified "as a rebel against society" and consequently the cross was a consequence of the activism embodied in the incarnation. Youthful Mennonites, outraged by the atrocities in Vietnam, were empowered by the new interpretation of Jesus. Meanwhile back at Goshen College, Kraus soon found himself pleading with students to cancel their plans to march to the local draft board and pour blood on the draft files.[22]

The revisions of nonresistance swirling about in the late sixties and early seventies were synthesized in John H. Yoder's *The Politics of Jesus*. Yoder's work, in process for many years, was directed toward an ecumenical audience, but it happily coincided with the needs of the hour in Mennonite circles. With a bold, almost audacious title, it established a new paradigm for Mennonite peacemaking—one that took nonresistance seriously but with a radical revision.

To link the word *politics* with the name of Jesus was virtually an outrage to meek, apolitical Mennonites. They argued that the nonresistant Jesus called them to quiet separatism, beyond the world of power politics. To suggest that Jesus so much as even cared about politics was to turn the tradition of passive nonresistance on its conceptual head.

Indeed, Yoder (1972:12) claimed that Jesus was "a model of radical political action." His radical political activity hung him on a cross. The paradigm shift cast the spotlight away from Jesus' nonresistant posture in front of the cross to the activism of his life that triggered the cross. "I'm glad you put in writing what some of us have been practicing for some time," activist Gene Stoltzfus told Yoder upon publication of the volume.[23]

While the notion of using Jesus to bless radical political action troubled conservative Mennonite souls, Yoder had to be reckoned with. In good Anabaptist fashion he argued that Jesus was not only relevant for social ethics but also normative. Further, Yoder took the New Testament Scriptures seriously. Although Yoder's Jesus was a political figure—a King crucified because of his political threat—he did not stoop to violence nor embrace conventional politics. Indeed this Jesus, in Yoder's (1972:241) word, "renounced the claim to govern history."

Thus while Yoder irked conservative Mennonites by legitimating radical political action in the name of Jesus, he also chastised progressive Mennonites eager to enter the corridors of political power and govern history. Such ambitions, Yoder might have argued, were an utter misunderstanding of the politics of Jesus.

Yoder's Jesus was an activist—fearless of the political consequences of provocative actions—and hardly a mild, nonresistant shepherd. But this Jesus was also sectarian. Refusing to embrace the conventional political system, he created instead a separate "messianic community"—though one with real political consequences.

The Politics of Jesus not only provided an ideological legitimation for Mennonite activism; it forever changed the character of passive nonresistance by giving Jesus' blessing to the use of provocative force, albeit short of violence. With penetrating biblical exegesis, Yoder made explicit and crystallized what was already inherent in Hershberger. In essence Yoder struck a middle ground between "withdrawal" and "responsibility" by focusing on the social and political consequences of nonresistance in the face of the cross.[24]

The politics of Jesus captured the imagination of Mennonites of many stripes. Within a year the MCC Peace Section Annual Report called readers to "embrace the politics of Jesus and confront the principalities and powers," and in 1976 MCC sponsored a major Peace Theology Colloquium which focused, of course, on "the Politics of Jesus."[25]

Peace and Justice for All

The politics of Jesus filtered into action as a wave of "Peace and Justice" thinking crested in Mennonite circles in the late seventies and early eighties. Although justice concerns had appeared occasionally in the sixties with the civil rights movement, Mennonites were increasingly inserting justice into their peacemaking vocabulary in the late seventies.[26] The embrace of justice was propelled by both ideological and social factors. On a theological level the emerging themes of "witness to the state," "the lordship of Christ," "the politics of Jesus," and the "principalities and powers," as well as the impact of liberation theology, provided a fertile ideological seedbed for social justice.

Changes in the social context of the Mennonite experience also created an affinity for justice. Mission and service assignments had scattered hundreds of Mennonites around the world. In such settings they experienced poverty and economic oppression firsthand and witnessed governments and multinational corporations often perpetuating injustice and oppression (Kreider and Goossen, 1988). In addition, through their growing involvement as managers and professionals in both secular structures and church organizations, Mennonites were becoming sensitized to "structural sins"—patterns of social organization that perpetuated oppression.

The first statement to incorporate justice into Mennonite peacemaking was endorsed at the 1971 GC general assembly. Titled "The Way of Peace," a subsection declared, "The Way of Peace is the Way of Justice."[27] The statement called Christians to "confront those who because of their greed cause injustice and oppression for others," and "to identify with the oppressed and participate in ministries of love and service in their behalf."

The statement cites the litany of traditional "peace Scriptures" but never uses the word nonresistance, nor quotes Matthew 5:39, "resist not evil." The Sermon on the Mount looms prominent—especially Matthew 5:9, "Happy are those who work for peace." But in a new twist, Mennonites searching for scriptural support for social justice were turning to the Old Testament prophets.

The focus on justice gained momentum in 1976 when MCC commissioned a three-year study of it. Major addresses at the 1978 Mennonite World Conference in Wichita also articulated concerns for justice. The International Peace Interest Group, meeting at the conference, called on Mennonite congregations around the world "to a study of the Biblical understanding of peace and justice."[28]

A 1979 MCC statement on "Militarism and Development" traced

the links between militarism and poverty and declared, "The way of peace and justice is at the heart of the Christian faith." Echoing sentiments from the 1978 Mennonite World Conference, it called on congregations to "seek justice for the oppressed, and witness against powers and principalities who trust in bombs and move toward nuclear holocaust."

The momentum for justice peaked in 1983 at a joint session of the GC and MC general assemblies in Bethlehem, Pennsylvania. Both groups approved a major statement, "Justice and the Christian Witness."[29] With the blessing of both denominations, the 1983 statement marked a major benchmark in the legacy of nonresistance. The statement incorporated many previous themes—"responsibility," "peace and love," "witness," "the politics of Jesus," and "nonviolent action."

Moreover Mennonites were now stretching their canopy of peacemaking, in the words of the statement, "to enlarge our understanding of peace with the dimension of biblical justice." Signaling the demise of nonresistance, the word appeared only once in the document, and then diluted in the phrase, "the biblical way of nonresistance, peace and love." But a new word—*shalom*—was floating to the surface. Shalom linked peace with justice as well as Old and New Testaments, providing a wholistic sense of peacemaking.

The peace vision reflected in the 1983 statement carried four distinctive accents. First, it was boldly *activist.* The statement overflows with strident language—radical witness, constructive confrontation, assert, empower, act, do, participate, challenge, nonviolent protest, and peacemaking. This was modern language that rang with rationality. Mennonites were taking initiatives, employing strategies.

Turning their backs on passive nonresistance, they were appealing to the politics of Jesus to "confront the principalities and powers." "In Jesus we see . . . a love which is far from passive but is active and aggressive." Moreover, "making peace is not always peaceful . . . the quest for peace with justice . . . can make people angry and upset . . . concern for the neighbor in some circumstances, therefore may call for public protest . . . or other controversial actions," including "nonviolent protest." Nonviolent protest, on the margins in the late sixties, now was receiving the blessing of official bodies.

Second, the new vision was *wholistic,* incorporating political and economic dimensions together with the biblical mandate. Mennonites were turning to the Old Testament, especially the prophets, for their view of "prophetic witness." The prophets exemplified how "God's love confronts injustice." Mennonite peace theology was rehabilitating the Old Testament, confirming Hershberger's 1944 argument that peace was threaded throughout the Old Testament. Shalom—blending peace with justice—became the operative biblical word for a new vision of Mennonite peacemaking.

Third, the 1983 statement had an *external* focus. The notion of justice shifted the target of peacemaking outside the Mennonite community. Mennonites were now talking about responsibility for *others.* Christians were called to "defend the fatherless, plead for the widow," indeed, "justice is acting for the oppressed." Mennonite followers of Christ were called to "strengthen the rights of the poor and powerless." The statement gives explicit guidelines for participation in and witness to "secular structures." In all these ways the spotlight of Mennonite peacemaking had shifted beyond the Mennonite fold.

Fourth, the focus on justice brought a *systemic* understanding of peacemaking, far exceeding the old posture of nonresistance that emphasized how an individual should respond to personal evil. The statement speaks of "structural injustice" and "fallen and rebellious . . . institutions," as well as "structures." Indeed the statement concludes with guidelines for relating to "secular structures."

In tone and language the statement was a modern document imbued with rationality, differentiation, and individuation. It talked of goals, actions, rights, and organizations. It allowed ample latitude for a plurality of peacemaking initiatives. The statement confessed that "involvement in justice issues may force us to rethink the meaning of peace."

This rethinking was a fundamental rethinking indeed. MC and GC bodies acting in unison in 1983 had tolled the death knell for the quiet nonresistance that had dominated much of Mennonite thinking throughout the twentieth century. To be sure Mennonites "with our Lord" continued to "renounce violence" but the long reign of passive nonresistance had succumbed to the winds of modernity.

Active Peacemaking

By the late 1980s the work of change agents and the theological revisions of the ideological brokers had clinched the focus on peacemaking. The word dominated the language Mennonites used to describe their peace convictions. Although nonresistance was still widely used by conservative groups and remained in partial currency among mainline Mennonites, peacemaking clearly occupied center stage. Not only significant as a linguistic tool, peacemaking reflected a major paradigm change in Mennonite consciousness and fittingly described a variety of activist ventures that blossomed in the eighties.

A New Language

A review of Mennonite publications and magazines confirms the rapid ascendance and dominance of "peacemaking" as the prominent rubric for pacifist impulses in the late eighties and nineties.[30] In 1986, peacemaking appeared for the first time in the index of the *Gospel Herald*, the same year nonresistance disappeared.[31] Swartley and Dyck's (1987) annotated bibliography of Mennonite peace writings devotes more pages to peacemaking than any other topic. Most of the entries that include peacemaking are fairly recent.

TABLE 6.1
Columns of Text in the Mennonite Encyclopedia by Time and Topic*

Concepts	1955	1990
Nonresistance	18	2
Conscientious Objector	15	7
Nonconformity	15	4
Church and State	14	7
Relief Work	14	6
Simplicity	5	0
Love	3	4
Litigation	3	0
Pacifism	1	0
Civil Disobedience	0	2
Justice	0	4
Development Work	0	6
Politics (and related)**	0	12
Peace (and related)***	0	13

*Note: 1955 includes Vol. 1-4, 1990 pertains only to Vol. 5.
** Includes Politics, Political Attitudes, and Political Activism.
*** Includes Peace, Peace Activism, Peace Education, Peace Studies, and Lobbying.

The shift of peace-related topics in *The Mennonite Encyclopedia* between 1955 and 1990 appears in Table 6.1. Although the 1955 edition has four volumes and the 1990 only one, the shift from nonresistance to activism is clearly obvious. Entries related to "Peace" are missing from the 1955 edition, whereas the 1990 volume devotes considerable attention to peace activities. Appearing for the first time in 1990 are

"Justice," "Politics," "Lobbying," and "Political Activism," along with other activist entries.

The dramatic transformation of the meek into activists is also captured in a 1986 brochure produced by MCC to describe its peace efforts. The three-page, twelve-panel pamphlet reflects a broad Mennonite consensus because MCC enjoys the support of the major Mennonite bodies as well as the Brethren in Christ. Titled "The Peacemaking Commitment," the publication mentions peacemaking twenty-seven times but never nonresistance.[32] The frequency of key words appears in Table 6.2.

Justice, reconciliation, and love assume major significance in the peacemaking scheme. The pamphlet defines in a simple but eloquent manner the contemporary view of Mennonite peacemaking at the dusk of the twentieth century. "Peacemakers reach out to all people caught in fear, suffering, hate, oppression, and violence. Peacemaking involves reflection, prayer, and an active nonviolent witness to the structures that cause and perpetuate injustices and violence." The legacy of nonresistance, stretching across some four and a half centuries since 1525, found its modern consummation under the umbrella of peacemaking.

New Vehicles of Peacemaking

Some of the enthusiasm for positive peacemaking became institutionalized into ongoing programs. The Victim Offender Reconciliation

---

TABLE 6.2
Word Frequency of an MCC Peacemaking Brochure

Concepts	Frequency of use
Peace	36
Peacemaking (ers)	27
Justice	16
Reconciling (ed)	13
Love	11
Nonviolence	4
Shalom	4
Nonresistance	0

Source: Mennonite Central Committee, Akron, Pa., 1986.

Program (VORP) expressed the sentiments of active peacemaking in the seventies and eighties in many Mennonite communities. Focused on the theme of restorative justice, VORP seeks to bring victims and criminal offenders together for reconciliation and healing. Offenders typically agree to make restitution directly to the victims of their crimes.

Since its inception in 1974, VORP projects have appeared in some seventy-five communities across North America. MCC offices in the U.S. and Canada have encouraged and supported the development of VORPs in many local communities. Mennonites are involved in at least thirty of the VORP projects, although the programs are not directly administered by churchwide agencies. Involvement in VORP has enabled many Mennonites to promote peacemaking and reconciliation in criminal justice in alternative ways to the traditional penal system.[33] The MCC offices in Canada and the U.S. are also involved in a variety of other criminal justice ministries.

The transition to active peacemaking in the eighties was also embodied in the work of Mennonite Conciliation Service. The idea surfaced in 1975 at a workshop on conflict resolution at Bethel College. Bill Keeney and others envisioned a Mennonite program that would remedy social disasters in the way that Mennonite Disaster Service had addressed the physical disasters that follow in the wake of tornadoes and hurricanes.

After a variety of consultations and meetings facilitated by MCC's Peace Section, Ronald Kraybill was appointed full-time director of the fledgling Mennonite Conciliation Services (MCS) in 1979. The ministry of MCS burgeoned in the eighties with a flurry of requests for training and conflict resolution both within and beyond Mennonite circles. Building on the national interest in new alternatives to dispute resolution, MCS trained mediators and established a number of community mediation centers. It also provided professional mediators for ethnic disputes as well as for conflicts in church, family, community, and businesses; published resource materials; and provided consulting services to many other groups. The services of MCS have reached beyond the U.S. and Canada through the efforts of persons like John Paul Lederach who spearheaded International Conciliation Services.[34]

The rise of Mennonite-related Peace Centers also signaled the flowering of activist peacemaking in the eighties. Summarizing the growth of local Peace Centers in both Canada and the U.S., John R. Burkholder found that some thirty Mennonite-related Peace Centers had blossomed by 1984.[35] The bulk of these had arisen since 1980, many in response to the growing threat of nuclear war.

The local centers were "Mennonite-related" because Mennonites were involved in some way in administration, funding, and staffing. The centers had some paid staff but most leaned heavily on volunteers, including non-Mennonites. Their annual budgets rarely topped $15,000. Although the centers initiated a wide range of peace and justice activities many of their efforts fell into four categories: education, networking, action, and resources. Whether the vitality of these centers will endure over time remains to be seen but they clearly signify a turnabout from passive nonresistance of earlier years.

At the 1984 Mennonite World Conference in Strasbourg, France, Ronald J. Sider urged Mennonites to develop a nonviolent peacemaking force to intervene in situations of international hostility. This plea gave rise to Christian Peacemaker Teams (CPT). Directed by Gene Stoltzfus since 1986, CPT organizes Peacemaker Teams which are dispatched to international settings of conflict, hosts an annual training/action conference, sponsors local peace initiatives, and encourages public vigils of protest and worship.

In recent years CPT has sponsored a variety of conferences and training seminars, witness vigils, and public protests. It has commissioned peacemaking envoys to hostile situations in Israel, the West Bank of Palestine, Jordan, Montreal, Quebec, Haiti, Los Angeles, and Iraq, among other places. In the early nineties CPT was developing plans to form an active CPT Peace Reserve. The reserve, consisting of twelve persons trained in the skills of nonviolent direct action and mediation, would be ready at any time for deployment to emergency situations and points of conflict around the world.[36] Duane Ruth-Heffelbower's (1991) *The Anabaptists Are Back* is a compelling introduction to activist peacemaking that includes vignettes and stories from the experience of CPT volunteers.

We have underscored several concrete programs that articulate the spirit of active peacemaking. These, however, are only a sample of some of the more prominent Mennonite initiatives. Many other activities designed to bear witness to the healing and reconciling ministry of Jesus Christ in peace and justice continue. Consider the outreach ministries of hundreds of local congregations, as well as the efforts of individuals in occupational and community projects. The witness of voluntary service workers in many branches of the Mennonite family also lend credence to the peacemaking calling.

Moreover, MCC workers around the world actively provide relief to the suffering and initiate long-term projects of community development. The MCC U.S. Office on Crime and Justice and the Committee on Women's Concerns, along with peace education efforts, typify the growing concerns for justice and an activist style of peacemaking. The MCC Women's Concerns Desk, established in 1973, has given significant leadership to gender related issues. In recent years the Desk has prepared information packets dealing with domestic violence and sexual abuse. Some 15,000 copies of these packets were printed and the Desk publishes a newsletter *Report*.[37]

The publications flowing off the Mennonite presses in recent years also confirm the embrace of a more positive stride in peacemaking. Ruth-Heffelbower's (1991:120) *The Anabaptists Are Back* links the spirit of activism to the legacy of the sixteenth-century Anabaptists. He argues that to characterize "their nonresistance in the beginning as passive is incorrect. Today, Mennonites are rediscovering the original Anabaptist vision in which nonresistance was a dynamic force for social transformation."

The fifteen books in the Herald Press "Peace and Justice" series illustrate the activist bent with titles such as *The Way God Fights*, *The Good News of Justice*, *Making War and Making Peace*, and *Jesus' Clear Call to Justice*. The peacemaking focus is heralded as well by *Seeking Peace* (Peachey and Peachey, 1991) and *A Christian Peacemaker's Journal* (Kreider, 1991). Such programs and publications confirm the substantial shift in the Mennonite consciousness that has occurred in the late twentieth century.

Summary

The language of peacemaking fit the sensibilities of modern Mennonites. It tied them to their past but also rang with plausibility in the context of a people who had largely become acclimated to modern life. The change agents who charted new trails of activist peacemaking were followed by theological brokers. The theologians found biblical legitimation for the transformation from passivity to activism by shifting their focus within Matthew 5. No longer leaning on verse 39, "resist not evil," they now highlighted verse 9, "happy are the peacemakers." Still anchored in the Sermon on the Mount as well as in the Old Testament prophets, peacemaking articulated the Mennonite legacy with integrity for a people amidst modernity.

The peacemaking rubric fit modern Mennonite consciousness for several reasons. It was *pluralistic*, providing cover for a wide panorama of peace thinking from biblical nonresistance—still alive among conservative sectors—to nonviolent resistance and political action among more strident members, from militarism to domestic violence. The elastic rubric sanctioned a plurality of initiatives in the modern spirit of diversity and individuation.

Peacemaking was *activistic*, truly modern in the sense that Mennonites were able to confront situations, address injustice, mediate conflict, and bring reconciliation. Unlike passive nonresistance, peacemaking provided the perception, at least, that things could be done, that Christians could take initiatives and make the larger world a better place.

In addition, the peacemaking label was *polite*. It provided easy access to ecumenical conversations for Mennonites who were weary of explaining the meaning of nonresistance and defending its negative and irresponsible tone. Acculturated Mennonites could embrace peacemaking with confidence and pride, leaving behind any traces of embarrassment.

In all of these ways peacemaking fit modern plausibility structures while also linking Mennonites to their heritage. Mennonites had stretched the peacemaking canopy to sanction witness against violence in all of its forms, from militarism to family voilence. But had individual members retained their historic rejection of force when faced with personal harm? That question, for which we lack empirical answers, is an intriguing riddle that lies beneath the transformation of Mennonite peacemaking.

We have traced the reconstruction of nonresistance in the twentieth century in the official documents and the writings of key leaders. Was the transformation confined to the intellectual elite? What of rank-and-file members? In the second part of the book we investigate the peacemaking attitudes of some 3,000 Mennonites tapped by the binational Church Member Profile of five denominations. This rich source of data to which we now turn provides documentation of the views and behavior of typical members.

PART II

Modern Visions

During the Vietnam War, some Mennonite men entered Canada to avoid cooperating with the U.S. Selective Service. Mennonite professor Walter Klaassen (L), of Conrad Grebel College, Ontario, and two other professors counsel two U.S. draft dodgers about alternatives to military service.

CHAPTER SEVEN

Alternative Service

Two historical developments dramatically changed the shape of Mennonite peacemaking in the twentieth century. One focused on in-group peace convictions and the other on political relationships with the larger society. A search for alternatives to military conscription began in the 1930s, when nine out of ten Mennonites were rural, confined mostly to farming, minimally educated and largely segregated from the larger world. Civilian Public Service was created in the context of World War II as a legitimate alternative to military service for COs. Chapter seven wrestles with current attitudes toward military service which Mennonites display despite being more urban, educated, modern, and not (as of this writing) facing conscription.

Chapter eight turns to Mennonite participation in the public political arena—a new arena of activity for Mennonites. In chapter nine we focus on contemporary dimensions of peacemaking which illustrate the plurality of present-day Mennonite thinking. The final chapter (10) ties together our historical sweep, reviews significant changes in the transformation of nonresistance, and highlights emerging Mennonite visions for peacemaking in the twenty-first century.

The Agonies of World War II
Alternative Service in Canada
The threat of war in the 1930s put pressure on Mennonites to address the question of what they would do if war broke out.

Bishop David Toews of Rosthern, Saskatchewan, took the initiative in calling a joint meeting of various branches of the Mennonite faith. On May 15, 1939, four months before Canada declared war against Germany, the historic meeting took place in Winkler, Manitoba. Nine groups were represented (Klippenstein, 1979:11).

The meeting revealed basic differences between the more conservative "Kanadier" who had migrated to the west in the 1870s, and the "Russlaender" who had come fifty years later in the 1920s. Earlier groups had been completely exempted from services in World War I by an Order-in-Council given in 1873 which applied to them but not to later Mennonite immigrants. The "Russlaender" who came from Russia in the 1920s had served in either forest camps or semi-military medical service during World War I in Russia. They were again willing to do so in Canada (Klippenstein, 1979:12).

On September 8, 1939, Canada declared war against Germany. Following many meetings and vigorous debate between the "Kanadier" and "Russlaender" of the west and the "Swiss" in Ontario, an alternative service program was established by June 1941. At that time the first 1,000 men with CO status were sent out on alternative service assignments (Janzen, 1990:49). By the end of the war some 7,500 Mennonites had served in the Canadian Alternative Service program (Toews, 1959; Regehr, 1992:463).

Alternative Service in the United States

The U.S. entered the war later than Canada, but Mennonites and others were also preparing for it.

> The 65 church representatives who met in Chicago during October 4 and 5, 1940, were no longer strangers to one another. Many of these had attended the historic Newton, Kansas, peace conference in 1935 and had been working on peace and conscientious objector plans since. Now the military conscription of their young men was no longer in the future. A plan had to be designed (Keim, 1990b:27).

In collaboration with government officials, religious leaders from several denominations established Civilian Public Service (CPS) as an alternative to military service for conscientious objectors.[1]

The first camp opened on May 15, 1941, seven months before Pearl Harbor. The program grew rapidly. Keim reports (1990b:33) that "by 1942, there were 3,738 men in CPS; 1,572 in 13 Mennonite camps, 1,035 in 12 Friends camps, 1,048 in 10 Brethren camps. Two Catholic camps had 68 men and a cooperative camp had 15."

The CPS projects included conservation and forestry camps, hospitals and training schools, university labs, agricultural experimental stations and farms, and as government survey crews. The CPSers built

roads, fought forest fires, constructed dams, planted trees, built con-
tour strips on farms, served as guinea pigs for medical and scientific
research, built sanitary facilities for communities, and cared for the
mentally ill and juvenile delinquents (Keim, 1990b:40; 1990a; 1990c).

Not all COs entered alternative service assignments. Some Mennonites entered noncombatant military service. This received limited
support from Swiss Mennonites, but Russian Mennonites were more
open to noncombatant service because it was more common in Russia.

By the end of the war in 1945, nearly 5,000 American COs had
served prison terms. Most of the imprisoned were Jehovah's Witnesses. Draft boards refused to give them ministerial exemption and
sent over 4,000 to jail (Keim, 1990b:34).

Service Choices in Canada

North American Mennonites in both Canada and the United
States faced hard choices with the military draft of World War II. Over
one-half (55%) of those drafted chose alternative service, while 45
percent entered military service. Almost two-thirds (62%) of the
12,036 Canadian Mennonites drafted chose alternative service. This
involved some 7,500 men and a few women as shown in Table 7.1
(Regehr, 1992:465; Gingerich, 1955).

The 4,508 Canadian Mennonites who entered the military represented more than one-third of those drafted. They included 3,905 who
joined the army, 316 in the air force, 232 in the navy, and fifty-five
who entered the women's corps (Regehr, 1992:465). Regehr
(1992:471) found no major generals, colonels, or lieutenant colonels
with Mennonite names, but there were five majors, nineteen captains,
twenty-four lieutenants, and nineteen second lieutenants. Swiss Mennonite names were more common among Canadian military leadership than Russian Mennonite names. We know relatively little about
those who opted for military service; even less about the 5,273 American Mennonites who entered the military (Janzen, 1990).

We also know relatively little about Mennonites who went to jail.
William Janzen and Frances Greaser (1990:7) report that at one time
as many as thirty COs were incarcerated at Headingly, Manitoba.
Some think there may have been many more.[2] Frank Peters was imprisoned for two and one-half years including six months in military
detention at the Fort Osborne Barracks in Winnipeg. In *Sam Martin
Went to Prison* Janzen and Greaser tell the story of a CO who wanted to
do alternative service but was jailed instead for nineteen months.

TABLE 7.1
Mennonite Participation in Alternative and Military Service During World War II

Service Choice		USA		Canada		Totals	
Alternative Service		4,536	46	7,500	62	12,036	55
Military Service		5,273	54	4,508	38	9,781	45
TOTALS	Number	9,809		12,008		21,817	
	Percent		100		100		100

Sources: Albert N. Keim, (1990c); T. D. Regehr, (1992:463-65).

CPS in the United States

South of the Canadian border, 151 camps were established in thirty-two states, with a heavy concentration in the northeast (Kreider, 1991; Thiesen, 1990). To underscore the significant role Mennonites played in alternative service, we present the religious affiliation of CPSers in World War II as shown in Table 7.2.

The three historic peace churches contributed roughly 7,000 of the 12,000 who served in CPS, representing well over half (58%) of all who served. The 4,665 Mennonites, by far the largest denominational group, represented almost four out of ten (39%) CPSers. The 1,353 CPSers affiliated with the Church of the Brethren constituted 11 percent, and the 951 Friends represented about 8 percent. Thus the heart of the CPS program was comprised of individuals with ties to the historic peace churches.

The remainder (42%) of CPSers came from other denominations or were unaffiliated with a religious denomination (Keim, 1990b:80). The 673 Methodists were the largest non-historic peace church contingent representing nearly 6 percent, followed by the Jehovah's Witness, who numbered 409. About 4 percent of the CPSers were unaffiliated with any religious group.

Current Mennonite Service Preferences

A study of Mennonites in North America, based on a sample of more than 3,000 Mennonites in 1972 and again in 1989, shows that most of them still hold the historic peace position.[3] Mennonite respondents, males and females as well as young and old, were asked how they would respond if faced with a military draft today. A large majority would prefer serving in an alternative to military service if drafted

TABLE 7.2
Conscientious Objectors in Civilian Public Service During
World War II by Religious Affiliation

Affiliation	Number	Percent	
Mennonite	4,665	39	
Church of the Brethren	1,353	11	
Friends	951	8	
			58
Methodist	673		
Jehovah's Witness	409		
Congregational Christian	209		
Presbyterian	192		
Baptist, Northern	178		
German Baptist Brethren	157		
Roman Catholic	149		
Christadelphian	127		
Lutheran	108		
Evangelical and Reformed	101		
Episcopal	88		
Church of Christ	78		
Disciples of Christ	78		
Russian Malokan	76		
Evangelical	50		
Baptist, Southern	45		
Unitarian	44		
Other Religious Groups	1,695		38
Unaffiliated	449		4
TOTALS	**11,875**		**100**

Source: Albert N. Keim, (1990b:81).

today. A sizable minority is willing to consider the more radical action of non-registration or refusal of induction.

Draft Choices by Denominations

The responses to a military draft are shown in Table 7.3. The alternative service option—by far the most popular preference of almost three-fourths (71%) in 1972—declined to less than two-thirds (62%)

TABLE 7.3
Draft Choices by Denomination in Percent

Which position would you take if faced with a military draft?	Denominations					Totals	
	EMC	BIC	MB	GC	MC	1972	1989
Refuse registration and/or induction	1	3	6	8	7	3	7
Alternative service	17	43	50	59	73	71	62
Uncertain	12	17	16	14	10	11	12
Noncombatant military service	38	21	20	14	7	10	13
Military service	32	16	8	6	3	5	6
TOTALS Number	50	249	548	811	1374	2990	3032
Percent	2	8	18	27	45	100	100

in 1989. There were significant differences by denomination. Respondents from larger denominations more strongly favored alternative service. Three-fourths of the respondents of the Mennonite Church (73%) in 1989, but only 17 percent of U.S. Evangelical Mennonite Church members chose alternative service.[4] Support for alternative service among GCs, MBs, and BICs respectively was 59, 50, and 43 percent.

While support for alternative service declined during the past generation, more radical forms of protest rose slightly. Seven percent in 1989 chose refusing registration (3%) or induction (4%). Twice as many in 1989 (7%) as in 1972 (3%) opted for these more radical positions. Historic nonresistance is represented by those selecting alternative service, refusing registration, or refusing induction. Throughout the chapter we sometimes refer to these three choices as "peaceful alternatives" to military service.

Three-fourths of the respondents in 1972 preferred one of the peaceful alternatives to the military draft. This support dropped to two-thirds by 1989. While 80 percent of the MC respondents chose these alternatives in 1989, only 18 percent of the EMCs and 46 percent of the BICs embraced them. These smaller denominations, with less than half of their members choosing peaceful alternatives, have a difficult task if they hope to strengthen peace convictions.

In Table 7.3 the denominational responses are ordered across a continuum from refusing to register, to the opposite pole—entering regular military service. Only 6 percent of our total sample in 1989 (5 percent in 1972) said they would choose regular military service. However, 13 percent of the sample in 1989 were willing to enter non-combatant military service so they would be excused from carrying weapons. Nearly three out of four of the EMC respondents chose a form of military service.

Again, respondents of the larger denominations were much less willing to enter any type of military service, with only one in ten of the MCs choosing this option. The denominational differences are rather dramatic. EMCs are seven times (70 vs. 10%) more likely than MCs to enter noncombatant or regular military service.

Those uncertain about their choice varied by denomination from ten to 17 percent. If we combine all those in 1972 who were uncertain (11%), chose noncombatant service (10%), or opted for military service (5%) fully one-fourth of the Mennonites and Brethren in Christ respondents did not endorse a historic peace position.

By 1989 each of these categories rose slightly, and when combined, we find that one-third of all respondents did not clearly reject military service—a rise of five percentage points over one generation. Support for peaceful alternatives to military service has seriously eroded among some denominations—down to 18 percent among the EMCs and to 46 percent among the BICs. It is only the larger denominations, who represent greater numbers in the sample, that keep the overall support for peace alternatives relatively high.

Theology and Draft Choices

While response to the draft varies greatly by denomination, theological orientation also differentiates choices. Kauffman and Driedger (1991) developed a scale of Anabaptism dealing with adult baptism, discipleship, nonswearing of oaths, reluctance to take others to court, and the like. Do Anabaptist beliefs make a difference in draft choices?

Table 7.4 presents the relationship between Anabaptist beliefs (low to high), and draft choices. While less than half who scored low on Anabaptism chose alternative service, nearly three-fourths of high scoring Anabaptists did. Four percent with low support for Anabaptism refused registration or induction, while 9 percent who scored high on Anabaptism did so. While 51 percent of low scoring Anabaptists chose peaceful options, four out of five of the committed Anabaptists did so. Anabaptist theology differentiates Mennonites almost as much as denomination.

TABLE 7.4
Draft Choices by Anabaptist Theological
Orientation in Percent

Which position would you take if faced with a military draft?	Anabaptist Theological Orientation		
	Low	Middle	High
Refuse registration and/or induction	4[a]	7	9
Alternative service	47	62	71
Uncertain	16	13	9
Noncombatant military service	17	13	10
Military service	15	6	2
TOTALS **Number**	556	1499	898
Percent	19	51	30

[a] "Four percent of those with a low Anabaptist orientation would refuse registration and/or induction."

Thirty-two percent of those who scored low on Anabaptism chose noncombatant (17%) or regular military service (15%). Few (12%) Anabaptist adherents chose noncombatant or military service. There is a strong overlap between Anabaptist beliefs and denominational affiliation. Respondents belonging to the Mennonite Church scored highest on Anabaptist beliefs. Evangelical Mennonites—scoring lowest on Anabaptism—were most willing to choose military service. Anabaptist beliefs undergirded Mennonite Church choices for alternatives to the military. The embrace of peaceful alternatives to military service is woven into both the denominational and theological fabric.

Draft Choices by Generation

Mennonites who served in the military or in alternative service in World War II are now in their seventies. They likely will make different choices than young Mennonites who have not faced the draft. After World War II, Mennonites in the United States continued to face difficult draft choices in the Korean and Vietnam wars. Vietnam veterans and service workers are now in their forties, and Korean war returnees in their fifties. We expect that younger Mennonites who have not struggled with draft choices may make different choices than their elders. Great efforts were made by American Mennonite leaders in the fifties and sixties to educate Mennonite youth by mailing peace literature, providing draft counseling, and hosting study conferences to promote alternative service. We expect that service choices may reflect age differentials, which we now examine.

Table 7.5 shows that as age rises, alternative service preferences increase. More radical choices—refusing registration or induction—vary little by age. Half of the teenagers chose peaceful alternatives to military service, while more than two-thirds over fifty made the same choice. Those under thirty were less likely to choose alternative service than respondents over thirty. With draft pressure subsiding, will peace convictions diminish among Mennonite youth?

Indeed, one-fourth of Mennonite teenagers selected one of the military options, with 8 percent choosing regular military service. Only 3 percent of the seventy- to ninety-year-olds selected that option. One out of four teenagers were uncertain how to respond to the draft. Some of this ambivalence is typical of teenagers and some likely arises from the absence of a draft. Combining the uncertain and military service options shows that nearly half of the teenagers have not embraced historic Mennonite teaching. This is a sizable proportion and if it continues, could erode support for peaceful alternatives to military service, if educational measures are not taken to stem the tide.

TABLE 7.5
Draft Choices by Age in Percent

Which position would you take if faced with a military draft?	Age of Respondent				
	13-19	20-29	30-49	50-69	70-94
Refuse registration and /or induction	7	11	7	5	7
Alternative service	46	49	63	67	61
Uncertain	23	19	11	10	14
Noncombatant military service	17	14	12	12	16
Military service	8	7	7	6	3
TOTALS　　Number	140	403	1195	947	328
Percent	5	13	40	31	11

Choices by Region and Nation
While theology and generational differences greatly influence draft choices, we expect that regional and national origin will also be

important. Mennonites in the eastern United States came much earlier, some 300 years ago, and settled in Pennsylvania along with other conservative groups—Amish, Dunkers, and others of German origin. They tended to remain rural and conservative theologically (Driedger, 1988). Eastern American Mennonites, largely affiliated with the Mennonite Church, were heavily influenced by such World War II pillars as H. S. Bender, G. F. Hershberger, and J. C. Wenger who promoted the Anabaptist Vision.

The fermenters of the fifties—J. L. Burkholder, J. H. Yoder, P. Peachey, and some other members of the Concern Group discussed in chapter four—hailed from the Mennonite Church east of the Mississippi. Early Mennonite settlers in eastern Canada, came from this same Swiss American East roughly 200 years ago. All of these eastern American Mennonites lived through the wars of independence and the American Civil War.

By contrast Mennonites in the western United States and Canada were mostly of Dutch North European origin, arriving little more than 100 years ago in the 1870s. The more liberal ones settled in Kansas, the more conservative in Manitoba. These Mennonites had gone through the Prussian and Russian revolutions. More Russian Mennonites came in the 1920s and 1950s, mainly to Canada. Twentieth-century migrants had lived through the Russian revolution and two world wars. They had seen their home territories invaded by waves of military forces from all sides. These different regional and national experiences, which influenced past Mennonite attitudes, still persist today.

In Table 7.6 we present four regions in which Mennonites reside, two in the United States and two in Canada. The Mississippi River divides east and west, and the American-Canadian border slices north and south. The alternative service choices of Americans and Canadians vary little—western Americans rank highest and western Canadians lowest. Although Canadians are more ready to refuse registration and induction, neither regional nor national differences are great.

Eastern Canadians were least willing to enter noncombatant service. While only 6 percent of all Mennonites in 1989 chose military service, American Mennonites were four times as likely to as Canadians (2%) to do so. Living in the United States, the strongest military power in the world, has influenced American Mennonite attitudes to-

TABLE 7.6
Draft Choices by Region and Nationality in Percent

Which position would you take if faced with a military draft?	Region and Nationality			
	American West	American East	Canadian West	Canadian East
Refuse registration and/or induction	6	6	9	10
Alternative service	65	63	55	60
Uncertain	8	11	20	20
Noncombatant military service	14	11	14	8
Military service	8	9	2	2
TOTALS Number	1360	695	666	263
TOTALS Percent	46	23	22	9

ward peacemaking. Does living in a small or middle power country with few armed forces press Canadian Mennonites away from military choices? Or have more recent Mennonite migrations to Canada been a factor? Causes of these differences are not easy to untangle. Why are those in eastern Canada less likely to choose military options?

The Impact of Modernization

In chapter two we predicted that the forces of modernization would likely mold Mennonite attitudes toward peacemaking. We have observed the formidable influence of denominational and theological factors. Will the structural changes in the Mennonite community related to urbanization, education, and occupation shape Mennonite responses to the draft? Will urban, educated, and professionalized Mennonites select peaceful alternatives to military service as much as their more rural, less professionalized counterparts?

Influences of Urbanization

Earlier we suggested that modernizing influences—urbanization, education, and socioeconomic status—might influence Mennonite attitudes toward peace. Before World War II most Mennonites lived in the country. By 1972 one-third had moved to cities of 2,500 population or more, and by 1989 one-half lived in urban areas (Kauffman and Driedger, 1991). Does urbanization erode historic Mennonite commitments to alternative service options?

Table 7.7 shows that farmers (66%) are slightly more willing to choose alternative service than residents of large cities (58%). However, more large city Mennonites are willing to refuse registration than their farm counterparts. Combining the three peaceful options (refusing registration, refusing induction, and alternative service), we find a little difference between farm (71%) and large city (64%) Mennonites, but for the most part urbanization does not greatly erode pacifist convictions.

TABLE 7.7
Draft Choices by Urbanization in Percent

Which position would you take if faced with a military draft?	Residence			
	Rural Farm	Rural Nonfarm	Small City	Large City
Refuse registration and/or induction	5	5	9	8
Alternative service	66	65	59	58
Uncertain	11	11	12	15
Noncombatant military service	12	12	14	13
Military service	5	7	7	6
TOTALS Number	672	898	616	811
Percent	22	30	21	27

Place of residence is also not a factor in acceptance of combatant and noncombatant military service. Twice as many in both city and farm preferred noncombatant over regular military service. We conclude that urbanization has little influence on the Mennonite response to the draft, except that a few more city Mennonites prefer activist alternatives or are more uncertain than rural Mennonites.

Influence of Education
Using education as a second indicator of modernization, Table 7.8 shows that those with graduate education were more likely to choose alternative service (67%) than Mennonites with elementary education

(61%). Interestingly, high school graduates (56%) were least likely to choose alternative service.

Educational differences among the first three levels of education were minor on the more radical choices (refusing registration/induction). However, those with graduate degrees were twice as likely as the rest to select the more activist choices. When we combine the alternatives to military service, graduate educated Mennonites were the most likely (78%) to endorse peaceful options. Uncertainty regarding draft choices declines as education rises. The better educated have firmer convictions either for or against military service.

TABLE 7.8
Draft Choices by Educational Level in Percent

| Which position would you take if faced with a military draft? | Educational Level | | | |
	Elementary	High School	College	Grad School
Refuse registration and/or induction	6	5	6	11
Alternative service	61	56	64	67
Uncertain	19	16	9	6
Noncombatant military service	12	14	13	9
Military service	1	7	8	5
TOTALS Number	342	1174	860	643
TOTALS Percent	11	39	28	21

While roughly the same number of elementary and graduate educated Mennonites chose military-related service, the graduate educated showed the least interest in noncombatant service. In 1989, almost one in five Mennonites chose one of the two military options—a matter of concern for those who want to keep the peace position alive.

Influence of Occupational Status
Urbanization and education had relatively little impact on the Mennonite response to the military draft. How does occupational status influence service preferences? In Table 7.9 we have arrayed six occupational categories from low to high preference for peaceful alter-

natives. One-half of the blue collar workers compared to three-fourths of the professionals chose alternative service as their first choice. Two-thirds of the blue collar Mennonites chose one of the peaceful alternatives and four out of five professionals agreed. Differences among occupational subgroups in refusing registration or induction were minimal, but 9 percent of the students and professionals chose that option. Overall, Mennonites in business were more similar to blue-collar workers, and farmers more like professionals.

TABLE 7.9
Draft Choices by Occupation in Percent

Which position would you take if faced with a military draft?		*Occupation*				
	Stu- dent	Blue Collar	Busi- ness	Home- maker	Farmer	Profes- sional
Refuse registration and/or induction	9	8	5	5	6	9
Alternative service	51	54	58	61	69	70
Uncertain	23	15	12	19	6	5
Noncombatant military service	12	14	14	13	14	11
Military service	5	10	10	3	5	6
TOTALS Number	180	422	600	737	214	824
Percent	6	14	20	25	7	28

On the other hand, one out of four blue-collar Mennonites chose a military alternative, while less than two out of ten professionals (17%) did so. Twice as many in blue-collar work and business (10%) chose military service as farmers (5%) did. Service choices varied only modestly by occupational status groups. As might be expected students demonstrated the greatest degree of uncertainty, whereas farmers and professionals were nearly alike in showing little ambiguity about their response to the draft.

When we combined the education, occupation, and income indicators into a scale of socioeconomic status, we found upper status Mennonites preferred alternative service options more. Lower status Mennonites leaned more toward military options. The differences, however, were not great.

Modernizing forces such as urbanization, education, and occupational status impacted draft choices only slightly. Despite a few variations, urban, educated, and professional Mennonites made similar draft choices as their rural, less educated, and blue-collar counterparts. We conclude that modernization only slightly affects—in a positive way—peaceful service choices. Attitudes toward service preferences relate more strongly to theology, age, and national region.

Regathering Under the Lordship Canopy

In the previous chapter we described how Mennonites had enlarged their witness by expanding their two-kingdom view into an all-encompassing canopy where Christ was Lord of both church and society. As we noted earlier, Peter Berger's (1967) notion of *Sacred Canopy* was reminiscent of a Jewish tent-like cover, with four stakes at each corner, under which sacred services are held. The canopy symbolizes the protection of sacred valuables from the secular onslaughts of a hostile world. The tent protects if stable stakes can be found to hold it in place.

For Mennonites, doctrinal beliefs, religious life, service to others, and ethnic culture have been important stakes in their sacred canopy. To what extent has the "lordship canopy"—propped up by such stakes—become a stable reality in contemporary life? Do these important elements protect the historic peace emphasis? What have been the effects of modernization—education, urbanization, professionalism, materialism, secularization, and individualism—on attitudes toward service choices?

Canopy Strength and Service Preferences

In Table 7.10 we present indicators of four religious stakes in the Mennonite lordship canopy—theological beliefs, religious life, service to others, and ethnic identity. We begin with three theological orientations (Anabaptism, Orthodoxy, and Fundamentalism) and explore their relationship to draft choices.[5] Four out of five respondents who scored high on Anabaptism chose peaceful alternatives to the draft. One in ten chose a military option. And one in ten was uncertain. Mennonites scoring high on fundamentalism chose peaceful alternatives less and military service significantly more. Anabaptist beliefs are a strong theological stake upholding peace convictions under the lordship canopy.

TABLE 7.10
Draft Choices by Religiosity and Modernization in Percent

| | *Draft Choices* | | |
	Peaceful Alternatives[a]	Uncertain	Military Related Service[b]
Percent Who Scored High On:	*Religiosity*		
Anabaptism	80[c]	9	12
Orthodoxy	69	12	19
Fundamentalism	64	14	22
Church Participation	78	7	15
Religious Life	76	7	18
Devotionalism	74	9	17
MCC Support	81	8	11
Serving Others	76	10	15
Evangelism	71	9	20
Ethnic Identity	80	10	11
	Modernization		
Occupational Status	60	23	17
Urbanization	66	15	19
Educational Status	78	6	15
Individualism	49	20	31
Secularization	55	18	28
Materialism	61	8	32

[a] Includes three choices: refusal to register, register but refuse induction, and alternative service.

[b] Includes noncombatant and regular military service.

[c] "Eighty percent of those who scored high on Anabaptism selected a peaceful alternative (refuse registration/induction or alternative service) to a military draft."

Associationalism (church attendance), religious life (spiritual vitality), and devotionalism (prayer, Bible reading) represent another religious stake supporting the canopy. Roughly three out of four who scored high in these measures chose alternatives to the draft and less than two out of ten opted for military service.[6] Few who scored high on these measures of religiosity showed uncertainty about their draft choice.

Service indicators such as support of the Mennonite Central Committee (MCC), serving others in the community (visiting the sick, etc.), and evangelism (inviting others to church, etc.) represented a third stake which upholds peaceful alternatives to the draft.[7] Those who scored high on these various forms of service were more likely to prefer alternatives to military service.

Ethnic identity—support of Mennonite culture, institutions, friends, marriage, and the like—undergirded peaceful alternatives to the draft as much as Anabaptism and MCC support, which are the highest indicators of commitment under the lordship canopy. Expressions of Mennonite culture and identity are supportive of peaceful alternatives to participation in war. Indeed, 80 percent of those who scored high on Mennonite identity selected peaceful alternatives to the draft.

Table 7.10 also summarizes the effects of modernization. Respondents who scored high on urbanization and worked in professional and business occupations chose nonmilitary alternatives to the draft (60-66%) somewhat less than those scoring high on religiosity and ethnicity discussed above. Urban and upper status Mennonites were somewhat uncertain about their response to the draft. This ambivalence also showed up among those scoring high on individualism, secularization, and materialism—where only a half to two-thirds chose peaceful alternatives to the draft and nearly a third opted for military service. This demonstrates the corrosive influence of individualism, secularism, and materialism on convictions for nonmilitary alternatives to the draft.

The impact of modernization is somewhat mixed. The structural forces of modernization—urbanization, occupation, and education—exert little impact on draft choices. However, the ideological influences of modernization—individualism, secularism, and materialism—are much more corrosive of historic peace convictions.

Influences of Service Experience

Do those who enter church service programs have a greater commitment to the church than those who join the military or do not enter a formal service program? Fortunately, our North American sample included 377 who had served in church programs—MCC, Civilian Public Service, Voluntary Service, etc.—as well as forty-six veterans of military service. This permitted us to compare the religious commitments of respondents who had served in church or military service with the 901 persons who had served in neither program.[8]

In Table 7.11 we see that those who participated in church service programs scored higher on Orthodoxy, much higher on Anabaptist beliefs, and lower on Fundamentalism than their military counterparts. Veterans of church service programs also scored higher on all of the other "sacred" variables—associationalism, religious life, devotionalism, serving others, MCC support, and evangelism. Those who served in the military always ranked lower. Those without either type of service experience resembled church service respondents more, although they scored a little lower.

These findings suggest that the choice of service programs has an enduring effect in helping to stabilize the "lordship canopy." Those entering church service programs are more likely to remain under the sacred Mennonite canopy than those who enter military service.

Those who entered the military scored somewhat lower on socioeconomic status and higher on individualism. The differences between church service workers and those who had no service experience are relatively small. Those who entered the military tend to score higher on materialism and individualism.

We also explored the impact of service assignments on present-day responses to the draft as shown in Table 7.12. Type of service experience was highly associated with the draft choices of the respondents. Nine out of ten church workers chose alternative service or refusal to register, while three out of four who had entered the military chose military alternatives. Indeed half of them chose military service again. The choices of those with no service experience ranged between the other two groups.

Military veterans showed no ambivalence about their response to another draft. None were uncertain! One-fourth had switched to peaceful alternatives despite their military record. Service experiences clearly have an enduring influence on attitudes toward the draft.

Summary

As the agony of World War II fades in the Mennonite memory, it is fitting to assess the state of peacemaking among Mennonites. The fiftieth anniversaries of those who served in alternative service in the forties were held in 1991. Numerous publications have documented how 22,000 North American Mennonites dealt with conscription in World

TABLE 7.11
Religiosity and Modernization Scores
by Service Experience in Percent

| | *Service Experience* | | |
	Church Service	No Service Experience	Military Service
Percent Who Scored High On:		*Religiosity*	
Orthodoxy	74[a]	73	65
Anabaptism	39	36	11
Fundamentalism	20	23	32
Church Participation	41	34	18
Religious life	27	23	21
Devotionalism	23	18	13
Serving others	34	27	24
MCC support	28	22	15
Evangelism	24	23	16
Ethnic Identity	34	23	16
		Modernization	
SES[b]	25	29	21
Education	30	29	17
Occupation	37	39	20
Urbanization	42	49	45
Materialism	15	14	20
Secularization	18	21	20
Individualism	22	13	30

[a] "Seventy-four percent of those who had participated in church service programs scored high on orthodoxy."
[b] Social-economic status determined by combining occupation, education, and income scores.

TABLE 7.12
Draft Choices by Service Experience in Percent

What position would you take if faced with a draft?	Service Experience		
	Church Service	**No Service Experience**	**Military Service**
Refuse Registration/Induction	7	9	6
Alternative Service	81	58	19
Uncertain	3	8	0
Noncombatant Service	4	15	25
Military Service	5	10	50

War II—12,000 in alternative service and roughly 10,000 in the military. The historic peace churches supplied over half of the persons who entered alternative service. Mennonites led the way along with many others who refused military service.

Today North American Mennonites continue to favor alternatives to military service, along with an increasing emphasis on greater witness and peacemaking. Some are willing to advocate more radical forms of protest such as refusing to register for the draft or to pay taxes underwriting military purposes. Socioeconomic status appears to make little difference in Mennonite attitudes toward peacemaking.

While three out of four Mennonites chose nonmilitary forms of service in 1972, by 1989 this choice had declined to two-thirds. In other words, one-third were uncertain of their position or willing to enter some form of military service. While only one in ten in some denominations chose military options, in other Mennonite groups over two-thirds were willing to enter the military. Indicators of modernization such as urbanization, education, and occupational status have little influence on service choices. However, denominational affiliation is a significant factor in shaping attitudes toward the draft.

While modernization played a minor role, theology, age, and nationality are important influences. Almost all Mennonites embracing Anabaptism chose some form of alternative service, while fundamentalists were more likely to enter the military. Theological commitments are one of the most potent forces shaping responses to the draft. Theology and denominational influences are mutually reinforcing because Anabaptist-leaning Mennonites more heavily populate the larger denominations.

Older Mennonites living during the Second, Korean, or Vietnam wars and their accompanying military drafts favor alternatives to military service more than Mennonites under thirty. Youth are less inclined toward peaceful alternatives, with noticeably higher choices for military programs. To a lesser degree these differences are also reflected in regional and national locations. It is clear that Mennonite conscientious objection to war has declined, a shift which may not bode well for Mennonite peacemaking in the future.

Those who gathered under the lordship canopy—staked upon Anabaptist beliefs, a strong religious and devotional life, high ethnic identity, and service to others via MCC and evangelism—were most likely to choose peaceful alternatives to the draft. Similarly those with church service experience were four times more likely to embrace alternative service than those with military experience. The lordship canopy does not deter upward socioeconomic mobility, but it does moderate the negative influences of modernization and thus keeps the forces of individualism, secularism, and materialism in check. The lordship of Christ, embroidered on the sacred canopy, provides a protective covering for peaceful alternatives to the draft.

Contemporary Mennonites still prefer alternatives to military involvement, but there are some signs of weariness. More recently Mennonites have shouldered greater political involvement in the wider societal arena. How will such entanglements in the public political order impact on Mennonite peace convictions? That is the question to which we now turn.

As Mennonites became more politically active they made increasing trips to national capitols in Washington and Ottawa. These MCC representatives spoke with government officials in Washington, D.C., about violence in rural areas of the Philippines. Standing on the steps of the Capitol (from L) are Earl Martin, Betsy Byler, Bert Lobe, and Patty Wagner.

CHAPTER EIGHT

Political
Participation

While participation in alternative service has been a cornerstone of Mennonite peace convictions, Mennonites had relatively little experience in political participation in the larger society until after World War II. To what extent are Mennonites now open to the calls of J. Lawrence Burkholder and Gordon Kaufman for social responsibility and political engagement? How do contemporary attitudes align with the earlier debates about political withdrawal and social responsibility? Will political participation dramatically change Mennonite understandings of peace? How will political engagement affect the contemporary "lordship canopy" as Mennonites approach the twenty-first century?

John H. Redekop suggests that Mennonites are moving from separatist apolitical stances to increasing involvement. This is happening faster among Dutch-Russian Mennonites, who became more involved in Russia and carried these tendencies to western North America, especially Canada. The Schleitheim confession of 1527 represents the Swiss-South German tendency to be more wary of politics. We therefore expect that Swiss members of the Mennonite Church will also be less willing to become involved, although they too are changing (Redekop, 1983).

We expect that increased education, income, and occupational status will inch Mennonites in the direction of greater political participation now that half are living in urban areas (Driedger, 1986, 1989). Elmer Neufeld in the fifties illustrated that Mennonite scholars of the

Dutch-Russian heritage were more willing to consider greater involvement with the state than Swiss-South German scholars. By the seventies the trend toward greater openness to work with the state was clearly illustrated by John H. Redekop, a Mennonite Brethren political scientist teaching at Wilfrid Laurier University in Waterloo, Ontario.

The Beginnings of State Involvement
MCC Washington and Ottawa Offices

Conscription and arrangements for alternative service during the 1940s and World War II required frequent contacts and hearings with many agencies in Washington and Ottawa. More recently Mennonites have testified periodically before congressional and parliamentary committees in Washington and Ottawa (Burkholder, 1990:837-383). MCC's Peace Section had lengthy discussions about the advantages and disadvantages of establishing more permanent offices, first in Washington and later in Ottawa.[1] In 1968 the Mennonite Central Committee (MCC) Peace Section opened an office in Washington and in 1975 MCC Canada established an office in Ottawa.

> These offices serve as "listening posts" for constituents. Staff members monitor legislation and policy developments that affect the life and work of Mennonite and Brethren in Christ churches at home and abroad. Refugee concerns, world hunger, human rights, the environment (ecology), criminal justice and nuclear arms are among the issues added to conscription as legitimate areas of concern by the churches. Information is published for interested constituents, contacts with government are facilitated, and seminars are conducted (Delton Franz, 1990:528).

The expanding Mennonite presence of missionaries and MCC personnel in over fifty countries prompted more and more requests for meetings with government officials in North America. Such meetings both enlightened governmental officials and smoothed the way for the work of mission, relief, and rehabilitation organizations. As Mennonites become more educated and involved in the media, their awareness of the relevance of human needs and governmental policy has expanded accordingly. Today some "6000 Mennonites receive the *Washington Memo* of the MCC Washington office, and the 'Ottawa Notebook' appears regularly in the *Mennonite Reporter*" (Franz, 1990:528).

Ted Koontz (1990:160-161) suggests that Mennonites moved away from a strict church-state dualism after World War II because of increased urbanization, education, and occupational change which were linked with a positive theology of mission and service. This "caused Mennonites to become more engaged with the world in a new way. This shift lies in the background of a growing acceptance of the state as a proper arena for Christian witness in both countries among most, though not all, Mennonites."

Interestingly, this stance of witness to government still assumes that Christians (at least Mennonites) are not themselves the government. In fact, more and more Mennonites have moved into the respective U.S. and Canadian capitols working in government lobbies as well as in various governmental positions.

Since the mid-1970s, MCC Canada has also received millions of dollars from the Canadian government, through the Canadian International Development Agency (CIDA). These funds have become a sizable part of its budget. The use of such monies has been on the MCC Canada agenda almost annually. Debates have erupted between more conservative members—uneasy about receiving government funds—and those who feel they have an opportunity to use their tax monies in constructive ways.

Setting up national Mennonite "listening posts" was a controversial issue in the 1960s. However, competent and trustworthy staff such as Delton Franz in the Washington office and William Janzen in the Ottawa office have slowly won the trust of most Mennonites. Table 8.1 shows that in 1972 only half of the Mennonites and Brethren in Christ favored such offices with a full one-third being neutral, and 12 percent opposing such a presence. By 1989, three-fourths favored such offices, one-fourth remained undecided, and only 4 percent opposed them.

When MCC set up its Washington office in 1968, it enjoyed only partial constituency support. But by 1989 most Mennonites willingly

TABLE 8.1
Support for MCC Offices
in National Capitols in Percent

Do you favor having MCC offices in Washington and Ottawa capitols?	Attitudes		
	Disfavor	Uncertain	Favor
1972	12	34	55
1989	4	24	72

accepted such a witness. These offices are becoming more active, so that by 1990 it was possible for Delton Franz of the Washington office to describe their work as "lobbying."[2] In less than twenty years passive listening posts had become active lobbies. Since 1987 William Janzen, in the MCC Ottawa office, has been required to register as a lobbyist.

Redekop's Call to Action

John H. Redekop, who served as moderator of the Mennonite Brethren Canadian Conference and president of the Evangelical Fellowship of Canada, reflects a political outreach with which Canadian Mennonites are comfortable. Canadian Mennonites tend to be more involved in church-state relations. This is because of their mostly Dutch background, because their governments are less militarily minded, and because Canadian governments are more involved in promoting social welfare. The Canadian state seems more friendly and compassionate than some others.[3] are stated clearly and unequivocally. He says that

> we have . . . largely overlooked the extent to which the concerns and actual activities of the faithful church and the concerns and actual activities of certain types of government now overlap. Even more important, we have hardly begun to probe the extent to which they could or should overlap. . . .
>
> Guy Franklin Hershberger's [1958:156] suggestion in 1958 that Anabaptists could be characterized as people who are "indifferent toward the state" may have been descriptively adequate at that time but it cannot be accepted as a sufficient prescription today or at any time, for that matter. To be indifferent to the policies and practices of the greatest concentration of human power, to suppress all judgment of government policies, and to neglect all opportunities for Christian impact in the governmental apparatus constitutes an unacceptable restriction of the Great Commission which Jesus gave His church (Redekop, 1976:179-195).

Redekop (1976:181) bases his call for state involvement in the evangelical-Anabaptist and free church tradition. "In at least some of his writings Menno Simons (1956:604) perceived a definite and positive role for government and if he had lived under an enlightened, democratic system he would probably have argued for the propriety of considerable cooperation." Redekop (1976:184) expands Harold Bender's call to discipleship to include more active participation in government as followers of Jesus in modern times.

One reason why we can properly speak of free church coercion is that the church has a biblical directive to exercise selective resistance as well as nonresistance. . . . Love is a basic trait of God but nonresistance in not! God resists evil (1 Peter 5:9), God resists the proud (James 4:6) and from Genesis to Revelation God resists the evil one. We can say that God is love but we cannot properly say that God is nonresistance.

Such prophetic witness to the state has a threefold purpose: (1) addressing itself to major problems, (2) helping society comprehend the ethical thrust of Christianity, and (3) facilitating the resolutions of specific problems (Redekop, 1976:184). This Christian call to *The Good News of Justice* is well expressed by Hugo Zorrilla (1988). Redekop advocates initiative and action by the church in political affairs, with fewer distinctions between church and state. He claims that both open and closed societies have changed so much—in size, scope, function, and process—that the entire stance of Mennonites toward the state must be reexamined because the state is increasingly involved in society (Redekop, 1988:61-72).

With increased urbanization and with governments becoming more entangled in all facets of society

> the option of fortifying ourselves in ideological and sociological compounds has come to an end. Like the New Testament churches which were organized in the cities we will have to put our witness to the test in modern urban settings where government bureaucracies thrive and tentacles of government penetrate everywhere (Redekop, 1976:186).

Redekop assumes that the scope of government influence will increase into more services and projects at national, state, provincial, and local levels. Christians will have no choice but to be involved one way or another. The problem then becomes, how does the church relate to the state? (Redekop, 1990b:349-351).

Obviously the church cannot speak on every issue, so it must be selective. When the church is divided and can't speak with one voice, individual Christians must speak out.

> Nor should our political activism, be it individual or corporate, be primarily self-centered. Traditionally, despite repeated protestations of political aloofness, we have usually not hesitated to seek justice or even special privileges for ourselves. . . . For too long we have doubly deceived ourselves: we have told one another that pressuring governments to further Christian causes does not constitute political activity and we have supposed that interactions with governments becomes political only at the point where our own individual or corporate self-interest is not immediately and obviously at stake. . . .

The temptation, as long as we are not the ones being disadvantaged, will be to say nothing. But who of us familiar with righteous indignation expressed by Jesus can remain silent in the face of injustice, exploitation, deception or barbarism? There comes a time when we must remind ourselves and others that opposition can be the highest form of true patriotism (Redekop, 1976:191-192).

Such involvement will of course be fraught with problems. Redekop in no way implies that the church should unreservedly throw in its lot with government, nor is he overly optimistic about the success that greater involvement promises. Redekop's recent evangelical call to witness is clearly presented in an Anabaptist frame (Wuthnow, 1989a, Wuthnow, 1989b). The objective is faithfulness to a call to witness, not to success. Redekop (1976) identifies many problems which need to be balanced as shown in Table 8.2.

Evolution of Officeholding

John Redekop (1990a:71-714; 1983:79-105; 1984) has outlined a succinct summary of Mennonite involvement in federal and state officeholding. In Russia, Mennonite migrants from northern Europe were fully involved in the political administration of their own Mennonite Commonwealth after arriving in the late 1700s (Toews, 1982). By the 1900s these Mennonites were electing their own representatives to the Duma, the Russian national parliament. Large numbers of these Mennonites later arrived in Kansas and Manitoba in 1874, locating largely west of the Mississippi.

Redekop (1990a:711) suggests that the principle of avoiding politics persisted among Mennonites in Canada and the United States, but the reality hardly reflected the theory. In Pennsylvania, Ohio, and Ontario some leaders were political activists. Mennonite leaders in Ontario petitioned for military exemption as early as 1793. In Waterloo, Abraham Erb was actively engaged in politics, and Moses Springer became the first mayor of the city when it was incorporated. Springer was elected to the provincial legislature a few years later. The 1873 Russian Mennonite delegation to Manitoba drove a hard bargain for land in that province, with considerable interaction with political representatives (Ens, 1979).

By the middle of the twentieth century political participation was on the rise. According to Redekop (1990a:712), while denominations debated political involvement, many individuals became politically involved. "In Canada early political activism included, at the provincial level, the election of Cornelius Hiebert . . . 1906-09, and Gerhard Enns in Saskatchewan . . . 1905-14."

TABLE 8.2
Issues Related to Involvement in Church-State Relations

---

1. How can the church be politically responsive without becoming partisan, especially petty partisan?

2. How can we speak clearly in opposition to capital punishment, racism, exploitation of women, and other stances we believe the Bible clearly rejects when there is opposition within the church?

3. How can the church find ways of assessing laudable government programs such as Social Security, public health insurance, etc., without undue effort and resources that divide the church?

4. How can the church retain awareness of its own responsibility to do welfare work and also urge government to use its tax resources for the same purpose?

5. In view of sharp disagreements, how can the church maintain openness about which government positions it endorses?

6. How can we ensure that Christian political involvement will not become an end in itself, since controlling wealth and fame are already problems?

7. How can we learn to live with the perpetual tensions and risks which invariably accompany prophetic Christian interaction with sociopolitical authorities?

8. How can we become politically informed and sensitive without becoming narrowly nationalistic or cynical?

9. How can we combine exhortations about ethical improvements with the evangelical commission to all to become transformed Christian disciples?

10. How can we be critical without becoming filled with hate and be supportive without unqualified allegiance to the state?

11. How can we learn to persevere in prophetic politicking with good will, humility, and Christian grace in face of both success and rejection?

12. How can Christians look to government as an agent to restrain evil, as well as an arena for potential service, without generating undue allegiance to it and dependency on it?

13. How can the free church as a whole learn to take politics seriously without giving it the status of ultimate seriousness?

Adapted from John H. Redekop (1976:193-194).

Redekop (1990a:712-713) lists others who served in provincial governments. Ray Ratzlaff, elected in Alberta in 1967, became Minister of Tourism. Also in Alberta, Robert Wiebe was elected in 1967 and Werner Schmidt became a leader of the Social Credit Party as well.

In British Columbia Harvey Schroeder was elected provincial legislator in 1972, served as minister in several departments, and became speaker of the House. Peter A. Dueck was elected the same year to the British Columbia legislature and became Minister of Health. He remains a member of the provincial legislature as of this writing.

In Manitoba Robert Banman won election in 1973 and served in six ministries, Jake Froese served from 1959-73, and Harry Enns, elected in 1966, served as minister in various departments in the Progressive Conservative government. Arnold Brown was elected in 1973, and Albert Driedger, elected in 1977, served as the Conservative Minister of Transportation. Victor Schroeder served a long time in various ministries, including Minister of Finance in the Manitoba NDP government.

In Saskatchewan David Boldt was elected in 1960 and served in various Liberal government ministries. Isaak Elias was elected in 1956 in Saskatchewan as well as John Thiessen. Allen Engel gained office in 1971, Herbert Swan, elected in 1978, also became Speaker, and Harold Martens won in 1982. Three Mennonites were in the Conservative cabinet in Saskatchewan in the 1980s and three have again been placed in cabinet portfolios in the new NDP government in the early 1990s.

Today, in any of the five most westerly Canadian provinces Mennonites run for office in all elections. This political activism has also extended to the federal level. Erhart Regier was elected in 1953 and served until 1962. Siefried Enns served 1962–68. Dean Whiteway served 1974-79. Jake Epp has been in federal politics since 1972, with numerous cabinet portfolios, including Minister of Health and Welfare.[4] Others include Benno Friesen, 1974–, Jake Froese 1979–80, and John Reimer 1979–80, 1984– (Redekop, 1990a:713). The Mennonites running in federal elections included sixteen in 1974 and eleven in 1980.

Canadian Mennonites serving in nonelected government appointments include Peter Thiessen (assistant to Manitoba Premier Edward Schreyer in the 1970s) and William Regehr (chief-of-staff to Manitoba Premier Howard Pauley in the 1980s). At the national level Peter Harder served as executive assistant to Party Leader Joe Clark (who later became Prime Minister, 1979-80) and in the 1990s became Associate Deputy Minister of Immigration. In Manitoba John Enns served as crown prosecutor. A 1965 General Conference Mennonite survey revealed that about one percent of the membership was employed in government services.

Mennonites in the U.S. have been less active in partisan politics, likely because of rural sectarian roots in the largely Swiss Mennonite Church, a more monolithic federal government in the most powerful nation in the world, and the fact that Mennonites are a much smaller portion of the U.S. population. However, William Ramseyer from Iowa (1915-33), Benjamin Welty from Ohio (1917-21), and Edward Clayton Eicher from Iowa all were members of Congress (Redekop, 1990a:713). Eicher became commissioner on the Securities and Exchange Commission in Washington, D.C. (1938-42) and chief justice of the U.S. District Court for the District of Columbia. James Juhnke ran unsuccessfully for the U.S. Congress in Kansas in 1970 and in 1980. In 1982 LeRoy Kennel ran in Illinois for the U.S. Congress.

Several Mennonites also campaigned for state legislatures including Peter Galle, elected in 1902; H. P. Krehbiel, 1908-10; J. A. Schowalter who served three terms beginning in 1934; Harold P. Dyck, who served nine terms 1970-88; and Ferdinand Funk elected in 1984.[5]

A. Kremer of Nebraska was first elected a senator in 1962, serving two terms, and Harvey Wollman served briefly as governor of Nebraska beginning in 1978. In 1984 South Dakota had two Mennonite state legislators, Terry Miller and Benny Gross. Interestingly, most of these political representatives lived west of the Mississippi, where Dutch-Russian Mennonites are more heavily represented. In the fall of 1992 at least eight Mennonites in the U.S. were holding or seeking political office at the state level or higher. Four of these were in Kansas, two in Pennsylvania, and one each in Indiana and Maryland.[6]

While churches and their leaders were passing statements about their reluctance to embrace politics, some Mennonites were getting elected as early as the turn of the century. However, most churches were sufficiently conservative that many early candidates did not retain their Mennonite membership because of hostility in their local churches. Many had already left the Mennonite scene when they entered politics, so they were in essence only "ethnic background" Mennonites.

This, however, is changing as Mennonites become more professional, more educated, and more urban. Many Mennonites elected to government more recently have remained active in Mennonite congregations. Although some who were Mennonites when they were elected, later jóined other denominations.

Attitudes toward Politics

Fortunately the 1972 and 1989 Church Member Profiles, which sampled over 3,000 North American Mennonites, provide us with an extensive variety of questions which probed Mennonite attitudes toward politics (Kauffman and Driedger, 1991). We can assess the impact of urbanization and rising socioeconomic status on political attitudes and behavior with the resources of these major data sets.

Political Participation

The surveys of 1972 and 1989 involved five Mennonite and Brethren in Christ denominations. Using the survey data we created two scales to track political involvement—Political Participation and Political Action. The Political Participation items include both attitudes and behavior as reported by individuals. The Political Action scale reports the level of congregational activity which respondents deem appropriate for political issues. The questions included in these two scales are presented in Table 8.3

As reported in Table 8.3, we see that in the span of one generation (1972-1989) Mennonites became more politically engaged. Whereas three-fourths in 1972 agreed that members should vote in state, provincial, and national elections, by 1989 some 84 percent favored voting.

Two-thirds in 1972 agreed that Mennonites could hold government office. This rose to 78 percent by 1989. While less than one-half voted in 1972, by 1989 two-thirds voted in most recent elections. Actual officeholding in either local, city, state, provincial, or national government also increased slightly from 3 to 4 percent. As Mennonite attitudes toward involvement change, members are becoming more actively engaged politically.

There are also significant denominational differences. Members of the Mennonite Church (MC) are always less politically engaged than Evangelical Mennonite Church (EMC) members. The Swiss-South German heritage deters MCs, while EMCs who have recruited more nonheritage members are more politically active. Mennonites of Dutch-Russian background are typically more politically engaged than those with a Swiss lineage. As the data in Table 8.3 demonstrate, denominational cultures exert an enormous influence in shaping the rate of political participation of their members.

TABLE 8.3
Political Participation and Action by Denomination in Percent

Issues	\multicolumn{5}{c|}{*Denominations*}					\multicolumn{2}{c}{*Totals*}	
	MC	BIC	GC	MB	EMC	1972	1989
Political Participation							
Agree members should vote in state, provincial, or national elections	72	88	94	95	96	76	84
Agree members may hold government office	63	83	90	92	95	64	78
Voted in all or most elections in recent years	45	64	84	85	87	46	65
Agree some political offices cannot be held by Christians	71	48	52	49	31	74	59
Held membership in major political groups	8	19	10	10	9	7	10
Held an elective or appointive political office	3	3	6	3	5	3	4
Political Action							
Congregations should . . .							
Encourage members to study political issues	69	87	87	89	95	68	79
Encourage members to engage in political action	43	71	62	67	79	32	55
Endorse particular candidates for office	32	48	43	47	56	25	39
Discuss political issues from pulpit	25	29	31	29	31	16	28

Urbanization and Participation

Before World War II, Mennonites in North America were almost all living in rural enclaves (Driedger, 1986). However, after the war many who had been exposed to the larger world began moving to the city. Many started new Mennonite churches in the city (Peachey, 1963). By 1972 one-third lived in towns of 2,500 or more, and by 1989 almost half were urban. We expect that this diaspora of Mennonites to the cities, exposing them to urban pressures and opportunities, has changed their political attitudes.

In Table 8.4 we discover that Mennonites scored higher in 1989 on several dimensions of political participation and action. The items of political participation tap general issues which Mennonites had debated in the fifties. The data show that voting and holding office, already acceptable in 1972, have become more generally endorsed today, except for a small minority. As expected, the data in Table 8.4 confirm that political participation rises with urbanization. Mennonites living in large cities are 20 percent more likely to have voted in recent elections than those on the farm. Nevertheless, even the majority (57%) of Mennonite farmers vote.

The last four items in Table 8.4 measured attitudes toward political action in the local congregation, where such action is less acceptable. Whereas two-thirds in 1972 favored study of political issues, only one-third wanted congregations to encourage political action, one-fourth wanted to endorse candidates, and few thought such partisan issues should be discussed from the pulpit.

More in 1989 were willing to engage in such activities, but congregational involvement was controversial. Nearly eight out of ten respondents thought congregations should encourage their members to study political issues. It is clear, however, that rural members were more reluctant about political activities than those living in larger cities. But even among Mennonites living in large cities only a third thought political issues should be discussed from the pulpit of their congregation.

The likelihood of actually holding political office is higher in rural areas where Mennonites may be better known and more likely elected to local posts on school boards, planning commissions, or other public groups. On all other dimensions, however, political participation and action clearly increases with urbanization. As more Mennonites move to the city in the future, political involvement will surely rise.

Education and Participation

Education was often emphasized in Mennonite circles. Literacy was important to read and understand the Bible. Educational levels among Mennonites have increased significantly since World War II in

TABLE 8.4
Political Participation and Action by Urbanization in Percent

	Urbanization				*Totals*	
Issues	Rural Farm	Rural Nonfarm	Small City	Large City	1972	1989
Political Participation						
Agree members should vote in state, provincial, or national elections	76	82	86	91	76	84
Agree members may hold government office	74	70	82	87	64	78
Voted in all or most elections in recent years	57	58	67	77	46	65
Agree some political offices cannot be held by Christians	61	63	60	53	74	59
Held membership in major political groups	10	9	9	12	7	10
Held an elective or appointive political office	5	5	4	2	3	4
Political Action						
Congregations should . . .						
Encourage members to study political issues	71	75	84	88	68	79
Encourage members to engage in political action	47	51	58	66	32	55
Endorse particular candidates for office	36	38	38	44	25	39
Discuss political issues from pulpit	22	23	31	36	16	28

order to compete in the modern economic fray. Before the 1940s relatively few finished high school, whereas by 1972 the average level of education had risen to several years of high school. By 1989 the average level had increased to the first year of college. We expect that as education expands awareness of the larger society, it will encourage Mennonites to be more politically aware and involved.

Table 8.5 confirms our expectations. As education increases so does political engagement. One-half to two-thirds of those with an elementary school education thought Mennonites should vote, hold office, and reported voting themselves. However, more than two-thirds of those with graduate education supported these actions. The influence of age and education likely overlap since older Mennonites are less highly educated. Nevertheless, education is a significant factor in arousing political awareness and action.

Education also affects views on political action. Respondents were asked whether congregations should study political issues, encourage involvement, endorse candidates, or discuss such action from the pulpit. Those with graduate school education favored all the activities more than members with elementary school education. Endorsing candidates and discussing issues from the pulpit received much less support regardless of educational levels. These activities could politicize the pulpit, which some have feared. Again, 1989 respondents scored significantly higher on the political action scale than 1972 respondents. More education will make Mennonites increasingly politically active in the future.

National Political Differences

We tend to think that Canada and the United States are similar, but political differences are considerable. The United States is a superpower with large military forces; Canada plays a relatively minor role in world affairs. Mennonites in Canada are mostly of Dutch-Russian origin, whereas Swiss-South German Mennonites dominate Mennonite communities in the eastern United States. Driedger and Kauffman (1982) found significant national differences among Mennonites, which we also expect to discover in their political participation.

TABLE 8.5
Political Participation and Action by Education in Percent

Issues	Education				Totals	
	Elementary School	High School	College	Grad School	1972	1989
Political Participation						
Agree members should vote in state, provincial, or national elections	64	81	91	91	76	84
Agree members may hold government office	55	73	86	87	64	78
Voted in all or most elections in recent years	47	58	73	77	46	65
Agree some political offices cannot be held by Christians	70	58	54	64	74	59
Held membership in major political groups	2	7	14	16	7	10
Held an elective or appointive political office	2	4	5	5	3	4
Political Action
Congregations should . . .						
Encourage members to study political issues	54	74	88	91	68	79
Encourage members to engage in political action	28	46	68	70	32	55
Endorse particular candidates for office	35	39	43	38	25	39
Discuss political issues from pulpit	13	20	35	40	16	28

Table 8.6 demonstrates that indeed U.S. Mennonites east of the Mississippi are generally more reluctant to participate in political activities than Canadians in the west. Generally U.S. Mennonites, both east and west, are not as involved in political issues as Canadians both east and west. When we controlled for Swiss-Dutch origins, we found that nationality was a significant factor (Kauffman and Driedger, 1991). However, the national differences have less influence on political attitudes than educational and urbanization factors.

Regional (east-west) differences in both countries are also significant. Dutch-Russian Mennonites moved mostly to areas west of the Mississippi River and are mostly affiliated with Mennonite Brethren and General Conference Mennonite congregations. Thus on all of the items western Mennonites in America are more politically engaged. The same trend is less evident in Canada, however, because Ontario Mennonites (East) are not as Swiss oriented as are Mennonites east of the Mississippi in the United States. We conclude that westerners in both countries, and Canadian Mennonites nationally, are the most politically engaged Mennonites as shown in Table 8.6.

Support of Parties and Leaders

While Mennonites are becoming increasingly involved in politics, they tend to do so in a conservative fashion. Perhaps this should not be surprising, since Mennonites have for centuries lived in rural communities outside the mainstream. As a minority they have also been concerned with preserving their faith within ethnic cloisters. While they are moving from their communities into the larger urban society—from farm to professional and business ventures—these changes are nevertheless recent and for many threatening (Juhnke, 1975:1-110). This general religious and ethnic conservatism is clearly reflected in their political alignments.

TABLE 8.6
Political Participation and Action by Region and Nationality
in Percent

Issues	United States		Canada	
	East	West	East	West
Political Participation				
Agree members should vote in state, provincial, or national elections	77	82	87	93
Agree members may hold government office	68	77	82	89
Voted in all or most elections in recent years	47	65	67	85
Agree some political offices cannot be held by Christians	66	59	60	53
Held membership in major political groups	12	12	5	6
Held an elective or appointive political office	3	6	2	3
Political Action Congregations should . . .				
Encourage members to study political issues	72	82	78	83
Encourage members to engage in political action	49	58	59	56
Endorse particular candidates for office	33	42	41	39
Discuss political issues from pulpit	25	29	36	26

Political Party Loyalties

Since the political parties and systems in the United States and Canada are different, we have separated them in Table 8.7. We have ranked the parties in each country from conservative to liberal, ordering them so they are somewhat comparable with respect to liberalism and conservatism. Note also that whereas Americans have only two party choices, Canadians have at least four. The Social Credit Party (SC) in Canada is farther right of center than the Republican mainstream, and the New Democratic Party (NDP) is farther left than the Democratic center. Thus we have segmented Republicans and Democrats into Conservative and Liberal sections to provide four political options for Americans as well.

We see at the bottom of Table 8.7 that in the U.S. one-third did not embrace a party position in 1972, but by 1989 the nonaligned had declined to one-fourth. Swiss respondents east of the Mississippi were heavily represented among these nonaligned respondents. With relatively few Swiss in Canada, the Canadian nonaligned Mennonites were fewer—representing 23 percent in 1972 and only 14 percent in 1989. Since Americans have so few party choices, 9 percent in 1972 and 3 percent in 1989 favored independent or other party choices. With more choices (four parties), very few Canadians opted for other parties.

TABLE 8.7
Political Orientation by Year and Nationality in Percent

Orientation	United States		Orientation	Canada	
	1972	1989		1972	1989
Conservative			Social Credit	15	6
Republicans	35	46	Progressive		
Conservative			Conservative	31	47
Democrats	5	10	Liberal	25	20
Liberal Republicans	9	8	New Democratic		
Liberal Democrats	6	9	Party	6	13
Independent/Other	9	3	Other	0	2
Hold no position	35	23	Hold no position	23	14
Total Percent	**100**	**100**		**100**	**100**

Examination of the four top choices in the United States shows that the largest number of American Mennonites aligned themselves with conservative Republicans in 1972 and 1989. Presumably some of those who took no position in 1972 voted conservative Republican in 1986, raising the conservative Republican preference half a generation later.

When we eliminate those who took no position in 1972 and 1989, we find that one-half in 1972 chose conservative Republican while two-thirds did in 1989. When we add conservative Democrat preferences, we find that most American Mennonites preferred conservative candidates and positions.

Only 15 percent favored liberal Democrats and liberal Republicans in 1972. This increased in 1989 to 17 percent (roughly one-fifth if those who took no position are eliminated). We conclude that for American Mennonites who took a position, more than three out of four held a conservative political orientation.

Canadian Mennonites are also politically conservative, although the patterns vary somewhat. Ultraconservative Social Credit Party preferences declined from 15 to 6 percent by 1989. However, these Social Creditors may have joined the Progressive Conservatives, which increased from 31 percent in 1972 to 47 percent in 1989.

When we combine the two parties and eliminate those who did not take positions (23% in 1972 and 14% in 1989), we find that over half of the Canadian Mennonites in 1972 had conservative leanings. This conservative tilt increased to two-thirds in 1989. Roughly one-third leaned left of center in 1972, and this remained about the same in 1989. Interestingly, however, the New Democratic Party (NDP) choices doubled from 6 to 13 percent over half a generation. The majority of Canadian Mennonites also preferred conservative parties in both 1972 and 1989, although ultraconservatives declined and the more socialist NDPers increased by 1989. We conclude that both American and Canadian Mennonites preferred conservative parties, but Canadians did so somewhat less.

National Political Candidates

The various candidates running for elections also shape the political preferences of voters. Both Americans and Canadians were involved in national elections in 1988, voting for president and prime minister. This enabled us to gather specific leadership preferences in our 1989 sample. One-fourth of the American respondents did not vote at all, while 10 percent of the Canadians bypassed the polls as seen in Table 8.8. Another 5 to 8 percent of our sample were too young to vote in national elections.

TABLE 8.8
Mennonite Voting for Candidates by Nationality in Percent

United States		Canada	
George Bush	49	Brian Mulroney	51
Michael Dukakis	19	John Turner	16
		Ed Broadbent	11
I did not vote at all	24	I did not vote at all	10
I do not qualify to vote	8	I do not qualify to vote	5
Someone else	1	Someone else	8
Total percentage	**100**		**100**

One-half of the U.S. Mennonites voted for Republican President George Bush—two-thirds, if we eliminate those who did not or could not vote. Only 19 percent voted for Democrat Michael Dukakis (one-fourth if nonvoters are eliminated). The conservative trend of Mennonites voting for Republicans is evident, although George Bush seemed to be somewhat more popular among Mennonites than his party. We do not have comparable data on how respondents voted for specific candidates in the seventies.

In the Canadian federal election in 1988, one-half of the respondents voted for Progressive Conservative Prime Minister Brian Mulroney (two-thirds if nonvoters are eliminated). About as many Canadians voted for the Liberal candidate, John Turner (16%), as U.S. Mennonites voted for Democrat candidate Dukakis (19%). Thus the first and second place outcomes were similar in both countries with three times as many Mennonites voting for conservative candidates.

However, one in ten Mennonites in Canada voted for a third party (New Democratic) candidate, Edward Broadbent, who represented a socialist alternative. A larger proportion of Canadians voted (90% versus 76%) than U.S. citizens, underscoring again the greater Canadian Mennonite involvement in politics.

With respect to voting for national candidates we conclude that Mennonites in both countries voted two and three times as often for the more conservative candidates. Canadian Mennonites did so somewhat less. However, a minority of Canadian Mennonites voted for a socialist candidate, and considerably more U.S. Mennonites than Canadians did not vote at all.

The Effects of Urbanization

As outlined earlier, we expect that as Mennonites move to urban areas and become more exposed to the influences of the larger society, they will also become more interested in politics and political decision-making. Mennonites in business become increasingly aware of market forces which affect them, and they begin to develop attitudes toward government policies. Schoolteachers are affected by governmental budgets, and social workers lean toward parties which have a more open ear to the welfare of others.

In Table 8.9 we note that 11 percent of the Mennonites living on farms have a graduate school education, while three times as many living in large metropolises of 250,000 have attended graduate school.[7] The same is true for socioeconomic status (a combination of education, occupation, and income). Three times as many of those residing in large centers score high on social economic status. We expect that urbanization and higher socioeconomic status will combine to influence attitudes toward political parties and leadership candidates.

Table 8.9 shows that five times as many Mennonites in large metropolises as farmers favored Liberal Democrats. The reverse was evident with respect to conservative Republicans. Mennonite farmers outvoted metropolitan Mennonites (52 vs. 31%) in their preference for conservative Republicans. Clearly U.S. urban Mennonites vote more toward the left. The same pattern is less obvious for Canadian Mennonites, where urban Mennonites favor NDP candidates only slightly more than farmers. Canadians living in small cities were most likely to favor the Progressive Conservative party.

With respect to presidential candidates, most U.S. Mennonites voted for Republican George Bush in 1988, and this varied little by place of residence. Urban Mennonites, however, were three times as likely as those on the farm to vote for Michael Dukakis, a more liberal Democratic candidate.

These trends are more complex historically in Canada. More metropolitan Mennonites (53%) voted for the Progressive Conservative Prime Minister Brian Mulroney than farmers (38%). Canadian Mennonites in large urban centers voted only slightly more for socialist New Democratic Party candidate Ed Broadbent than the others.

Urbanization does affect voting behavior and political preferences but this is more evident in political orientation than in leadership choice. The conservative political attitudes of Mennonites are entangled with their long history of segregated rural life as well as their recent rise in economic status. All things considered, they are

FIGURE 8.9
Political Orientation and Behavior by Urbanization in Percent

Issues	Rural Farm (3 acres plus)	Rural Non-farm (under 3 acres)	Urbanization			
			Village or town (under 2,500)	Urban (2,500-25,000)	City (25,000-250,000)	Metropolis (250,000-plus)
Graduate school education	11	16	20	23	30	36
High socioeconomic status	12	23	22	27	37	37
Favor Liberal Democratic position	5	4	4	13	19	26
Favor Conservative Republican position	52	49	52	41	42	31
Favor New Democratic Party position	10	4	9	8	18	15
Favor Progressive Conservative position	42	47	43	54	44	52
Voted for . . .						
George Bush	46	49	57	47	49	45
Michael Dukakis	11	12	17	24	25	37
Brian Mulroney	38	63	41	58	52	53
Ed Broadbent	10	3	7	6	14	13
TOTALS Percent	21	17	13	22	15	12
Number	(640)	(516)	(382)	(667)	(470)	(373)

generally inclined toward more conservative preferences but urbanization will likely increase their preferences for more liberal politics.

Age and Party Preferences

Normally we assume older persons are more conservative than youth. Is this true with political preferences? Do youth prefer more liberal parties and vote for more liberal candidates?

The data in Table 8.10 show that two-thirds of U.S. Mennonites are oriented toward conservative Republicans. However, only half of the teenage respondents share this orientation compared to three-fourths of those over seventy. The reverse is also true. Those under fifty are more likely to prefer liberal Democrats and liberal Republicans than those over fifty. Whereas three-fourths of our U.S. sample preferred conservative candidates in the two parties, voters under fifty were more likely to prefer liberal affiliations than those over fifty.

TABLE 8.10
Political Orientation by Age and Nationality in Percent

Political Orientation	Age					Total
	13-19	20-29	30-49	50-69	70+	
United States						
Conservative Republicans	56	61	56	69	76	63
Conservative Democrats	15	12	16	12	11	14
Liberal Republicans	18	13	12	9	7	11
Liberal Democrats	11	15	16	10	5	13
Canadian						
Social Credit	-	5	5	10	9	7
Progressive Conservatives	57	57	57	54	45	55
Liberal Party	19	21	19	27	34	23
New Democratic Party	24	17	18	9	11	15

The trends were similar in Canada, except the choice of four parties provided more interesting variations. Twice as many over fifty preferred the ultraconservative Social Credit Party as those under fifty. On the other hand, twice as many under fifty leaned toward the New Democratic Party (more socialist and left of center) than those over fifty.

These trends were less evident in the two centrist parties (similar to Republicans and Democrats). Those over fifty preferred the Liberal Party more because it was the party which helped many older Mennonites to immigrate to Canada, and they have remained loyal. More than one-third of the Canadians endorsed parties left of center, suggesting they are somewhat less conservative than their American Mennonite counterparts.

Since both the U.S. and Canada held federal elections in 1988, we asked respondents who they voted for as shown in Table 8.11. Three-fourths of the U.S. Mennonites who voted cast their ballot for George Bush and one-fourth for presidential contender Michael Dukakis. Age was not a large factor, although respondents over seventy voted more heavily for Bush (82%) and less for Dukakis (16%) than on the average. Mennonites who were politically active in 1988 overwhelmingly voted for Republican George Bush.

TABLE 8.11
Voting Patterns by Age and Nationality in Percent[a]

Voted for	Age of Respondents				Total
	20-29	30-49	50-69	70+	
United States					
George Bush	72	68	72	82	72
Michael Dukakis	28	31	26	17	27
Other	0	1	2	1	1
Canadian					
Brian Mulroney	61	58	61	54	59
John Turner	17	17	22	24	19
Ed Broadbent	15	16	8	8	13
Other	8	9	9	14	9

[a] Percentages are based on total number of persons who voted in 1988 and thus exclude nonvoters.

Again, Canadian voting patterns for prime minister were more varied, with twice as many under fifty as over fifty voting for Socialist Ed Broadbent. Those over fifty voted more for Liberal candidate John Turner than their younger cohorts, again following Liberal Party preferences because of early immigration policies. Age was not a factor in

Mennonite votes for Progressive Conservative Brian Mulroney who won the 1988 election. These voting patterns appear to follow party preference. Again, well over one-third voted for candidates left of center in Canada.

Religious Commitment and Party Preferences

Anabaptism began as a religious movement, and religious commitment remains a major stake in its sacred canopy. In Table 8.12 we present beliefs, religious participation, devotionalism, and religious experience as four indicators of religious commitment to assess how religion effects political orientation. Anabaptist beliefs weakly correlate with political orientation. Low Anabaptist beliefs are slightly associated with more liberal politics, but these trends are hardly significant. The same pattern holds for church participation.

TABLE 8.12
Political Orientation by Religious Commitment in Percent

Political Orientation	Anabaptist Beliefs		Church Participation		Religious Experience		Devotionalism	
	Low	High	Low	High	Low	High	Low	High
United States								
Conservative Republican	40[a]	47	42	47	40	50	37	55
Conservative Democrat	11	10	9	12	12	9	10	9
Liberal Republicans	12	4	10	8	9	6	12	5
Liberal Democrats	12	10	12	10	14	6	15	4
Canadian								
Social Credit	4	9	5	7	3	6	2	8
Progressive Conservative	42	49	41	47	43	50	40	49
Liberal Party	20	20	20	19	21	22	25	22
New Democratic Party	15	9	13	13	18	12	18	6

[a] "Forty percent who scored low in Anabaptist beliefs held a conservative Republican orientation."

Religious experience and devotionalism, however, are much better predictors of political orientation. Those with an active devotional life of prayer and Bible reading preferred conservative Republican (55 vs. 37%) and Social Credit more than those who scored low in devotionalism. Less inner-oriented Mennonites were two and three times more likely to endorse liberal Republicans, liberal Democrats, or the New Democratic Party than the devotionally active. Religious experience, another indicator of the inner life, followed the same trend, although the differences were not quite as great.

These findings underscore a tie between the inner religious life and political conservatism. On the other hand, those who focus less on the inner life tend to align themselves more with politically liberal causes.

In Table 8.13 we have summarized many of the relationships between political involvement and a variety of social and theological variables. The Pearson (r) measures the strength of relationship between two variables. A positive value means the two factors increase or decrease together. A negative (r) indicates that one variable is rising and the other is falling. In Table 8.13 the r values show that education, socioeconomic status, and urbanization are positively associated with greater political involvement. On the other hand, ethnicity, separatism, and various religious variables are negatively associated with political participation and political action.

The pattern of relationship is rather consistent and striking. The forces of modernization—urbanization, education, professional status, and individualism clearly encourage greater political participation. Religious activities and theological factors tend to deter participation in the political order. As Mennonites become more urban, educated, and of higher social status, we expect that their political participation will continue to increase.

Summary

Our discussion in earlier chapters traced the history of Mennonite wariness of political participation. However, World War II forced many into service projects outside their communities. By the fifties Mennonite leaders were seriously debating their social responsibility in the larger society. This chapter charts the willingness of Mennonites to engage in a greater variety of political activities.

We found that in one generation (1972-1989) more Mennonites were willing to participate in voting, witness to government, and permit members to run for election. These changes, however, varied by denomination. Members of the Mennonite Church were least willing to engage in such political action and Evangelical Mennonite Church members were most willing to do so. Urban, more educated, western U.S., and Canadian Mennonites were more willing to participate in

TABLE 8.13
Correlations* between Political Scales and Other Variables

Variable	Political Participation	Political Action
Education	.25	.25
Socioeconomic status	.21	.20
Urbanization	.15	.17
Age	.05	-.18
Church Participation	-.12	-.02
Devotionalism	-.16	-.14
Orthodoxy	-.13	-.16
Fundamentalism	-.18	-.21
Anabaptist	-.26	-.11
Individualism	.10	.01
Religious life	-.12	-.10
Separatism	-.33	-.12
Ethnicity	-.34	-.17

*A Pearson r over .045 (plus or minus) is statistically significant at the .01 level.

politics than rural, less educated, and eastern U.S. Mennonites. Increased modernization has brought greater political involvement.

While Mennonites increased their participation in politics, they did so conservatively. U.S. Mennonites were more reluctant to affiliate with political parties than Canadians. Of those who had political preferences, two-thirds of the U.S. Mennonites preferred conservative Republicans in 1989, and only one in seven chose liberal Democrats.

The trend was similar in Canada, with two-thirds endorsing Progressive Conservatives or Social Credit, and one-third left-of-center Liberals and the New Democratic Party. Mennonites vigorously voted for conservative candidates President Bush and Prime Minister Mulroney in the 1988 election. Urbanization again was a factor. Mennonites in rural areas voted more conservatively than urban ones. The rising economic status of Mennonites undoubtedly also bolsters conservative attitudes.

Interesting patterns of political participation and action have de-

Mennonite Marian Franz (L) serves as executive director of the National Campaign for a Peace Tax Fund. Here she talks with the bill's lead co-sponsors, Sen. Mark Hatfield, R-Ore., center, and Rep. Andy Jacobs, D-Ind., at the Peace Tax Fund Bill hearing, May 21, 1992.

veloped. Modern urban Mennonites who are more educated, with higher status occupations and growing incomes, are definitely more active in politics than their rural, less educated, lower-income counterparts. On the other hand, Mennonites who scored high on Anabaptist religious beliefs, and who are more devotionally inclined, tend to be less politically involved. This varies somewhat with age—younger Mennonites more than their elders want greater political action in their local churches. More younger Mennonites also voted for social democratic parties and candidates than older members did.

How do the changing patterns of political participation relate to the transformation of Mennonite peacemaking? That is the question which we explore in the following chapter.

Mennonite peacemaking efforts have become internationalized in many ways. John A. Lapp, executive secretary of Mennonite Central Committee (MCC), talks with Mother Teresa in Calcutta. A long-time friend of MCC ministries, she helped to celebrate 50 years of MCC work in India.

CHAPTER NINE

Contemporary Dimensions of Peacemaking

The previous two chapters have examined Mennonite responses to alternate service and growing Mennonite participation in the larger political arena. Throughout the book we have argued that Mennonite theological thinking and the language of official statements have shifted from passive nonresistance to activist peacemaking. Expressions of the activist mode are embodied in such ventures as Mennonite Conciliation Services, Christian Peacemaker Teams, the Victim Offender Reconciliation Program, and various programs of the Mennonite Central Committee as well as many local and regional peacemaking efforts.

To what extent do typical Mennonites support the more active modes of peacemaking? The rich resources of the 3,000 respondents in the Church Member Profile enable us to answer that question and to explore the contemporary profile of Mennonite attitudes.

For purposes of analysis we conceptualized three dimensions of peacemaking: *nonresistance, witness,* and *activism*. Questions from the Church Member Profile were used to tap each of these dimensions. Thus we are able to assess the level of support for each dimension and to monitor the impact of social and theological variables on the three dimensions of peacemaking as well.

Finally we created a *composite* peacemaking scale—consisting of five questions—to provide an overall measure of Mennonite commitment to peacemaking. The composite peacemaking scale enables us to measure the ties between peacemaking and a variety of other relevant variables. We begin the analysis with an examination of present-day attitudes toward classic nonresistance.

Dimensions of Peacemaking
Classic Nonresistance

The historical section of this volume identified the growing discomfort of many Mennonites with the negative and passive implication of the term nonresistance. Despite a growing sense of activism, the meaning of the term nonresistance has not entirely evaporated from Mennonite thinking. Our respondents were asked if members of their congregations interpret the principle of peace and nonresistance primarily as "conscientious objection to participation in military service and war" *or* as "nonviolent acts of protest against militarism and preparation for war." Given the forced choice, four out of five (81%) of the respondents selected the more traditional response—suggesting that their fellow parishioners view peace and nonresistance primarily as conscientious objection to war.

The working draft of a new Mennonite confession of faith jointly prepared by MC and GC representatives has a subsection titled "Peace, Justice, and Nonresistance" which among other things calls on believers to do justice and practice "nonresistance in the face of violence and warfare." The commentary for this section of the proposed confession of faith notes that "nonresistance and nonviolence, rightly understood, contribute to justice." Moreover, nonresistance can mean a "nonviolent confronting of offenders with the effects of their behavior."[1] Although the term nonresistance is retained in the draft of the new confession, its meaning is interpreted in a more active sense.

Ruth-Heffelbower (1991:88) also resuscitates nonresistance and reinterprets it as relevant for activist peacemaking. "Nonresistance, to be faithful to its heritage and to Jesus, must include the possibility of nonviolent direct action challenging rulers in God's name." How do typical Mennonites view nonresistance today?

We used four questions (displayed in Table 9.1) to probe attitudes toward classic nonresistance—entering military service, participating in war promoting activities, filing lawsuits, and holding political office. Although all four of these items tapped key issues entailed by classic nonresistance, none of the questions used the word itself. As we have seen in chapter 7, when faced by a military draft two thirds of the respondents would opt for a peaceful alternative to military service. A similar proportion agree that Christians should not participate in war or promote it.

Thus two of three Mennonites endorse these cardinal tenets of nonresistance. However, as shown in Table 9.1, support for these beliefs has dropped about 6 percent since 1972. There are other traces of erosion as well. The five denominations vary dramatically in their enthusiasm for historic nonresistance. Support for alternative service peaks at 80 percent among MCs but plummets to 18 percent among EMCs. A similar pattern (78 vs. 11%) emerges between MCs and EMCs regarding their willingness to outrightly reject war-promoting activities.

Classical nonresistance, as we have seen, considered lawsuits and political officeholding as worldly entanglements that entailed an ex-

TABLE 9.1
Nonresistance Dimension by Denomination:
Percent "Agreeing"

Nonresistance Items	Denominations					Totals	
	MC	GC	MB	BIC	EMC	1972	1989
Would enter alternate service or refuse registration if drafted.	80	67	56	46	18	74	68
Christians should take no part in war or war-promoting activities.	78	65	56	39	11	73	66
A Christian should *not* bring a suit in a court of law.	41	31	32	30	28	36	35
Mennonites should not hold *any* political office.	14	4	3	6	2	13	9
Percent high on nonresistance scale	34	15	10	9	1		

cessive use of force, incongruent with the spirit of Christ. Although two-thirds of Mennonites would continue to refuse induction into the military, their view of officeholding and filing lawsuits has changed dramatically. Only one-third believe a Christian should *not* file a lawsuit if faced with a legitimate claim of property damages.

Of all the nonresistance items, litigation produced the most ambivalence. Nearly one-third were undecided if Christians were justified in filing lawsuits, but 34 percent were willing to endorse litigation for property damage. Attitudes toward the use of the law remained virtually unchanged between 1972 and 1989.

As we noted in the previous chapter, resistance to officeholding has also succumbed to modernity. Fewer than one in ten agree that members, "should not hold *any* local, state, provincial, or national government office." Supporters for this rather severe statement would prohibit officeholding even on the local level. Although 14 percent of the MCs reject officeholding, opposition to it among all groups had already dipped to 13 percent in 1972, and the erosion continued into the eighties. Denominational differences are minimal in regard to both officeholding and filing lawsuits.

In the process of modernization, two classic expressions of nonresistance—opposition to filing lawsuits and holding political office—have faded across all five denominations. However, on two other aspects of nonresistance—alternative service and rejecting war—the groups have not responded in a uniform fashion, as seen in Table 9.1. Indeed, the rejection of military service and war-promoting activities varies dramatically between the denominations—four of five MCs reject military service compared to less than one of five EMCs.

Although Mennonites have been willing to embrace the use of political and legal force as they entered business and professional life, most members of the three largest bodies (MC, GC, MB) continue to shun personal involvement in the military forces. The seventeen-year trend, however, shows a continuing, small erosion of opposition to military service.

The pattern of support for nonresistance across the four questions constituting the nonresistance scale, as seen in Table 9.1, ranks the five denominations from high to low in this order: MC, GC, MB, BIC, and EMC. Despite their rootage in the legacy of nonresistance, the denominational cultures of the various groups appear to exercise an inordinate impact on their members' views of peacemaking.

Witness for Peace

Despite the decline of enthusiasm for classic nonresistance, three questions probing support for "witness to the state" enjoyed a rise ranging from 13 to 17 percentage points between 1972 and 1989 as shown in Table 9.2. Fully three-quarters of all Mennonites agreed that "church members should witness directly to the state (nation) by writing to legislators and testifying before legislative committees, etc." Indeed "witnessing to the state" enjoyed the highest (75%) support of any item on all three dimensions of peacemaking. It ranged from a low of 73 percent among MCs to a high of 83 percent among EMCs.

TABLE 9.2
Witness Dimension by Denomination: Percent "Agreeing"

Witness Items	Denominations					Totals	
	GC	EMC	MB	BIC	MC	1972	1989
Church members should witness directly to the state (nation) by writing to legislators, testifying before legislative committees.	79	83	77	74	73	61	75
The church should influence the actions of government in war and peace, race relations, etc.	75	68	74	68	64	56	69
Favor MCC offices in Washington and Ottawa, that present church concerns on war and peace, etc.	75	61	72	69	71	55	72
Percent high on witness scale	26	22	21	17	17		

Differences between MCs and EMCs provide an intriguing comparison. Although 80 percent of the MCs embraced alternate service, only 73 percent supported "witnessing to the state." By contrast, only

18 percent of EMC members opted for alternate service, but 83 percent—the highest of any group—endorsed "witnessing to the state."[2]

In other words, EMCs, the Mennonite group most willing to enter military service, were also the most willing to witness to the state, raising questions about the content of their "witness." Political action, legitimated by the word "witness," may carry a smorgasbord of concerns which do not necessarily coincide with historic interpretations of Mennonite peacemaking. In any event, three of four Mennonites are standing under the lordship of Christ canopy—willing to witness directly to the state.

When asked if "the church should influence the actions of government in regard to . . . war and peace," 69 percent of our respondents agreed—an endorsement that rose by thirteen points since 1972. Although denominations varied little, the GCs at 75 percent showed the highest support for the statement. As we noted earlier, MCC had opened offices in Washington, D.C., and in Ottawa to monitor national policies and "witness" to government officials about the church's concerns for war and peace as well as other issues. Nearly three-quarters, of Mennonites today favor these offices, which "present the concerns of our churches on matters of war and peace, the draft, and various social issues." Variation between denominations on this question, as on the other witness issues, is quite small.

Activist Peacemaking

As shown in Table 9.3, three questions on the survey measured the dimension of active peacemaking. Two-thirds of the respondents agree that Mennonites and Brethren in Christ should "actively promote the peace position and attempt to win as many supporters to the position as possible from the larger society." Denominational support however diverged on this question. The high tide of support (75%) among the GCs dropped thirty-three points to 42 percent among the EMCs. Enthusiasm for promoting the "peace position" rose by some nine percentage points from 1972 to 1989 across all the groups, as seen in Table 9.3.

As we noted in chapter five, noncooperation with the draft was a contentious issue in many of the Mennonite bodies in the late sixties and early seventies. Support for noncooperation with the draft rose from 3 to 15 percent in the seventeen-year period after 1972. Although only a small minority of Mennonites in all the denominations support noncooperation, sharp denominational differences are evident. More than one out of five GCs support noncooperation with the draft, in contrast to only one percent among the EMCs.

TABLE 9.3
Activism Dimension by Denomination: Percent "Agreeing"

Activism Items	*Denominations*					*Totals*	
	GC	MC	MB	BIC	EMC	1972	1989
Mennonites should actively promote peace and win supporters.	75	68	53	55	42	56	65
Mennonite youth should refuse to register with selective service.	21	12	15	8	1	3	15
Mennonites should not pay income taxes for military purposes.	15	11	9	6	5	12	11
Percent high on activism scale	41	30	27	16	5		

The payment of war taxes nags the conscience of some Mennonites—11 percent. That, at least is the number who agree that members, "ought not pay the proportion of income taxes that goes for military purposes." Support for withholding war taxes climbs to 15 percent among GCs and dips to 5 percent for EMCs, confirming a stable pattern between denominations. Of all the groups, the GCs scored the highest on all the "witness" and "activism" questions except one. The EMCs, by contrast, ranked lowest on four of the six questions in these two dimensions. In any event two-thirds of our respondents were happy to "actively promote" peace but fewer than one out of five were willing to promote noncooperation with the draft or withhold their military taxes.

A Composite Peacemaking Scale
The five questions appearing in Table 9.4 were combined into a composite peacemaking scale. The issue of holding stock in companies producing war goods was added to four previous questions involving nonresistance, witness, and activism. These five questions

TABLE 9.4
Composite Peacemaking Scale by Denomination:
Percent "Agreeing"

Peacemaking Items	Denominations					Totals	
	MC	GC	MB	BIC	EMC	1972	1989
Christians should take no part in war or war-promoting activities.	78	65	56	39	11	73	66
Mennonites should actively promote peace and win supporters.	68	75	53	55	42	56	65
Mennonites should not pay income taxes for military purposes.	11	15	8	6	5	12	11
Would enter alternative service or refuse registration if drafted.	80	67	56	46	18	74	68
Owning stock in companies producing war goods is wrong.	81	78	72	64	55	69	77
Percent high on peacemaking scale	36	34	20	12	2		

form a composite peacemaking scale which undergirds the remainder of this chapter.

Before we explore the relationship of this composite peacemaking scale with other variables, a word about responses to the questions on the scale.

As reported in Table 9.4, only 11 percent think Christians should withhold taxes for military purposes, but some 77 percent believe it is always or sometimes wrong to own stock in companies producing war goods. Thus apart from withholding war taxes, two-thirds of Mennonites and Brethren in Christ support peacemaking activities, although the level of endorsement, as noted above, varies considerably by denomination. The other third of the sample are either undecided or disagree with the peacemaking statements. Ambivalence soars regarding withholding war taxes—two out of five are uncertain what to do.

The five items in Table 9.4 were combined into a composite peacemaking scale. Those scoring high on the scale support peacemaking activities. Scores on the scale could range from a low of 4 to a high of 23. The median score was 13.0. Nearly a third of all respondents scored high by falling into the top range (18-23). Although more than one-third of the MCs and GCs scored high on the peacemaking scale the number dropped to 2 percent among the EMCs. This chapter explores the factors that produce high commitments to peacemaking as well as high endorsements for the nonresistance, witness, and activism scales. Which social and religious forces encourage or dampen peacemaking impulses?

The Effects of Modernization

In chapter two we proposed that three particular aspects of modernization—differentiation, rationalization, and individuation—might unravel Mennonite commitments to peacemaking. Differentiation has touched Mennonite communities as the timid have become urbanized and professionalized. Mennonites who once lived in homogeneous rural settings are now scattered from suburb to city and across social class boundaries as well. As Mennonites encountered modernity they became diversified—socially, politically, and religiously. How have historic Mennonite commitments to peacemaking fared in the midst of modernity? Is nonresistance a residual of rural life that vanishes in the vise of urban plausibility structures?

The data in Table 9.5 shed some light on these questions. The percentage of respondents scoring high on nonresistance, witness, and activism as well as on the composite peacemaking scale are cross-tabulated with various indicators of modernization. By scanning down the column under activism, for example, the variation in percentages shows the influence of variables such as urbanization, education, etc. Comparing the differences between extreme levels of urbanization allow us to trace in a rough way its "effect" on activism or nonresistance, as the case may be. We will focus on the composite peacemaking scale (in the last column) but also comment on the three dimensions as appropriate.

TABLE 9.5
Percent High on Peacemaking Dimensions by Modernization

Modernization Items		*Three Dimensions*			*Composite*
		Nonre-sistance	Witness	Activism	Peace-making
Urbanization					
Rural		25*	16	26	27
Large city		15	30	38	34
	(r)	(-.10)	(.16)	(.12)	(.04)
Socioeconomic Status (SES)					
Lower		23	14	24	24
Upper		21	39	38	40
	(r)	(-.04)	(.28)	(.06)	(.08)
Education					
Elementary		33	6	37	31
Graduate School		25	38	39	43
	(r)	(-.05)	(.36)	(.04)	(.09)
Individualism					
Low		37	35	35	44
High		11	14	32	23
	(r)	(-.25)	(-.18)	(.01)	(-.15)
Materialism					
Low		33	28	40	42
High		13	19	28	23
	(r)	(-.21)	(-.09)	(-.09)	(-.17)

*"Twenty-five percent of those living in rural scored high on the nonresistance scale."
r=Pearson correlation coefficient with a range of -1.0 to +1.0.

Urbanization and Socioeconomic Status

Beginning with urbanization, we discover that support for peace-making actually rises from 27 to 34 percent as Mennonites move from farms to large cities. This contradicts the common sense notion that urbanization demolishes peacemaking convictions. Support for non-resistance, however, declines by ten percentage points in the urban transition. Endorsement of both the witness and activism dimensions rise with urbanization. Urban Mennonites are twice as likely (30 vs. 16%) to witness for peace than their rural counterparts.

The data in Table 9.5 consistently confirm that urbanization transforms Mennonite pacifist impulses—nonresistance declines, but witness and activism rise as Mennonites move into the city. Moreover, the overall commitment to peacemaking as measured by our composite scale actually strengthens. On all of the indicators except nonresistance, the move to urban areas bolsters peacemaking convictions.

Coupled with urbanization, the move into professions and business has stretched the socioeconomic diversity of Mennonites. Socioeconomic status (SES) reflects a respondent's combined scores on income, occupation, and education.

How does rising social mobility impact on Mennonite peacemaking? As seen in Table 9.5, peacemaking ascends in tandem with socioeconomic status. Those higher on the social status ladder are sixteen percentage points more likely to score high on peacemaking than those on the lower rungs. Commitments to peace witness and activism also rise with SES. Indeed, convictions for witnessing for peace nearly triple with a rise in SES. Nonresistant beliefs, however, remain stable despite fluctuations in SES. Thus the surge in Mennonite social status propelled by professional and business involvements, rather than weakening, appears to fortify general peacemaking sentiments.

Education

Education is one component of SES which we isolated for special analysis since it clearly reflects the rationalization inherent in modernity. Respondents were sorted into four levels of educational attainment based on their experience at a given level. For example, those at the college level did not necessarily graduate from college but had taken at least one year of college work. Those with only secondary educational experience scored the lowest on peacemaking while those with graduate training ranked the highest.

Table 9.5 shows the two extreme education levels. Respondents with graduate school experience exhibited high (43%) peacemaking commitments—virtually the highest of any subgroup in Table 9.5. About 22 percent of those with graduate education were pastors who likely helped to spike the peacemaking scores in this group. Among respondents with graduate education, 59 percent of the pastors and 38 percent of the lay persons scored high on peacemaking—reducing peacemaking support at the graduate level from 43 to 38 percent if pastors are extracted.

Nonresistance declines as education increases (r=-.05), except among those with graduate training. A commitment to witnessing for peace soars directly with education (r=.36). Those with graduate training are six times more likely to support witness efforts than those who only attended elementary school. Thus although nonresistance declines somewhat in the face of education, peacemaking in general rises to rather high levels among the better educated. The evidence presented in Table 9.5 suggests that the rationalization of modernity embodied in education has a positive impact on peacemaking (with the exception of nonresistance).

Individualism and Materialism

A major dimension of modernity, discussed in chapter two, was individualism. Historically, at least in the Swiss tradition, nonresistance was a firm expectation for members; those who rejected nonresistant ways could expect excommunication. Growing individualism is a pervasive aspect of the modernization process. In recent years, greater credence in the church is given to "individual conscience" and persons are allotted considerable latitude to make up their own minds about a variety of moral questions including peacemaking.

The responses in Table 9.5 confirm the pervasive impact of individualism in the Mennonite experience. Peacemaking responses were cross-tabulated with an "individualism" scale developed by Kauffman and Driedger (1991). Individualism was tapped by asking if the church has any business to be "directly involved in my personal affairs" and if faith is "a private matter for each to decide and practice," as well as other similar questions.

A glance at the data in Table 9.5 shows a consistent pattern—individualism correlates negatively with peacemaking convictions. High support for the composite peacemaking scale drops in half among those inclined toward individualism. Nonresistance fares even worse. As we suggested in chapter two, nonresistance with its giving up of personal rights is a rather unmodern idea. Support for nonresistance vanishes from 37 to 11 percent as individualism rises (r=-.25).

A similar pattern occurs with witness to the state. However, as might be expected, interest in peace activism does not wane with individualism. In terms of the general peacemaking scale, however, the influence of individualism levies a heavy toll with a drop of some twenty-one percentage points (44 to 23). Those who clamor after individual rights are less likely to be enthusiastic about peacemaking.

We also explored the relationship between peacemaking and materialism using a scale developed by Kauffman and Driedger (1991). Respondents were asked questions about "earning as much money as possible," "the simple life," "working hard to get ahead financially," and "getting the nicest home and furnishings I can afford." The results in Table 9.5 show that materialism also dampens peacemaking convictions. Those with scant material interests score the highest in nonresistance, witness, and activism as well as on the composite peacemaking scale. Exerting a similar influence as individualism, materialism weakens the peacemaking resolve by nearly twenty percentage points.

The evidence seems clear. Modernization levies a rather heavy toll on historic nonresistance. Nonresistant beliefs wither along all the dimensions of modernization tapped in our analysis (with a slight exception, as we have noted, among graduate school respondents). Urbanization, individualism, and materialism have the strongest corrosive impact on passive nonresistance. There is good news, however, for peacemakers. Urbanization, socioeconomic diversity, and education all boost Mennonite commitments to peacemaking, peace witness, and activism. Upward mobility and the move to the city, rather than threatening peacemaking values, appear to fortify them.

Thus our data suggest that modernization has indeed transformed the timid. As Mennonites grappled with the forces of modernization they underwent an ideological transformation that changed the content and posture of their peacemaking. Leaving nonresistance behind, but not abandoning their peaceful heritage, they have transformed it into a more activist peacemaking posture, one they could embrace with enthusiasm in the modern world. The real menace to peacemaking, however, comes not from *structural* changes—urbanization and professionalization—but from *ideological* threats. Individualism and materialism riding on the coattails of modernity appear to diminish the peacemaking impulse.

Religious Influences
Religious Life and Peacemaking

How do peacemaking convictions relate to spirituality? We explored the ties between the various dimensions of peacemaking with three barometers of spirituality—religiosity, devotionalism, and church participation. Some twelve questions tapping many areas of spiritual vitality—Bible study, closeness to God, spiritual goals, etc.—were combined into a scale of religious life. The devotionalism scale incorporated questions related to prayer and Bible study, grace before meals, and family worship. Responses to questions of church attendance, holding church office, and participation in congregational activities were combined into a church participation scale.

Table 9.6 presents the connections between peacemaking and religious life. Nonresistant commitments are clearly tied in a positive manner to all three aspects of religious vitality (r=.23 to .25). Indeed the religiously vigorous, on all three indicators, are three times more likely than the spiritually lethargic to score high on nonresistance. For example, 32 percent who were high on devotionalism scored high on nonresistance in contrast to only 11 percent for the devotionally negligent. Likewise the composite peacemaking scale corresponds positively with higher levels of religiosity (r.= .09 to .12) but the tie is somewhat weaker than with nonresistance. Nevertheless, support for peacemaking rises as piety flourishes on all three dimensions of religiosity.

TABLE 9.6
Percent High on Peacemaking Dimensions by Religious Factors

| Religious Factors | | *Three Dimensions* | | *Composite* |
	Nonre-sistance	Witness	Activism	Peace-making
Religious Life				
Low	10*	19	31	25
High	31	23	30	33
(r)	(.23)	(.00)	(-.05)	(.09)
Devotionalism				
Low	11	24	32	26
High	32	22	31	33
(r)	(.25)	(-.05)	(-.03)	(.10)
Church Participation				
Low	11	17	30	22
High	31	23	29	36
(r)	(.24)	(.10)	(-.04)	(.12)

*"Ten percent of those low on religious life scored high on the nonresistance scale."

Peace witness and peace activism, however, appear somewhat independent of the measures of religious life and devotion, with one exception. Support for witness does rise (r.=10) with church participation, but apart from that tie witness and activism do not fluctuate systematically with the religious indicators. These results should not be interpreted to suggest that those championing witness or activist peacemaking activities are not religious. The findings simply suggest witness and activism are not tied to the three aspects of religious life in a systematic fashion.

Theological Orientation and Peacemaking

The maze of relationships between peacemaking and theological orientation shows some interesting but not surprising results, as reported in Table 9.7. Theological orientations were clustered into five scales—Anabaptism, Orthodoxy, Fundamentalism, Charismatic, and Evangelism. The Anabaptist scale encompassed questions dealing with infant baptism, following Christ, the practice of church discipline, and swearing oaths, etc.

As the results in Table 9.7 confirm, all the dimensions of peacemaking correspond positively with Anabaptist beliefs. Indeed Anabaptism is the most influential of all the theological factors. The tie between Anabaptism and nonresistance is particularly strong (r.=.39). Stalwart Anabaptists are six times more likely than lax ones to score high on nonresistance. A similar pattern holds for the composite peacemaking scale (r=.28) where 44 percent of those high on Anabaptism endorse peacemaking compared to only 16 percent among those indifferent to Anabaptism. Anabaptism also produces a positive effect on witness (r.=.05) and activism (r.=.14) although the ties are weaker.

Not surprisingly fundamentalist beliefs corrode all the dimensions of peacemaking except nonresistance. The fundamentalism scale was formed from five questions dealing with issues such as biblical inerrancy, the virgin birth, a literal twenty-four hour creation, and eternal damnation for the unsaved. Ardent fundamentalists are slightly higher on nonresistance than milder ones, but the tie is quite weak.

On the other dimensions of pacifism an unmistakable negative relationship emerges. As fundamentalism rises, peacemaking declines. On both the peacemaking and activist scale, strident fundamentalists consistently score lower than others by a margin of twenty-five percentage points. "Low" fundamentalists are more than three times as likely (40 vs. 14) as committed ones to endorse "witnessing for peace."

TABLE 9.7
Percent High on Peacemaking Dimensions
by Theological Orientation

Theological Orientation		Nonre-sistance	Three Dimensions Witness	Activism	Composite Peace-making
Anabaptist					
Low		6*	19	22	16
High		37	26	37	44
	(r)	(.39)	(.05)	(.14)	(.28)
Fundamentalist					
Low		22	40	50	49
High		28	14	25	25
	(r)	(.03)	(-.24)	(-.23)	(-.19)
Orthodox					
Low		14	37	52	47
High		22	18	27	28
	(r)	(.07)	(-.08)	(-.15)	(-.09)
Charismatic					
Low		18	20	30	29
High		27	20	26	30
	(r)	(.09)	(.05)	(-.04)	(.00)
Evangelical					
Low		17	20	30	29
High		25	25	30	32
	(r)	(.08)	(.01)	(-.06)	(.01)

*"Six percent of those low on Anabaptism scored high on the nonresistance scale."

Apart from nonresistance, the evidence is rather persuasive—a fundamentalist orientation dilutes peacemaking convictions.

A general orthodoxy scale composed of seven questions tapped beliefs about the existence of God, the divinity of Christ, the resurrection and return of Christ, and life after death, among other things. Basic orthodoxy relates positively to peacemaking (r=.09) and nonresistance (r=.07), but negatively to witness (r=-.09) and activism (r=-.15). Thus commitments to peacemaking and nonresistance rise somewhat with orthodoxy, while support for witness and activism decline. The ties of peacemaking to orthodoxy are weaker than its ties to Fundamentalism and Anabaptism.

We also constructed measures of charismatic and evangelical theological orientations. As reported in Table 9.7 both charismatic and evangelical beliefs show virtually no relationship to peacemaking with one slight exception. Nonresistance correlates in a weak but positive way with both evangelical (r=.08) and charismatic convictions (r=.09). Again this does not mean that those with charismatic and evangelical commitments are disinterested in peacemaking. The evidence does suggest, however, that charismatic and evangelical convictions neither weaken nor invigorate peacemaking, at least in any systematic fashion.

Other Influential Factors

Demography and Ethnicity

How does peacemaking relate to demographic factors? Do gender, age, ethnicity, and nationality shape commitments to peacemaking? The results appearing in Table 9.8 are mixed. Unlike many studies that show stronger support for peacemaking among women, within the Mennonite fold gender seems to make little difference on any dimension of peacemaking. From nonresistance to activism, Mennonite men and women share similar beliefs about peace.

Moreover, age differences also matter little on the composite peacemaking scale. As anticipated, support for nonresistance does increase with age while witness and activism decline. Thus on the composite peacemaking scale, age and gender are impotent. Variations in peacemaking attitudes must be traced to factors other than age and gender.

The data in Table 9.8 suggest, however, that nationality and ethnicity do make a difference. Canadian Mennonites carry the peacemaking banner higher than Mennonites south of the border on all dimensions except nonresistance. Indeed Canadian Mennonites are twice as likely as their U.S. cousins to advocate an activist peace stance. U.S. Mennonites, influenced more heavily by the Swiss tradition, favor nonresistance by five percentage points. The strong Dutch-Russian influence, as well as a milder national military culture, likely contribute to the stronger support for peacemaking among Canadians. The activist bent among Canadian Mennonites may also derive from their longer history of political involvement.

TABLE 9.8
Percent High on Peacemaking Dimensions
by Demographic Factors

Factors	*Three Dimensions*			*Composite*
	Nonre-sistance	Witness	Activism	Peace-making
Gender				
Male	23*	22	29	30
Female	20	19	32	30
Age				
-29	16	24	37	28
30-49	20	25	29	31
50-69	26	18	29	30
70-94	25	9	32	30
Nationality				
Canada	18	24	48	36
U.S.	23	19	23	27
Ethnicity				
Dutch	16	22	35	30
Swiss	32	21	28	37
British/other	9	19	24	17

*"Twenty-three percent of males scored high on the nonresistance scale."

We have made many references to the cultural differences flowing from the Swiss and Dutch-Russian experiences. These ethnic traditions did impact, somewhat slightly, the three dimensions of peacemaking as shown in Table 9.8. As expected, respondents with a Swiss heritage are twice as likely (32 vs. 16%) to support nonresistance as those in the Dutch-Russian vein. The Dutch, however, are more activist, but only by a seven point margin. The two ancestries coincide in their levels of support for witnessing for peace. On the composite measure of peacemaking the Swiss lead only slightly—by seven percentage points. Thus although gender and age exert little influence on peacemaking, nationality and ethnicity do make a mild difference.

TABLE 9.9
Percent High on Peacemaking Dimensions by Nationality and Ethnicity

| | Canada | | U.S. | |
Dimensions	Swiss	Dutch	Swiss	Dutch
Nonresistance	32*	16	31	16
Witness	31	25	19	19
Activism	56	47	24	23
Peacemaking (composite)	53	34	34	25

*"Thirty-two percent of Canadian Mennonites with a Swiss background scored high on the nonresistance scale."

To tease out the simultaneous impact on peacemaking of ethnic roots and national identity, we constructed Table 9.9. We discovered that variations in the support of nonresistance are shaped not by nationality but by ethnic ancestry. Those with Swiss roots, regardless of where they live, are twice as likely to favor nonresistance as those with Dutch-Russian ancestry. Moreover, support for nonresistance is constant regardless of nation. On the composite peacemaking scale the same ethnic pattern emerges—the Swiss are more likely to score higher than the Dutch.

But with peacemaking, unlike nonresistance, nationality does matter. Among the Swiss, Canadians are more inclined (53 vs. 34%) to support peacemaking than U.S. citizens. The combined impact of ethnicity and nationality is quite potent on the peacemaking scale. Canadian Swiss are more than twice (53 vs. 25%) as likely as U.S. Dutch to score high on peacemaking. Thus we can conclude that ethnicity primarily influences nonresistance and peacemaking. Nationality touches Mennonite attitudes toward witness, activism, and peacemaking—Canadians, regardless of ethnic roots, are considerably higher on all three of these dimensions.

Trying to unravel the combined effects of ethnicity and denomination, we constructed Table 9.10. Both MC and GC bodies had enough respondents with Dutch or Swiss roots to permit comparison, but the numbers were too small in the other three groups for analysis. With regard to nonresistance, denominational effects clearly overwhelm ethnic ones. Comparing GC and MC members with Swiss roots we discover that the Swiss in the MC fold are three times as likely (39 vs.

TABLE 9.10
Percent High on Peacemaking Dimensions by Denomination and Ethnicity

Dimensions	MC		GC	
	Swiss	Dutch	Swiss	Dutch
Nonresistance	39*	30	12	15
Witness	19	13	28	26
Activism	31	32	28	44
Peacemaking (composite)	41	34	33	36

*"Thirty-nine percent of MC members with a Swiss background scored high on the nonresistance scale."

12) to support nonresistance as GC Swiss. A similar pattern emerges with the Dutch in both groups—MCs are twice (30 vs. 15) as likely to endorse nonresistance.

On the composite peacemaking scale, the denominational effects diminish. About one-third of the Dutch score high on peacemaking regardless of their denominational ties. Among the Swiss, MCs are slightly higher than GCs, but only by eight percentage points (41 vs. 33). Thus we conclude that the denominational effects are more pronounced with nonresistance than with the other dimensions of peacemaking. Denominational and ethnic influences are relatively mild on the composite scale of peacemaking.

Denominational Factors

When summarizing the responses to particular survey items we have already noted wide diversity between the five Mennonite groups. To what extent do denominational cultures and traditions embellish or erode the peacemaking convictions of their members? Since all of these groups historically have carried the "peace church" banner, our survey data allow us to tease out the influence of a denomination's ethos on peacemaking. In addition to denominational affiliation, Table 9.11 presents cross-tabulations that pinpoint the impact of leadership, attendance at Mennonite colleges, and length of membership in a Mennonite body.

Denominational influences are unmistakable. MC and GC members are seventeen times as likely to score high on the composite index of peacemaking as are EMC members. Those affiliated with the

TABLE 9.11
Percent High on Peacemaking Dimensions
by Denominational Factors

Factors	Nonre-sistance	Witness	Activism	Composite Peace-making
	Three Dimensions			*Composite*
Denomination				
MC	34*	17	30	36
GC	15	26	41	34
MB	10	21	27	20
BIC	9	17	16	12
EMC	1	22	5	2
Mennonite Identity				
High	39	23	42	46
Low	7	25	21	17
Leadership				
Pastor	43	33	52	58
Lay	20	20	29	28
Mennonite College Attendance				
Only Mennonite College	21	22	31	46
Never Mennonite College	12	26	29	24
Always Mennonite				
Yes	25	21	33	34
No	12	20	24	19

*"Thirty-four percent of MC members scored high on the nonresistance scale."

MC are three times more likely to score high on peacemaking than BIC members. MC members are twice as likely to rank high on nonresistance than GCs, but on both the witness and activism scales GCs edge out MCs by a margin of nearly ten percentage points. However, on the general peacemaking scale, MCs and GCs are, for all practical purposes, identical. MBs, BICs, and EMCs rank third, fourth, and last, respectively, on all of the measures except witness. On witnessing for peace, EMC members are slightly higher than both BIC and MB respondents. In any event, the data suggest that denominational culture makes a difference—a considerable one—in cultivating or thwarting peacemaking within particular Mennonite groups.

We then investigated the linkage between Mennonite identity and peacemaking. Are enthusiastic Mennonites more likely to be ardent peacemakers? With one exception the answer is a resounding yes. Ten questions regarding a respondent's embrace of Mennonite life were combined into an identity scale. It included questions about the importance of having Mennonite friends, marrying within the church, attending Mennonite schools, and receiving church periodicals.

As noted in Table 9.11 Mennonite enthusiasts were more than five times as likely to endorse nonresistance as Mennonite laggards. On peacemaking, Mennonite cheerleaders ranked higher than the lax by a margin of nearly 30 percentage points (46 to 17%). Support for activism doubled (21 to 42%) from the bottom to the top of the ethnicity ladder. Witness attitudes, however, appear unrelated to identity. In sum, peacemaking, nonresistance, and activism rise in concert with affirmations of Mennonite identity.

Another interesting difference emerged when we contrasted the beliefs of pastors and lay members. Without exception, on all four measures of peacemaking in Table 9.11, pastors, as expected, scored substantially higher than other members. Nearly two-thirds of the pastors scored high on the composite index—some thirty points ahead of lay members. Pastors were more than twice as likely as lay persons to affirm nonresistance. In the area of witness, the gap shrank with lay members lagging only thirteen points behind pastors.

Several factors likely undergird the strong peacemaking commitments of pastors. First, we already noted that peacemaking convictions jell with higher education. Second, in their theological training pastors are more likely than lay persons to have given serious study to peace issues. Finally, as leaders of denominations whose identities are entangled with peacemaking, those with peace convictions are most likely to seek leadership roles and, once in leadership, to feel compelled to fly the flag of peace.

Table 9.11 also traces the ties between higher education and peacemaking. Those who have attended a Mennonite college are twice as likely to score high on peacemaking as those who never attended one. The real impact of Mennonite colleges on peacemaking is difficult to untangle because church colleges may attract the more peaceful in the first place. Witness and activism are weakly related to Mennonite higher education. But in any event there is a sizable bond between attendance at a Mennonite college and positive attitudes on the composite peacemaking scale.

How do newcomers and old-timers in the Mennonite family differ in peacemaking? Do those coming into the Mennonite fold from other religious backgrounds weaken the resolve for peacemaking? Or perhaps the Mennonite flag attracts peace advocates from other religious traditions. The survey asked if respondents had ever been members of a different denomination. The newcomers may have been members of other Anabaptist groups or other religious denominations.

In any event, as shown in Table 9.11, newcomers were fifteen percentage points (19 vs. 34) less likely than old-timers to score high on the composite peacemaking scale. This of course does not mean that all newcomers bring diluted peace convictions. It merely suggests that all things considered, newcomers on the average are somewhat less likely to embrace peacemaking than old-timers.

Social Involvement

In the first portion of this book we suggested that a two-kingdom theology, emphasizing separation from the world, provided a plausible legitimation for passive nonresistance. Do modern Mennonites continue to uphold separatist ideas? Is separatism related to peacemaking in the modern world? The data in Table 9.12 summarize the linkage between social involvement and peacemaking. Attitudes toward involvement in the "kingdoms of this world" make little difference in the response of Mennonites toward peacemaking in general or toward their views of activism. But as expected, those supporting involvement are less likely than the separatists to endorse nonresistance and more likely to advocate witness.

The same pattern persists when the separatism scale is crosstabulated with the four dimensions of peacemaking. Nonresistance moves in tandem with separatism—the higher the separatism, the higher the support for nonresistance (r=.28). Indeed the separatists are more than three times as likely (36 vs. 10) to embrace a nonresistant posture. And, of course, those high on separatism score lower (r=-.16) on activism.

What impact does political participation exert on peacemaking? Are the politically active more or less likely to endorse pacifism? The

TABLE 9.12
Percent High on Peacemaking Dimensions
by Social Involvement

Involvement		*Three Dimensions*			*Composite*
		Nonre-sistance	Witness	Activism	Peace-making
Christians should be involved in Kingdoms of this world					
Yes		17*	31	32	34
No		26	17	30	30
Separatism Scale					
High		36	17	33	34
Low		10	29	30	30
	(r)	(.28)	(-.16)	(.04)	(.12)
Held Political Office					
Yes		15	23	20	25
No		22	20	32	31
Political Participation Scale					
High		5	33	23	18
Low		56	8	29	38
	(r)	(-.58)	(.29)	(-.12)	(-.33)

*"Seventeen percent of the respondents who think Christians should be involved in the Kingdoms of this world scored high on nonresistance."

results in Table 9.12 show that holding political office lowers scores on all the peacemaking scales except witness. When our more general scale of political participation—consisting of some six questions—is used, a clear pattern emerges. The political participation scale includes attitudes toward officeholding, frequency of voting, and membership in political groups. As political participation rises, support plummets for nonresistance (r=-.58), for peacemaking (r=-.33), and for activism (r=-.12). Those politically *inactive*, for instance, are eleven times more likely (56 vs. 5 %) to endorse nonresistance.

In contrast to these results, support for peace witness activities rise directly (r=.29) with political participation. The political enthusiasts are four times as likely (33 vs. 8%) as the separatists to support peace witness ventures. Thus many of the politically active apparently envision their activism fitting under the rubric of witness. The negative relationship between political participation and the other dimensions of peacemaking raise some concern about the motivation and message of political enthusiasts.

Summary

To focus our results, we selected variables that demonstrated the greatest impact on the composite peacemaking scale. Variables were selected which induced an impact of twenty percentage points or greater on the peacemaking scale. The nine factors meeting this criterion appear in Table 9.13. Influences such as ethnicity, nationality, and urbanization likely shape peacemaking attitudes. But any such influences with an impact less than twenty percentage points were excluded. Moreover, variables such as gender and evangelical orientation which have a negligible impact are also missing.

What are the positive sources of variation in peacemaking attitudes? As Table 9.13 displays and as we have already noted, denomi-

TABLE 9.13
Key Factors That Impact Peacemaking Attitudes

Factors	Percentage point difference on composite peacemaking scale
Positive	
Denomination: MC-EMC (36 vs. 2)	34*
Leadership: Pastor-Lay (58 vs. 28)	30
Identity: High-Low (46 vs. 17)	29
Anabaptism: High-Low (44 vs. 16)	28
Mennonite College: Menn/Non-Menn (46 vs. 24)	22
Education: Grad-Sec (43 vs. 21)	22
Negative	
Political Participation: High-Low (18 vs. 38)	-20
Individualism: High-Low (23 vs. 44)	-21
Fundamentalism: High-Low (25 vs. 49)	-24

*"MCs scored 34 percentage points higher than EMCs on the composite peacemaking scale."
(Note: Includes only those factors which had a 20 percent or greater impact on the composite peacemaking scale.)

national effects (34%) are the most pronounced. Pastoral leadership (30%), Mennonite identity (29%), Anabaptist beliefs (28%), Education (22%), and Mennonite college attendance (22%) are all positively associated with peacemaking. Interestingly, these forces impact more strongly than urbanization and socioeconomic status.

The most significant negative influences come from fundamentalism (-24%), individualism (-21%), and political participation (-20%). All three of these factors—two ideological and one more behavioral—diminish enthusiasm for peacemaking. The striking differences between Mennonite groups suggest that denominational cultures do matter. The considerable diversity within the Mennonite fold suggests that denominational efforts to fortify peacemaking can be rather significant in perpetuating it in the midst of modernity.

Finally, the evidence of this chapter suggests that the peacemaking patterns of the meek and mild have indeed been transformed by modernity. The *structural* influences of modernity—urbanization, education, and professionalism—have not diminished the peacemaking impulse and, in some cases, especially with education, have encouraged it. On the other hand, the *ideological* components of modernity—especially individualism and materialism—have indeed eroded peacemaking committments. The process of modernization has levied a heavy toll on passive nonresistance. But the evidence shows that for the most part Mennonites have not abandoned their peacemaking heritage.[3] Although nonresistance lacks credibility in the context of modern plausibility structures, Mennonite pacifist impulses have been restructured into active peacemaking—which for many Mennonites not only articulates their historic tradition but also offers credibility within the plausibility structures of the modern world.

CHAPTER TEN

Visions for the Future

The Mennonite peace paradigm has undergone a major shift in the last fifty years as Mennonites turned from nonresistance to social engagement. World War II, as we have seen, was a key turning point. In Part I we traced the historical stages in the development of this shift. Hershberger, Yoder, Burkholder, and Kaufman were some of the key ideological brokers in the ferment of the forties and fifties. In Part II we reviewed the empirical evidence supporting the transformation to active peacemaking. Mennonites are increasingly pursuing witness and activist projects as well as becoming politically engaged.

Having traced the underlying trends, we now summarize some of the major factors shaping the dynamics of Mennonite peacemaking in the nineties. Who are the brokers seeking to create new ideological formulations for the new social realities? Hershberger brought Mennonites together in the forties. Who will issue the call today? Or are Mennonites, in the words of Stephen Leacock, "quickly mounting their steeds and riding in all directions at once?"

Factors Which Matter

Following our sweeping historical and survey analysis we can summarize some of the major factors which shape Mennonite peacemaking. In Table 10.1 a multiple regression analysis pinpoints the factors which influence peacemaking and political participation. In previous chapters we focused on simple relationships between two factors without considering the simultaneous impact of other variables. Multiple regression considers the simultaneous influence of several variables and identifies the distinctive impact of a particular variable on our composite scales of peacemaking and political participation.[1]

Theology and ethnicity are key factors which matter. Surprisingly, religiosity and modernization contribute little to peacemaking and political participation after the influence of theological and ethnic factors. The data in Table 10.1 show how these four factors shape peacemaking attitudes and political participation in the Mennonite experience. In earlier discussions, we noted that when modernization was considered alone, its *ideological* influences eroded peacemaking. However, when modernization variables are considered simultaneously with other factors, the influence of modernity is overshadowed by theological and ethnic forces.

TABLE 10.1
Influences on Peacemaking and Political Participation:
Multiple Regression

Influences	Peacemaking (composite)	Political Participation
Theology		
Anabaptism	.24*	-.13
Fundamentalism	-.29	.01
Solidarity		
Ethnicity	.30	-.22
Separatism	.05	-.18
Religiosity		
Church Participation	.06	-.08
Religious Life	-.03	.07
Modernization		
Education	.03	.11
Urbanization	.02	.02
Individualism	-.02	-.02
SES	-.01	-.01
Multiple R	.54	.46

*Standardized beta regression coefficients summarize the unique influence of a variable beyond the combined influence of other variables.

Theology: Anabaptism vs. Fundamentalism

Our earlier discussions noted that Anabaptist theology undergirds peacemaking, and this remains evident in Table 10.1. A strong positive correlation between Anabaptism and the peacemaking scale (beta .24) holds after the influences of modernization and religiosity are taken into account. This suggests that an Anabaptist theological orientation remains integral to peacemaking. In the past Mennonites have been reluctant to engage in politics, and this negative relationship between Anabaptist theology and political participation (beta .13) continues. Mennonites strong in Anabaptist theology wish to promote peace but tend to be reluctant participants in the larger political order.

Our previous analyses also demonstrated that Fundamentalist Mennonites disparaged peacemaking, and this pattern continues in Table 10.1. Fundamentalism is negatively correlated with peacemaking (beta .29), but not related to political participation (beta .01). Thus theological orientation remains a formidable factor in peacemaking; Anabaptists promote it, while Fundamentalists discourage it. Anabaptists on the other hand tend to discourage political participation, while Fundamentalists remain neutral. These important theological differences deserve additional analysis. The data in Figure 10.1 permit us to compare the larger ramifications of the two theological orientations.

We see in Figure 10.1 that Anabaptists and Fundamentalists are both positively associated with evangelism (r =.30 and .24). However, Anabaptism is positively associated with peacemaking (r =.28), while Fundamentalism correlates negatively with it (r = -.19). Anabaptists are committed to both evangelism and peacemaking; Fundamentalists only to the first. This, we suggest, represents two different perspectives which Robert Wuthnow (1981) calls *dualist* and *holist* concepts of the world.[2] These two perspectives also clash within the bosom of the Mennonite churches. The basic theological task, it seems to us, requires careful reflection on the consequences of these divergent world views of the kingdom of God.[3]

Compared with Fundamentalists, Anabaptist Mennonites see their theological task in a more wholistic way, which includes evangelism (.30), serving others (.26), working through MCC (.09), assisting the welfare of others (.07), promoting racial justice (.07), and peacemaking (.28).[4] Many early Anabaptists incorporated peacemaking into discipleship along with evangelism and encouraged their followers to take both church and world seriously. This wholistic theology meant that early Anabaptists were viewed as socially and politically danger

FIGURE 10.1
Comparison of Anabaptist and Fundamentalist Theologies and Their Associations (Pearson r) with Six Issues

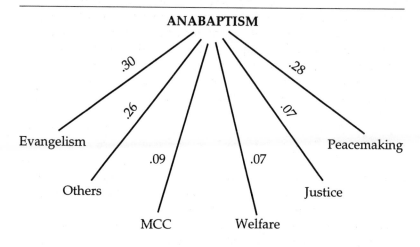

ANABAPTISM

.30 .26 .09 .07 .07 .28

Evangelism   Others   MCC   Welfare   Justice   Peacemaking

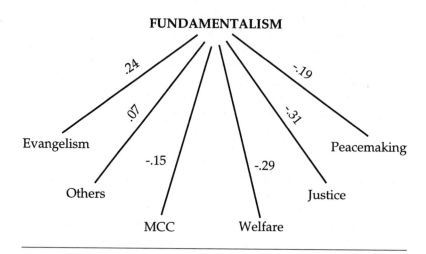

FUNDAMENTALISM

.24 .07 -.15 -.29 -.31 -.19

Evangelism   Others   MCC   Welfare   Justice   Peacemaking

ous, and many Anabaptists paid the dear price of exile and martyrdom.

In later centuries, when faced with war, Mennonites even in isolated communities were forced to deal with imprisonment or alternative service—experiences which, according to Keim (1990b) and Klippenstein (1979), incurred considerable social costs during World War II. While many youth in the forties were ill-prepared to give reasons for their faith, they were forced out of their communities and required to demonstrate their convictions. Since then, the embers of wholistic Anabaptist theology have flamed into an annual $35 million outreach effort involving 1,000 workers in fifty countries serving in the "Name of Christ" under the auspices of the Mennonite Central Committee.

Military conscription in World War II nourished Christian service programs which have flourished in the following decades. MCC workers—observing the injustices of war, famine, racial discrimination, and despair—have returned to their congregations for the last fifty years, interpreting anew the larger vision of Christ.

Figure 10.1 also shows that Mennonite Fundamentalists, like Mennonite Anabaptists, are committed to evangelism (.24) but much less to serving others (.07). Contrary to the positive linkages between Anabaptism, societal service, and outreach, Fundamentalism correlates negatively with MCC service (-.15), welfare for others (-.29), racial justice (-.31), and peacemaking (-.19). Service to society and the world beyond the church is minimized in Fundamentalist understandings of the gospel. More seriously, Fundamentalists sometimes oppose social services—viewing them outside the mandate of the gospel. Fundamentalists tend to accent personal salvation, while Anabaptists emphasize not only religious salvation but also active love and social assistance.

More recently evangelicals such as Ronald J. Sider and others are working to integrate evangelism, social service, and peacemaking (Marsden, 1991; Hunter, 1987; Rawlyk, 1990; Dayton and Johnston, 1991). Many Mennonites are also seeking to maintain a healthy Anabaptist dialectic between service and evangelism by balancing care for the soul with compassion for the needy. Mennonite leaders in the recent past—the Benders, Millers, Hieberts, Thiessens, Janzs, and Dycks—who had "courage to spare," encouraged a vital church-world tension. While that dialectic in the past was often seen in two kingdom terms (emerging out of rural settings) the delicate relationships between evangelism, service, relief, welfare, justice, politics, and peacemaking need continual fine-tuning in the context of political engagement.

Our research clearly documents that Mennonites are becoming more educated and urban, pluralistic, and increasingly open to political involvement. This openness to the larger world offers many opportunities for service and peacemaking. However, it remains to be seen how Mennonites will fare with the new challenges. Fundamentalist Mennonites tend to focus on personal evangelism and neglect the work of MCC, welfare services, social justice, and peacemaking. Anabaptist-oriented Mennonites also affirm evangelism, but view it as part of a larger fabric of concern for others, of MCC service, and of peace and justice. As Mennonites become more urban and educated they will need to continually update the precarious balance between evangelism and peacemaking.

Solidarity: Community Support for Peace

Through the centuries Mennonites have developed a strong sense of community and peoplehood which sustained their in-group identity. Dimensions of group identity measured in the Church Member Profile included Low German and Swiss German dialects, in-group newspapers and literature, choice of in-group friends and spouses, as well as support of churches, parochial schools, and other Mennonite organizations often confined to segregated Mennonite settlements. These ethnic communities often focused their faith and practice inward, and thus nonresistance rather than active peacemaking became the norm over centuries.

Both the Swiss sectarians and the Dutch activists were for centuries boxed into rural and sometimes segregated ethnic communities, which they are now in the process of leaving. The writings of the Concern Group flowing out of the ferment of the fifties criticized the excessive ethnicity of the Mennonite Church. The Concern Group members were only recently removed from their rural roots—three out of four MCs were still living in the country. The youthful scholars critiqued Bender and Hershberger for not implementing a radical "Anabaptist Vision" in rural congregations as the early vision demanded. But could rural congregations be renewed and revitalized with a radical vision?

Paul Peachey (1954) had already traced the urbanization of Swiss Anabaptists in his doctoral dissertation, and in 1963 offered a treatise on *The Church in the City* where he traced Mennonite urbanization and city evangelism, hoping for an urban rebirth. Peachey (1963:103) concludes,

> We simply cannot follow Christ in the industrial society—and which society we cannot wave out of existence—and hope to retain our former comforts. . . . The new communities struggling to be born will spring, not full-blown from a sudden blueprint of scheme, devised by some virtuoso

more clever than mortals, but from the pangs which new life always brings. To be sure, here and there, prophets may be granted us whose vision will penetrate some of the nearby mists. Yet if any offer us merely novel and externally reduplicable schemes, we do well to reject their word. Certainly the crucial task is the building of the new, not the dismantling of the old.

Peachey later served as peace ambassador to missionaries in Japan, as well as with the Church Peace Mission in Washington. There he worked with other denominations in the ecumenical arena—seeking to extend the Mennonite peace influence beyond the ethnic boundaries of his rural heritage. Others have continued to probe extensions into the city (Driedger, 1975; 1988; 1990).

Consider Table 10.1 again. The data show that ethnicity correlates even more strongly with peacemaking (beta .30) than does Anabaptism (beta .24). Those who support Mennonite institutions and ingroup practices are also most likely to endorse peacemaking. The peace child may vanish if Mennonites throw out their ethnic bathwater too quickly. On the other hand, ethnicity is more negatively associated with political participation (beta -.22) than is Anabaptism (beta -.13). Stalwart supporters of Mennonite ways are reluctant participants in the larger political order.

How will Mennonites who enter the larger social arena maintain community-sustaining values that support peacemaking? Will modern Mennonites be able to juggle the dialectic between peacemaking and political participation? This question circumscribes the Mennonite move from nonresistance to peacemaking and social responsibility. Will Mennonite urbanites lose their sense of solidarity and peoplehood which nourished nonresistance over the years?

A separatism scale was created to tap conflict between Mennonites and society, and to identify differences between the two kingdoms and societal avoidance. Table 10.1 shows that separatism does not affect peacemaking (beta .05). However, separatism does correlate negatively with political participation (beta -.18). Although separatists' attitudes deter political participation, they have a neutral influence on peacemaking. It is not surprising that the Mennonite Brethren who have become most urban have been forced to wrestle with the issue of ethnic solidarity.

John H. Redekop (1987) faced the ethnicity dilemma head-on in *A People Apart: Ethnicity and the Mennonite Brethren.* His survey of Mennonite Brethren churches found that in 1986, seventy-two of their 173 churches did not use "Mennonite" in their name. In recent years 75 percent of their new congregations do not call themselves Mennonite (Redekop, 1987:1). In 1972 over half of the Mennonite Brethren were urban, by 1989 three out of four were urban, and they scored the highest of all Mennonite groups on socioeconomic status. With the sharp rise in urbanization and status, Redekop suspected that many MBs thought the "Mennonite" label portrayed ethnic traditions which hindered evangelism. What then happened to their peace theology?

Redekop (1987:17) concluded that if the Mennonite Brethren do not take prompt corrective action, the retention of Anabaptist theology will be difficult if not impossible. Redekop agreed with anthropologist Jacob Loewen (1986), who said,

> When we look at the MBs in regard to the peace stance *per se*—one of the original Mennonite distinctives which MBs have consistently reaffirmed—we see that loyalty to this Anabaptist bedrock has been greatly weakened, and in many cases, totally lost. . . . This erosion of the peace stance has progressed to the degree that today in Western and Central U.S.A., it seems to me, many MBs probably would feel more drawn to Moral Majority and militarism than even mainstream evangelicalism.

Redekop and Loewen attribute the erosion of the MB peace witness to a decline of Anabaptist theology, and to a view that the "Mennonite" identification is an ethnic millstone which retards evangelism.

John E. Toews (1985:62), in reviewing the 1972 survey conducted by Kauffman and Harder (1975) as well as a 1982 MB survey, wrote,

> The response indicated a progressive weakening of Mennonite Brethren commitment to Anabaptist-Mennonite faith. . . . Only 42 percent of Mennonite Brethren believed Jesus was normative for daily living. . . . Only 54 percent of Mennonite Brethren in 1972 and 1982 rejected participation in war. . . . The profile pictures an ethno-religious group losing its historic religious group identity as it is assimilated into American cultural religion.

In contrast, J. B. Toews observed that "our forefathers did not distinguish between faith and culture" (cited in Redekop 1987:155). John H. Redekop (1986) found that MBs were declining in Anabaptist theology and denominational commitment, with many no longer regarding themselves as Mennonite. Thus, Redekop recommended that since Anabaptist theology was essential for peace, and since new urban congregations chaffed under the Mennonite label, that a name change to Anabaptist or something else was in order. MC and GC denominations appear less inclined to separate Anabaptist, Mennonite, peace, and ethnicity. But this may change as these denominations become more urban and recruit a larger proportion of members from non-Mennonite backgrounds.

Insignificance: Two Surprises

We expected that religious and devotional activities would support Mennonite peacemaking. However, our data in Table 10.1 show a weak but positive association (beta .06) between church participation and peacemaking which remains *after* the influence of other factors is removed. Furthermore, church participation slightly deters political participation (beta -.08). The various indicators of religious life such as Bible study, prayer, devotions, and a close relationship to God also have a weak effect on both peacemaking (beta -.03) and political participation (beta .07). This suggests that theological orientation, more than religiosity, decisively shapes attitudes toward both peacemaking and political engagement.

The minimal effects of modernization may also surprise those who are afraid to leave their rural communities. Whether Mennonites live in the country or the city, are of high or low social status, or score high or low on individualism appears to matter little *after* the effects of other variables are considered. Educated Mennonites, however, are more inclined to become politically engaged (beta .11). Modernization in any event does not seem to erode commitments to Mennonite peacemaking, nor does it influence political participation, except among the more highly educated.

We conclude that theological orientation and ethnic solidarity more powerfully shape Mennonite peacemaking than do religious practices and modernization. Modernization and religiosity are overshadowed by the decisive influence of theological orientation and ethnic solidarity when all of the variables are considered simultaneously. Mennonites who remain anchored in Anabaptist convictions and are conversant with their ethnic heritage should be resilient peacemakers in modern urban settings.

Peacemaking Arenas

In the early pages of this book we proposed that historic nonresistance, although passive in nature, affected many types of social relationships within the Mennonite community. The recent more activist modes of Mennonite peacemaking are also relevant to a wide array of settings, both within and without the church. Indeed the transformation of nonresistance has not only resulted in more active tactics but also in a greatly expanded scope of peacemaking, which, as we have seen, includes political involvement. Although participation in the political order has become a legitimate expression of Mennonite peacemaking in recent years, it is only one of many contemporary arenas.

In chapter 9 we noted that Mennonites are working at peacemaking in many ways. Some continue to embrace the nonresistant ideals outlined by Guy Hershberger in the forties. Other Mennonites—second- and third-generation urbanites—are more active politically and some seek structural changes. Still others call for revolutionary changes in the face of staggering oppression in less developed areas of the world. Between these options fall a variety of other peacemaking ventures. The plurality of urbanism requires the acceptance of Mennonites working in the modes and arenas of peacemaking most suited to their situation, ability, and conviction. The Christian peace presence takes many forms—not all are called to the same style or mode of involvement.

Modern societies with their variegated social structures offer numerous opportunities for peacemaking initiatives. We have identified six peacemaking arenas as shown in Table 10.2.[5] These are not mutually exclusive domains. Persons may frequently work in several arenas simultaneously and some conceivably in all of them. A person may sense a particular "calling" to a particular arena, but we nevertheless believe that all six constitute legitimate domains for peacemaking initiatives. We place the highest accent on peacemaking within the church—the community of faith—because it is the religious womb that nurtures Christian faith over the generations and should be an exemplar of the ways of peace.

Within the six arenas peacemaking initiatives should proceed at two levels: *ethos* and *structure*. Creating a peaceful ethos involves the cultivation of values, ideas, and sentiments that support the peaceful resolution of conflict. An enduring commitment to conciliation must be espoused in the church as well as in the political order. But peacemaking involves more than words and sentiments; it also entails the creation of just structures which impact on the well-being of humans in significant ways. Thus Christian peacemakers must also seek to support and create just political and economic systems of social behavior in the six arenas which we now consider.

Church Communities

The church—especially the local congregation—is the most basic arena of peacemaking. This community nurtures the Christian faith over the generations, guides our interpretation of Scripture, and seeks

TABLE 10.2
Arenas for Peacemaking Initiatives: Ethos and Structure

Arena	Initiative
1. Church communities	Create communities of faith that model shalom and justice in their values and structure.
2. Interpersonal networks	Demonstrate a conciliatory spirit and practice peaceful habits in family and interpersonal relations.
3. Vocational opportunities	Articulate values and shape structures that promote peace and justice in the workplace.
4. Church agencies	Support and participate in church agencies sponsoring peacemaking initiatives.
5. Voluntary organizations	Support and participate in voluntary agencies devoted to peacemaking projects.
6. Government agencies	Articulate the values of peace and urge political structures and policies to promote justice.

to incarnate the values of God's kingdom. The church, argues Duane Friesen (1986), has a special role in teaching children the values of nonviolence and in cultivating an ethos that supports peaceful means of conflict resolution. The first task, according to Friesen, is to challenge the legitimacy of prevailing institutions and belief structures which implicitly assume that violence is the best and most efficient means of resolving conflict. The educational efforts of the church can be instrumental in shaping a nonviolent ethos. The church, in essence, should create a worldview that values the dignity of each person and heralds the blessings of shalom.

But the church must do more than talk of peace. It must seek to create peaceful and just structures within its own orbit. The witness of the church to political structures will be muted and will ring hollow if congregations do not embody the values that they preach. Thus a strong commitment to conciliation and just relationships within both congregations and church institutions is essential for a credible witness in the larger world. Addressing inequalities in the church community created by gender, race, privilege, and position can model the biblical vision of shalom. Such initiatives are appropriate not only for local congregations but also for church agencies and bureaucracies.

The Hutterites and Amish have committed themselves to creating lifetime communities that care for all members (children, youth, the disabled, the aged). Such enduring expressions of care entice millions of tourists each year to the prairies, Pennsylvania, Ohio, and Ontario. Beyond these traditional groups, intentional communities such as Reba Place in Chicago and Koininia Farms in Georgia have attempted to model justice in their internal structure as well as in outreach.

But most Mennonites today find themselves in traditional congregations which are often tempted to adopt values and structures from the surrounding culture which are not conducive to peace. In its many missions and forms, the church is called to be the church—to demonstrate by example the values and structures of peace and justice.

Interpersonal Networks

It may be enticing to embark on crusades for justice in faraway places. But one of the most demanding arenas of peacemaking unfolds within the family and in the networks of daily relationships. In the heat of daily routines, love and hate converge to spark the fires of greed, jealousy, and competition. In the web of interpersonal ties, in family and beyond, peacemakers will seek to practice the virtues of reconciliation amidst the drudgery of everyday life. Interpersonal styles that embrace confession rather than arrogance, that encourage cooperation rather than competition, and that embody forgiveness instead of conceit, can be the conduits of peace in the maze of daily living. Respect for the dignity of spouse, sibling, friend, and colleague must replace abuse and degradation in the private corners of life. Peacemaking in the interpersonal arena goes largely unnoticed, yet it provides the essential infrastructure undergirding our larger efforts in the public eye.

Vocational Opportunities

Some church members working in church agencies or in the MCC Washington and Ottawa offices have peacemaking in their formal job portfolios. Peacemaking is their prime vocation, and their efforts are greatly needed. MCC personnel pursue peace and justice—seeking to bring about reconciliation and love in the midst of pain and oppression around the globe. Rank-and-file Mennonites, however, represent a vast corps of potential peacemakers as they embrace the ways of peace in daily work. This far-flung corps of vocational peacemakers will include farmers who contribute livestock to relief auctions, teachers who demonstrate justice in the classroom, administrators who de-emphasize status, lawyers who seek alternatives to legal confrontation, and politicians who speak the truth.

Today many Mennonites serve in leadership roles—heading up academic departments at universities, managing business organizations, leading professional groups, and administering public agencies, including government programs. Mennonites in these vocational realms have ample opportunities to influence public policy and to practice vocational peacemaking. In these settings, Mennonites well rooted in their faith can work daily for justice and reconciliation.

Vocational peacemaking easily becomes humdrum, commonplace, and forgotten. Mennonites in the past encouraged farmers to sow their wheat as a service to God. Now that four times as many are in professions as in farming, peacemaking efforts need to focus on school, hospital, business, and office. The Mennonite rural mentality is not easily transformed into active peacemaking in the city. The church needs to explore new ways to challenge its members to be active peacemakers in daily vocations. Ordinary members can make a great impact if they cultivate commitments to love and peace in their vocational pursuits. If the Anabaptist view of the priesthood of every believer is actualized the church can make a significant collective impact.

Church Agencies

Beyond vocational peacemaking on an individual basis, many persons may choose to participate as volunteers or full-time workers in agencies organized by the church to promote peace and justice. The church, according to Duane Friesen (1986), should create innovative institutions to meet human needs. Such ventures can model creative alternatives to mainstream culture and traditional public institutions.

The two world wars were often perceived by Mennonites as disasters, but out of these ashes grew the Mennonite Central Committee

(MCC), founded in 1920 to feed and rescue victims of the Russian Revolution. Especially after World War II, Mennonites turned to serve the needs of others so that now some 1,000 volunteers work in fifty countries around the world under the auspices of MCC. Dozens of annual MCC relief auctions generate millions of dollars for relief and refugee assistance. The core of MCC work has always centered around relief in the form of food, clothes, and shelter (Kreider and Goossen, 1988).

The Food Grains Bank in Canada has expanded to include most of the major denominations. Farmers deliver grain to designated elevators which is matched severalfold by governments for shipment to famine-stricken countries, especially in Africa and Asia. In many cases food is sent into war-ravished regions. This is truly food for peace. In recent years MCC has also spearheaded social and economic development efforts.

New service programs, begun after World War II, include efforts such as Mennonite Disaster Service, where Mennonites move within hours to communities devastated by tornadoes, floods, and fires. The Victim Offender Reconciliation Programs provide opportunities for restitution and interaction between victims and criminal offenders. Young people enter voluntary service programs for the summer or longer to teach children, supervise play, and provide social services, often in inner-city communities where community-building is especially needed. Newer programs work with the disabled, create jobs for the poor, and provide scholarships to promote racial equality and justice.

Mennonite Conciliation Service trains mediators to supervise dispute resolution in a multitude of settings—family, church, ethnic, business, and legal. The Christian Peacemaker Teams provide opportunities for witness and intervention in the midst of conflict situations around the world. In all these ways the church has organized creative, alternative institutions to meet human need. In so doing, the church has been a responsible moral agent alongside and often outside the traditional political structure.

Voluntary Organizations

In addition to church sponsored agencies, many peacemakers support a host of voluntary agencies with their time, ideas, and finances. Voluntary agencies such as the Fellowship of Reconciliation, The Center for Defense Information, Habitat for Humanity, Bread for the World, Witness for Peace, the Red Cross, the Peace Tax Fund, Amnesty International, and the War Tax Resisters (to name but a few), have been instrumental in alleviating suffering, promoting just economic structures, and heralding the peaceful resolution of conflict.

Many of these voluntary agencies are supported by churches and individual Christians, but these and a myriad of other voluntary efforts have created structures outside traditional political channels to promote peace and justice, sometimes in the crossfire of violence. These ventures, relying on voluntary gifts, have made a real difference in cultivating an international network and ethos that supports justice and serves the immediate needs of the victims of starvation and the refugees of war. Many of these agencies also actively seek to influence government policies and structures in ways that benefit the economically disenfranchised.

Government Agencies

As we have frequently noted, Mennonite interest in political participation continues to grow. Government provides still another legitimate arena for Christian peacemaking in at least three capacities: (1) as citizens give a witness to their convictions, (2) as appointed officials serve in various levels of government, and (3) as elected officeholders represent their constituencies. In all of these roles Mennonite peacemakers will seek to create an ethos that sustains peacemaking and implements structures to alleviate injustice and oppression.

Attempts to cultivate the values of peace will include not only witness and persuasion but also assertive moves to formulate new policies. The Peace Tax Fund exemplifies a serious attempt to shape legislation in ways that would permit conscientious objectors to allocate the military portion of their federal taxes to constructive purposes. Such legislative attempts help to ease the conscience of the faithful, but other efforts are also needed to develop policies and enact legislation that promote social and economic justice for others as well.

Beyond the witness of Christian citizens and appointed officials, elected leaders who retain their allegiance to the kingdom of God can also make a difference in nudging government in peaceful directions. While the political arena is fraught with ethical compromise and temptations to play to the fads and fears of the moment, politicians of conscience and conviction can make a difference in promoting the values and vehicles of peace. Political policies and programs tend to reflect the economic outlook and vested interests of those who create the legislation.

Mennonite officeholders who have not sold their souls for a pot of political porridge can exert constructive influence in highlighting the special needs of those who barely survive on the fringe of the political system. In less democratic settings, peacemakers may heed the call for structural surgery and help to shape alternative policies and programs at considerable personal risk.

New Century Voices

Guy Hershberger solidified a Mennonite rationale for nonresistance in the context of World War II and its aftermath. The Concern Group and other theological brokers in the fifties prepared Mennonites for a more engaged witness in the strident sixties and seventies amidst racial upheavals and the Vietnam War.

Who are the brokers of the nineties, when North American Mennonites no longer face conscription, when the prospects of nuclear war wane, and when the Soviet giant no longer threatens? The ferment in the fifties is brewing again in the nineties, as Mennonite brokers wrestle with new challenges to peacemaking (Burkholder, 1991a and Driedger, 1992). John R. Burkholder (1991a) has identified ten different streams of Mennonite peacemaking which grapple with a wide range of contemporary issues. Which voices will lead the way into the twenty-first century and articulate a relevant theology of peacemaking?

Realistic Peacemaking

Duane Friesen's *Christian Peacemaking and International Conflict* (1986), the most comprehensive work by a Mennonite scholar (forty-four years after Hershberger), blends recent scholarship in theology with insights from the social sciences. While Hershberger's classic in the forties grew out of the Goshen (Indiana) Swiss community, Friesen's work flows from the Newton (Kansas) Dutch-Russian tradition, which has emphasized a culturally engaged approach to peacemaking. Friesen's (1986:19-20) work is subtitled *A Realist Pacifist Perspective*. He explains,

> Realist means two things: 1) a pacifism that takes seriously the nature of human sinfulness as it expresses itself in the egoistic self-interest and exploitation of political and economic systems; and 2) a pacifism that is political, that seeks to apply its ethic to resolution of practical, economic and political issues within human institutions.
>
> My position has grown out of three traditions of human thought that have deeply influenced me the past 20 years: 1) the pacifist tradition of the Bible, the historic peace churches, and the political nonviolence

movement exemplified by such persons as Mohandas K. Gandhi and Martin L. King; 2) the just war tradition from St. Augustine through Paul Ramsey and Ralph Potter, and 3) the peace research tradition of the past thirty years, particularly the study and research done by a growing number of social scientists on human conflict. . . .

For Friesen, (1986:22), peace is both (1) the goal of justice, and (2) the use of nonviolent means to achieve justice. Peace is not merely the maintenance of social order or the absence of war. Peace also entails just social conditions conducive to human development. Thus peacemakers seek to maintain just social orders and change unjust ones. These attempts to induce change must always be done nonviolently—the use of violence to maintain or change structures is unacceptable. Friesen (1986:99) calls Niebuhr's approach a

> serious distortion of the Christian faith because it does not sufficiently emphasize . . . God's redemptive activity [in forming] . . . a new people . . . given new possibilities of obedience to God's will. Niebuhr is so preoccupied by the question of what human possibilities are that he underemphasizes the possibilities of God's redemption. In contrast to liberalism which was too optimistic about human possibilities (and which Niebuhr battled against), Niebuhr was too pessimistic about human possibilities. . . . In this respect both are distorted by a common failure: lack of trust and faith in God as the energizer, the redeemer, the one who acts creatively through human culture who frees persons from sin (that means the principalities and powers) and gives to human beings new possibilities of obedience.

Those who assert the inevitability of sin, Friesen contends, tend to subtly justify it and therefore compromise too quickly. To assume that sin is inevitable is to deny God's redemptive action in history.

Friesen poses two partially overlapping circles to illustrate the relationship between the community of faith and the political community. The area of overlap is the arena where the church cooperates with the political community to pursue common goals. Even outside the area of overlap, the church can exert a critical influence. The size of overlap demonstrates the relative range of Mennonite positions. Sectarians see little overlap, whereas realists contend there is substantial overlap between the church and political order. Interactionists and liberationists (to be discussed later), also argue for a large arena where Christians can work with governments and seek to change them in substantial ways.

Friesen (1986:155-156) agrees with John H. Yoder that the cross and resurrection point to an inherent connection between means and ends. Immoral means cannot be used to attain good ends. He also concurs with Martin Luther King, Jr., (1958) that "Constructive ends can never give absolute moral justification to destructive means, because in the final analysis the end is preexistent in the means."

Supporting John H. Yoder, Friesen notes that Christians cannot · manage history to make it come out their way, for that is beyond the power of humans. Nevertheless, on a practical level Christian peacemakers must assess the effectiveness of their actions and the impact of government policies on the welfare of persons both within and without their borders. Friesen proposes various levels of action for implementing the vision of peacemaking.

Thus we have in Friesen's realistic pacifism a call to actively promote peace and justice within the structures of society with nonviolent means of action. This position is considerably more active than historic nonresistance. A recently developed Mennonite position, his work flows in continuity with the Dutch-Russian tradition of culturally engaged pacifism.

Modified Dualism

Earlier Mennonite peace theology, best represented by Hershberger, was shaped by a two-kingdom outlook. As we noted earlier, the use of the lordship of Christ encouraged the acceptance of a single moral standard that blurred the two-kingdom ethic. In a recent autobiographical essay, Ted Koontz (1988) proposes a modified, dual ethic.

John R. Burkholder (1991a:7) describes Koontz's view as "a sophisticated return to a modified two-kingdom ethic, recognizing the moral necessity for occasional state violence, but supporting nonviolence (even radical nonviolent action) as the Christian ethic." Daniel Schipani (1991:78) summarizes, "Koontz's recent work . . . in most respects stands within the Guy F. Hershberger (first generation—'Historic Nonresistance') and John H. Yoder's (second generation—'Messianic Community') traditions of Mennonite peace theology. Yet his work and thought reflect a different setting and vantage point. . . ."

Koontz in essence proposes a floating ethical standard for the state which acknowledges the state's necessity to use violence to protect the innocent and to maintain order. The necessity to use violence arises because of the violence perpetuated by others, not because the state itself is inherently violent in nature.

Koontz (1988) makes a clear difference between two forms of state violence. One form is state force to limit the violence of those that threaten the common order and the welfare of the innocent. The other form is violence which perpetuates political oppression and economic injustice. Hence there may be times the state is too pacifistic—refusing to restrain troublemakers—and other times when the state uses excessive violence to curb threats or uses force to promote political and social injustice. Koontz thus proposes a floating ethic for the state that rises and falls with the tide of violence in particular situations.[6]

Such a formulation reflects the earlier Mennonite understanding of dual norms for church and state but also acknowledges the relativity of ethical standards for different political situations. Although it builds on the older dichotomy it is not separatist in stance. Rather, it provides the church ample room to critique a particular government. Koontz (1988) has brokered an ethical formulation that bridges between classic Mennonite understandings and the ethical complexities of modern states in different settings. Additional refinement is needed at two levels. First, how are the criteria for the floating ethic to be determined. Second, to what extent, if any, can Christian peacemakers participate in the state's use of violence to protect the innocent?

In correspondence Koontz proposes the use of "kingdom" as an important third category in ethical reflection. In a letter cited by Schipani (1991:79), Koontz says.

> I am increasingly convinced that we must always think not in "dualist" terms (i.e. either church/world or old age/new age—other labels could be used) but in terms that take account of three fundamental realities—the "world" (the present order which is "fallen" and does not profess to accept the lordship of Christ), the church (that body which in the present does acknowledge the lordship of Christ) . . . and the kingdom (the in-breaking of God's reign through the church). . . .

Political Interactionists

Most contemporary peacebrokers have cast their lot in the direction of greater societal engagement. This is especially true of political interactionists and those who call for more radical expressions of nonviolence and liberationist justice. Political interactionists, such as John H. Redekop (a political scientist) and the late Frank Epp, who ran for political office, tend to "see the modern democratic state as a positive arena for Christian participation" (Burkholder, 1991a:7). Both are Canadian.

Redekop (1991:60-61) sees three basic differences between Canadian and American Mennonites. (1) Canadians have a more positive view of the state and are less suspicious of governmental power. (2)

Canadian Mennonites more readily enter into joint ventures with governments. (3) Canadians have entered high elective political offices more extensively. Thus the area of overlap or common ground between church and state may vary considerably by national context.

Our earlier review of the extensive involvement of Canadian Mennonites in political offices illustrates the point. In the 1991 Saskatchewan provincial election, three Mennonites in the cabinet of the losing Conservative government were replaced by three new Mennonites in the cabinet of the New Democratic Party (NDP) which won the election. Canadian Mennonites often run for office and a goodly portion are successful.

Redekop (1991:61-62) views the Dutch-Russian factor as one reason for greater political participation in Canada. Canada is also a small (twenty-six million population) middle power nation with a relatively modest military budget—although Ernie Regehr (1975, 1980) would argue that militarism still persists. Canada has also developed socialist programs of universal health care, provincial insurance plans, and transportation systems (Air Canada, VIA Rail), all of which make it appear a more friendly, albeit smaller, giant than the U.S. This smaller scale government, with less involvement in armaments, may thus seem less threatening to peacemakers.

Redekop (1991:64-65) also suggests that Canadian founders, holidays, and buildings have little ideological or religious ceremonial content. This reduces potential conflict between religion and politics. The smaller Canadian government seems to demand less ultimate allegiance because of relatively weak nationalism and its political escapades rarely become religious crusades. Redekop (1972, 1988) proposes that Canadian socialism, rooted more in Methodism than in Marxist socialism, urges government to be an economic leveler and welfare provider. Thus Canadian Mennonites may readily participate in government for a variety of reasons: (1) their Dutch-Russian origin, (2) the smaller size and structure of the government, (3) fewer expenditures for military arms, and (4) the socialist content of political policy.

National location does make a difference in political participation. This underscores the necessity of being sensitive to various expressions of the state in different settings when articulating a Christian ethic of political involvement. In settings with more common ground between church and state, such as in Canada, the political interactionist can cheer extensive participation in the political realm. However, other national settings, where states deliberately use violence to perpetuate social and economic injustice, may call for a radically different strategy.

Activist Nonviolence

The more radical forms of peacemaking level serious critiques at theological, economic, and political systems which perpetuate oppression. Ronald J. Sider (1979:89) dreams of a time when denominational leaders proclaim, "Sisters and brothers, if we are to be faithful to Christ and our heritage of peacemaking, we must confront the terrible reality of systemic injustice." In *Christ and Violence* (1979), Sider outlines biblical and theological reasons for an activist, radical pacifism that, according to Burkholder (1991a:6), "affiliates the rigorous nonviolent ethic of Jesus with aggressive social and political action (a la Gandhi and Gene Sharp)." Sider sees no ethical problem in applying faith-rooted nonviolent means to the public political realm, but he is somewhat less optimistic than the "realists" and "interactionists" as to the results.

Sider also applies a biblical nonviolent activism to a variety of issues illustrated in *Rich Christians in an Age of Hunger: A Biblical Study* (1990), *Completely Pro-Life: Building a Consistent Stance* (1987), and *Non-Violence, the Invincible Weapon?* (1989). He contends that active nonviolence must seek structural changes as well as personal salvation.

Gingerich (1991:43) notes that Sider points to biblical principles for change—"The sovereign Lord of this universe is always at work liberating the poor and oppressed and destroying the rich and mighty because of their injustice"; "God is on the side of the poor"; "Extremes of wealth and poverty are displeasing to the God of the Bible"; "Private property is legitimate, but since God is the only absolute owner, our right to acquire and use property is definitely limited."

There is little evidence of ethical dualism in Sider's theology. The same morality applies to everyone, Christians and others alike. "In *Rich Christians* Sider explicitly addresses the issue of applying a single, biblically-derived standard to both church and society" (Gingerich, 1991:45). Active nonviolence rather than nonresistance is appropriate as a more faithful application of biblical teaching, and the use of economic and political power is compatible with the gospel (Sider, 1979:44).

Sider (1979:46-47) interprets Matthew 5:39, the classic text of nonresistance, in the context of several incidents in Jesus' life. The cleansing of the temple and Jesus' response when struck during his trial suggest to Sider that Jesus could not have been advocating absolute nonresistance to evil. "Do not resist one who is evil," means for Sider that one should not exact equal damages for injury suffered, and one should not treat evil persons as enemies.

Thus Sider is able to endorse peace activism including lobbying, political action committees, boycotts, civil disobedience, demonstrations, and tax resistance—a Christian witness earlier advocated by Donald Kaufman (1969). At the Mennonite World Conference in Strasbourg, France, in 1984, Sider introduced the idea of sending Christians into areas of world conflict to act as mediators and reconcilers—a proposal which eventually took shape in the Christian Peacemaker Teams of the late eighties and nineties. This activist form of nonviolence seeks to press political leaders and structures toward justice in the name of biblical faith and conviction.

Dorothy Friesen (1990:295) contends that it is easy to equate the Gospel with "niceness." The peacemaker's resolve to "confront the powers and principalities is muted unless we throw ourselves into the fray with the complete range of emotions. . . . By its nature, action for peace suggests change. It is disturbing. . . . It may be messy sometimes, but grace can only abound where people sin boldly."

Political Liberation

John R. Burkholder (1991a:7) labels the more radical forms of peacemaking Liberation Pacifism and points to Arnold Snyder (1984), Mark Neufeld (1988), Perry Yoder, and LaVerne Rutschman as some of its main proponents. Such "liberationists," who stand in solidarity with the poor and oppressed, sometimes emphasize justice over peace. They may at times be reluctant to recognize nonviolence as an absolute norm. Robert Suderman (1991:69-77) reviews the work of Neufeld, who bases his position on critical knowledge:

> "Critical Knowledge" is interested in emancipation "from structurally-generated distortions of human interaction" (257). Its tools are critical social sciences, and its purpose is critique. "What the critical social sciences all share is the premise that distortions in human interaction are rooted in socially-structured inequalities (e.g., of wealth and power) (258)."

The restructuring of inequalities is often not possible without considerable conflict. In the past Mennonites have shied away from provocative actions which liberationist theologians deem crucial for rectifying social injustice. Suderman (1991:70) contends that

Neufeld's approach is realistic about the nature of social interaction; it recognizes that social conflict cannot always be harmonized through understanding and mediation. Sometimes resolution only comes by structural transformation, by revolutionary organized struggle (259). The advantage of this model for Christian service is that it coincides with the heart of the Christian gospel, i.e., salvation, liberation, emancipation from sin. "Here peacemaking is conceived not as enforcing order nor as helpful impartial mediation, but rather as participating in a struggle for social justice; not as manipulating the oppressed, nor even standing with and listening to the oppressed, but as working alongside the oppressed for radical change" (260). Neufeld exhorts Christian service organizations, including MCC, to adopt this emancipatory approach even if it means losing some constituency support.

Perhaps the most sustained attempt at blending Anabaptist and liberationist theology has come from former Mennonite Brethren, Colombian missionary, and theologian Hugo Zorrilla, now located in Madrid. Zorrilla represents new Mennonite voices in the third world, which will likely become increasingly strident in the twenty-first century. Zorrilla (1988) dedicates his book, *The Good News of Justice: Share the Gospel: Live Justly*, "to those brothers and sisters in affluent and materialistic societies who are living out the justice of God in solidarity with the poor of the earth." Zorrilla (1988:35) continues,

One cannot really grasp the biblical message of evangelism without a mature understanding of justice. Perhaps this is why many churches seem not to care about injustice. They fail to realize that justice is the cornerstone of the gospel.

In the richer countries, too many Christians live indifferently, in spite of a world that is torn apart by crises and injustices. For example, 10 percent of the military expenses of the richer countries in 1986 could have ended hunger in the whole world.

Zorrilla's message to middle-class North Americans clearly challenges upward mobility, and its erosion of empathy and identification with the less fortunate and the poor. Zorrilla proclaims a costly gospel which combines evangelism and the good news of justice. He calls for an integrated faith, for "actions that create life," in the midst of oppression (Zorrilla, 1988:64). Such wholistic evangelism includes five aspects illustrated in Table 10.3 which deserve attention.

TABLE 10.3
Dimensions of Zorrilla's Call to Wholistic Evangelism

Sees the effects of exploitation and injustice
through the eyes of the poor;

   Participates in and feels the cruel anxieties
   of those who suffer,
     because of personal sin
     and because of the sins of others;

      Denounces unjust practices and structures
        that impoverish,
        dehumanize,
        and kill;

         Identifies the systems and structures
           that produce death . . .
             Poverty is not voluntary . . .
             but caused by centers of power;

            Sees the gospel of the kingdom
              to the poor in correct perspective.
              The good news of justice is for all . . .
              who have systematically lost everything,
                even their hope of a better life.

Source: Zorrilla (1988:64).

Zorrilla's Anabaptist call for justice will be costly.

Many times Christians behave as if they have the gospel in their pocket, like a passport to heaven. This is why any act of justice has little or no value in their relationship with God. They consider their salvation so close at hand that they feel no need to receive more of the gospel (Zorrilla, 1988:76).

Will rich North American Christians hear the call and leave comfortable suburbs to serve the North American inner city, or enter foreign service under the many opportunities provided by MCC and mission agencies? God shook Mennonites out of their deep slumber in the forties and provided them with new service opportunities. But will they hear the contemporary call to a wholistic gospel of peace that the brokers of Mennonite peace theology are sounding in the nineties?

Summary

Throughout these pages we have provided ample evidence for a transformation of Mennonite peacemaking—a shift from passivity to activism, from isolation to engagement. The earlier Mennonite view that nonresistance was primarily objection to warfare has been replaced by an activist mode of constructive conciliation with a wide scope of involvement that stretches over at least six arenas of peacemaking. The empirical evidence suggests that the transformed Mennonite commitments to peacemaking remain, for the most part, robust. But the transformation to an activist mode, we believe, can only be sustained over the long haul by an inner transformation—a renewing of our mind that enables us to discern the good, the acceptable, and the perfect ways of God (Rom. 12:2).

Jesus had words of blessing for peacemakers. But Mennonite peacemaker Zorilla reminds us that Christian peacemakers must see the effects of exploitation, must participate with those who suffer, must denounce unjust structures, must identify systems that produce death, and must announce that the gospel of the kingdom is the good news of justice for all.

Such peacemaking may agitate and irritate those who squat on the oppressed, and in some political situations it will entail considerable personal risk. Nevertheless, compassionate peacemakers heeding the call of Jesus will seek engagement, not benign neglect. Such activism, however, will not stoop to the use of violence, for in the blunt words of Menno Simons written in 1539

> . . ."Spears and swords
> we leave to those who, alas,
> REGARD HUMAN BLOOD AND SWINE'S BLOOD
> about alike."[7]

But the rejection of violent means dare never be an excuse for withdrawal, isolation, and irresponsibility for "true evangelical faith" again in the words of Menno Simons

. . . cannot lie dormant . . .
it clothes the naked;
it feeds the hungry;
it comforts the sorrowful;
it shelters the destitute;
it aids and consoles the sad;
it returns good for evil;
it serves those that harm it;
it prays for those that persecute it
. . . it binds up that which is wounded
. . . it has become all things to all.[8]

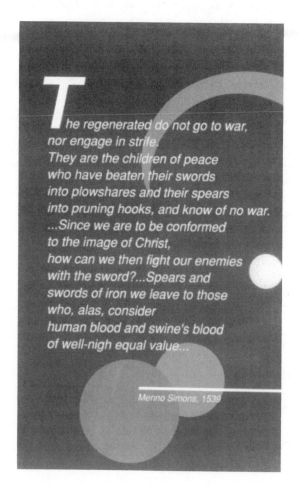

The regenerated do not go to war,
nor engage in strife.
They are the children of peace
who have beaten their swords
into plowshares and their spears
into pruning hooks, and know of no war.
...Since we are to be conformed
to the image of Christ,
how can we then fight our enemies
with the sword?...Spears and
swords of iron we leave to those
who, alas, consider
human blood and swine's blood
of well-nigh equal value...

Menno Simons, 1539

Epilogue

Enduring Dilemmas

Tracing the transformation of Mennonite peacemaking underscores several enduring dilemmas endemic not only to the Mennonite experience but to other religious traditions as well. These perennial quandaries have framed the dialogue of preceding generations and will likely persist into the future as new generations struggle with the moral issues of their time. Here we reflect on several enduring dilemmas which we believe require continuing dialogue and discernment within the Christian community. We summarize these issues to provoke discussion and to underscore their continuing complexity.

1. The Use of Force

Historic nonresistance was anchored on the words of Jesus, "resist not evil," and on Jesus' meek posture in the face of the cross. Mennonites, as we have shown, have shifted toward activist modes of peacemaking—sometimes employing forceful tactics, albeit short of violence.

Qualms about using the law and entering politics have subsided as Mennonites swam into the social mainstream. Litigation and malicious use of the law are certainly discouraged, but nevertheless in both personal and professional life Mennonites have increasingly turned to legal and other forceful means to defend their rights and protect their interests. Mennonite activists are willing to demonstrate in forceful ways—even to disobey civil laws if necessary—to raise concerns about social justice and oppression.

Yet Mennonites who take the Scriptures seriously sometimes feel a contradiction between the use of force and the spirit of agape love. Is force ever appropriate to protect the interests of others, of oneself? At what point will the use of force slide down the slippery slope to violence? As Mennonites become more comfortable with the use of force in litigation, political life, business affairs, and campaigns for justice are they inching ever slowly toward the legitimation of violence?

The use of force stretches across a conceptual spectrum from persuasion to coercion. Force may be used to protect oneself, to protect others, to reduce injustice, to induce change, and to retaliate. Striking a distinction between force and violence, Duane Friesen (1986) argues that violence occurs when the use of force (1) injures persons' dignity, (2) harms their body, or (3) kills them.

Force, according to Friesen, can be expressed in both violent and nonviolent ways. Verbal persuasion turns violent when it injures a person's dignity—an oral assault on their beliefs or character. On the other hand, physical coercion may be expressed nonviolently if it protects the dignity of the person in the long run. Spanking a child, intervening in a suicide attempt, and limited police action—all of which use physical coercion to restrain behavior—may be done nonviolently if the action does not injure the person's dignity, permanently harm the body, or take a life.

Nonresistant Mennonites may have acted violently when spanking their children or excommunicating members in ways that violated the dignity of the person. But what does it mean to violate the dignity of a person? Is there a qualitative difference between using force to protect one's self, to protect the interests of others, or to improve the welfare of others? Are some forms of evil so destructive that they can only be restrained by the threat and use of violence? Does it matter if the dignity of a few is violated or even if their lives are taken to save the lives of many innocent?

Certain situations—uncontrolled riots, career killers, malicious dictators, ruthless drug lords, expansionist nations—may require violent force to restore order and protect the innocent. When nonviolent solutions have been exhausted, the threat or use of physical force may be the only means of ending rampant violence. Yet violence often begets violence. The use of physical force typically triggers a new spiral of violence.

The use of violence clearly violates the spirit of love exemplified by Jesus. The gospels portray a nonviolent, although sometimes assertive, Jesus. Yet in the face of the cross Jesus willingly absorbed the barbs of evil in the spirit of suffering love. A ready endorsement of violence will mean that nonviolent solutions are not pursued seriously, thus eliminating the opportunity to experiment with the powerful witness of suffering love.

As Mennonites increasingly embrace the use of force, albeit short of violence, are they squandering the genius of their soul—the ability to absorb hostility without resistance? And do forceful nonviolent protests make them just one of many political interest groups? And yet injustice and oppression beg for forceful action from the compassionate. Moreover, rampant violence may sometimes require counter violence to protect the innocent.

Initial assumptions make all the difference. If one begins with the witness of the New Testament Scriptures and the life and teachings of Jesus, faithfulness surely requires a categorical rejection of the use of violence, even to maintain order. Yet on the other hand the harsh realities of some situations—a destructive riot, a vicious villain, a ruthless dictator, the systematic torture of innocent civilians—may necessitate counterviolence to protect the innocent, with the risk that such responses may flare into even greater destruction.[1] The enduring questions of this quandary concern our definition of what it means to violate the dignity of a person—and under what circumstances, if any, that is permissible and by whom.

2. Multiple Ethical Standards

If Mennonites cannot conscientiously participate in violence yet agree certain situations require coercive and violent means to restrain evil, they are in essence endorsing two ethical standards—one for the church and another for the state. Mennonite sectarians espousing a two-kingdom view of the world have argued that the state, in God's economy, is "outside the perfection of Christ" and thus may legitimately use the sword—but Christians may not. Sectarians solved the dilemma by emphasizing separation from the world. Governments could use force to restrain evil, but Christians would avoid politics and have little to say to government, for they were citizens of a different kingdom. The sectarian solution left the harsh work of restraining violence in the hands of government officials, some of whom were Christians.

As we have seen, the concept of the lordship of Christ over both church and world shifted Mennonite thought toward a single moral norm that condemned the use of violence even for governments. The single norm eroded sectarian boundaries and permitted Christians to "witness" to government officials about their accountability to the righteousness of God. Officials were urged to use minimal violence and to feel guilty for what they did use.

The embrace of a single ethic legitimated Mennonite witness to government and encouraged Mennonites to participate in government themselves. However, the appeal to a single moral standard is an optimistic view of human affairs that may overlook the depth of evil in the world and the necessity of violence to restrain it. Thus Mennonites may have implied that force is not necessary to maintain social order and those using it should feel guilty.

The modified dual ethic proposed by Koontz (1988) argues for different ethical standards for church and state without giving the state unqualified license to use violence. The state's floating ethic rises and falls with the tide of violence. Christians under this scheme appreciate the need for the harsh work of restraint even though they refuse to dirty their own hands in it. Unlike sectarians, however, they have something to say to the state since the state's floating ethic—its response to evil—must be proportional to the level of violence. Christians can urge the state to use more violence when its response is too lenient to protect the innocent, or less violence if its response exceeds the levels required to restrain the violent.

The notion of a floating ethic for the state permits sensitivity to various national conditions under which different states may function. It can also make distinctions between the use of police force to maintain internal order and the conduct of war across national boundaries. This view respects the grubby work of coercive restraint but urges pacifist Christians to abstain from it—though they may hope to advise the state on its appropriate response.

The question of ethical standards is an enduring dilemma. To argue that the state should never use violence paints a naive veneer of optimism on the reality of sin in a vicious world. But to assert that Christians cannot participate in the violence yet have the wisdom to tell the state when and how to restrain evil makes them unwelcome advisers in the corridors of power. Any blessing of violence quickly leads to a just war logic, which historically has only justified violence for all sides in a conflict.

Is it possible to recognize the sometimes necessary use of physical coercion to restrain violence without legitimating its wide use? Can Christians at the same time refrain from participating in violence and still advise or "witness" to state officials concerning its appropriate use? These difficult questions undergird the enduring dilemma of multiple ethical standards.

3. Social Responsibility

Sectarian reluctance to participate in the political order focuses the question of social responsibility—another enduring dilemma encapsulated in the Mennonite story. Turn-of-the-century sociologist Max Weber (1958) noted that, in contrast to Jesus' instruction "resist not evil," the reverse holds true for the politician—thou shalt resist evil by force or else take responsibility for evil winning out. Thus, pacifists who withdraw from political life are held responsible for the triumph of evil.

Weber described the pacifist ethic as one of "ultimate ends"—an ethic which disregards consequences. The pacifist behaves faithfully, does rightly, and leaves the results to the Lord. Moreover, if pure intentions lead to bad results, then the world, the stupidity of others, or even God is held culpable. Weber also talked of an "ethic of responsibility"—action oriented to foreseeable consequences. A "responsible" ethic calculates anticipated results and acts accordingly. Moreover it understands that the attainment of good ends may sometimes require the use of dubious means.

Moral responsibility in the political realm thus assumes that outcomes are predictable, when in fact they may be products of unexpected conditions, unknown causes, or unique coalitions of power. Discussions of responsibility often castigate pacifists as irrelevant and irresponsible. Beneath the rhetoric about responsibility lie two assumptions: (1) rural nonresistant Mennonites are socially irrelevant and irresponsible, and (2) politically active ones are relevant and responsible. These assumptions suggest that social responsibilities are only discharged in the public realm of politics, and that greater involvement in politics attests to greater moral responsibility. Should the Amish feel rather guilty? And should the many American Mennonites who voted for Ronald Reagan and George Bush feel satisfied that they have acted responsibly?

The real issue in this dilemma is the nature of the believer's civic obligations and how those duties are best discharged. Such obligations include constructive work to enhance the welfare of society as well as the dangerous work of restraining evil—in other words, positive responsibilities to improve the public welfare and coercive responsibilities to maintain order.

Does shouldering moral responsibility mean that Christians are accountable for everything that happens, or does it mean that they seek to live in ways that empower others, enhance the environment, and contribute to the common good? A plethora of avenues for discharging social responsibilities are available in many voluntary organizations in the private sector including the church. But restraint functions are, of course, only legitimate under government authority.

Responsible living does not necessarily entail political participation. There are a multitude of ways to contribute to the public good outside of government agencies. Indeed, one of the prime ways of acting responsibly is to create families, communities, and lifestyles that do not contribute to the decay of social order. Stable communities that give meaning, belonging, and identity to individuals—exemplified by many Amish, Hutterite, and Mennonite congregations—are bonafide acts of social responsibility that toss little social litter on public streets.

Beyond creating stable communities, responsible persons may improve the public welfare via volunteer organizations—the Red Cross and Habitat For Humanity, to name two of many. Others may contribute in personal ways by assisting refugees, providing homes for foster children, and assisting needy neighbors.

Historically the Christian church as well as many Mennonite congregations have shouldered enormous responsibilities for the needy around the world. Mennonite Central Committee administers multi-million dollar relief efforts with hundreds of volunteers working in many countries—feeding the hungry, clothing refugees, sheltering the homeless, guiding development projects, and giving the marginalized a voice. Moreover, these services are provided under the international flag of God's kingdom rather than the parochial flag of a sovereign state. All of these nonpolitical vehicles are responsible ways of making a significant difference in the lives of the destitute, while also contributing to the larger public good.

Church agencies that work to prevent and alleviate suffering are concerned about the consequences of their efforts—they hope to heal the wounds of the needy. Politicians, however, tend to focus on the consequences of policies for their particular nation and its vested interests. U.S. diplomats in the Persian Gulf War considered the vested interests of U.S. citizens—not the consequences for the estimated 150,000 Iraqis who died in the conflict and the thousands of others who suffered devastation. "Consequences" in the discussion of moral responsibility are typically defined from the perspective of the parochial interests of a particular state. Collective Christian action can transcend the narrow interests of nations and raise the specter of consequences for the larger international community.

Social responsibilities can also be discharged through service in numerous welfare functions of government which regulate public safety, assure equality of access, provide education, care for the infirm and disabled, and oversee a host of other health and welfare functions.

Christians can function as responsible moral agents in all the above spheres—from creating stable communities to serving in government programs for human betterment. It is a false dichotomy that assumes that separatists are irresponsible when in fact they are creating emotionally stable communities which scatter little social refuse over the larger society. Moreover, the politically active are not necessarily acting responsibly just because they vote for the popular candidate of the moment.

But just because Christians contribute in a responsible fashion to the public good both within and without political channels doesn't take them off the horns of the dilemma. Although Mennonite rates of political participation are on the rise, Mennonites may still be charged with irresponsibility if they refuse to fight in defense of the nation. Despite responsible acts to improve the public welfare, Mennonites may nonetheless be viewed as moral parasites if they refuse to take up arms. They may act responsibly to improve the social welfare, yet be held irresponsible if they let evil triumph by refusing to assist the state to restrain violence.

Moreover, what does moral responsibility mean when their own state becomes belligerent? If they stand by while their own government conducts campaigns of excessive violence—are they then irresponsible? Some U.S. Mennonites "sat out the Persian Gulf War," refusing to speak out against the actions of their government (Miller, 1992).[2] Are such bystanders who offered no protest to the Persian Gulf War morally responsible for the 150,000 Iraqi deaths? And what about the Mennonites who silently cheered the U.S. triumph in Iraq—do they hold responsibility? Or must evildoers of all stripes hold responsibility for their own actions along with those who could have tamed them?

4. Peacemaking Convictions

Are peace convictions integral to the Christian faith or mere peripherals—optional accessories susceptible to the whims of personal preference? If peace convictions are essentials of the gospel, should they be incorporated into baptismal vows, prescribed in membership covenants, and made a test of membership? Perhaps such explicit expectations violate—even do violence to—the very spirit of the gospel by contradicting its message of unconditional love.

On the other hand, to treat peacemaking as a matter of individual conscience, as one of many items on the smorgasbord of modern beliefs, is a capitulation to the forces of modernity—to excessive individualism and tolerance. Surely the church would not take that stance toward murder, adultery, fraud, drug abuse, and alcoholism.

Are peace convictions best cultivated by persuasion or by explicit requirements? Many Mennonite congregations struggle with this enduring dilemma. Expressions of nonresistance, central to Mennonite self-understanding over the centuries, have shaped Mennonite views of God, salvation, the nature of the church, and social relations within the faith community as well as those with the state.

Does the decline of nonresistance signal the demise of a distinctive Mennonite identity and the marginalization of peace convictions? At first blush this may appear to be the case. Mennonites are indeed using force, albeit in civil ways, but force nonetheless in their institutional and professional lives. And congregations shy from insisting on peace convictions as a membership requirement for fear of offending members or losing potential converts.

Yet at the same time, peacemaking language in Mennonite circles is trumpeted at virtually every turn—from international relations to sibling quarrels, from child rearing to economic injustice, from sexual abuse to racial hatred, from organizational conflict to personal differences. Such a widespread embrace of peacemaking surely honors the faithful of bygone days whose nonresistance was woven into a seamless web of social relations.

But does squeezing all human relations under the tent of peacemaking threaten to evaporate its meaning? If peacemaking entails everything, does it mean anything? A glib and careless use of the term threatens to erode its meaning. And will Mennonites who tout peacemaking at every turn still pass the litmus test and refuse to use force when threatened with personal harm?

Peacemaking sounds like a natural, noble expression of the gospel which Christians of many stripes and even most diplomats will applaud. Its modern ring, however, may have more to do with assuring social and ecumenical acceptance than with a willingness to make a costly and distinctive witness for the gospel. Many Christians may be willing to extol the virtues of peacemaking, but few are willing to sit in jail for refusing to pay taxes for warfare. And how many would be willing to suffer persecution if faced with conscription in a nondemocratic society without provisions for alternative service?

Does the modern version of peacemaking have the steely character of nonresistance that would willingly, without complaint and struggle, face imprisonment for refusing military service? Will the pleasant veneer of contemporary peacemaking crack under the stress of harsh political conditions?

Although Mennonites have generously pasted the label of peace-making on a host of wide-ranging efforts, few congregations have been willing to require a firm commitment to peacemaking at baptism or even make it a requirement for church membership. In the spirit of tolerance and respect for individual conscience leaders are reluctant to make peacemaking a prerequisite for church membership.

This raises the question of its centrality to the gospel. If peace is indeed integral to the gospel, at the very heart of the incarnation, and not merely the fluff and froth of individual preference, why is it not taken more seriously and made an explicit requirement in church membership classes, baptismal vows, and membership expectations—even a test of membership?[3]

Such firm expectations might hinder evangelism, alienate prospective members, and anger present ones. And such stipulations might even contradict the essential message of the gospel—unconditional acceptance through God's forgiving grace.

Thus Mennonites face the ultimate dilemma—if peace convictions are central to the gospel they surely should be made explicit for baptism and membership. But legalistic expectations easily violate the very essence of the gospel itself.

Notes

Chapter 1

1. Documentary evidence of Burkhart's case is available in the Irvin E. Burkhart Collection, Hist. Mss. 1-57, Box 1, File 62, AMC. This quote is found on p. 3 of his application for citizenship dated 1 May 1938.

2. Martha Graber Landis, born in Alsace-Lorraine, came to this country at age eleven and was denied citizenship because she would not bear arms to defend the U.S. After losing two appeals for naturalization she was granted citizenship in 1930 after a year and a half of legal skirmishes.

John P. Klassen and Anna Klassen were also denied citizenship for refusing to bear arms. John P. Klassen, born in Russia in 1888, married Anna Dyck. They emigrated to Canada in 1922 and then came to Bluffton College (Ohio) in 1924 where he taught art. His application for citizenship was denied in 1931 because of his refusal to pledge to bear arms. Eventually in 1933 he was granted citizenship. His wife, Anna, was denied citizenship at a later date for the same reason but eventually she also received U.S. citizenship. Documentation of the Landis and Klassen cases is available in the Mennonite Historical Library of Bluffton College, Bluffton, Ohio.

3. For a discussion of the issues surrounding the shift from total to limited high-tech warfare exemplified in the Persian Gulf War see Juhnke's (1991) essay.

4. This term has been used since 1935 to refer to the Friends, Mennonites, and Brethren groups which have cooperated in peace activities.

5. Introductions to Anabaptist history are provided by Dyck (1993) and Weaver (1987) as well as numerous articles in the *ME*. For excellent updates see "Anabaptism" and "Historiography, Anabaptist" in *ME* V.

6. The suffering and persecution recorded in Van Braght's *Martyrs Mirror* is also described by Dyck (1985), Jackson and Jackson (1989), Kreider (1984), and Oyer and Kreider (1990).

7. For a comprehensive review of the various and sometimes conflicting Anabaptist views toward the use of the sword in the first decade of Anabaptism, see Brock (1972 and 1991a), Stayer (1976), and Weaver (1987).

8. Brock (1991a:269-271) and Stayer (1976:325,335) agree that despite

the conflicting views on the use of the sword in the early years, by the 1560s what Brock calls "separational nonresistance" and Stayer (1976) dubs "separatist nonresistance" had become normative for second generation Anabaptists.

9. This is the wording in a recent translation and commentary of the Dordrecht Confession by Horst (1988:33). Emphasis added.

10. For discussions of the history and use of the term nonresistance consult the entries on "nonresistance" in *ME* III and *ME* V, Lowry (1990), and Hershberger (1979:133-134).

11. The appearance of "defenseless Christians" in the various titles and editions of the *Martyrs Mirror* is traced by Lowry (1990) and Kreider (1984).

12. Our sources for the size and location of the various Mennonite bodies are derived from Horsch (1992), Lichdi (1990), and Miller (1993).

13. The first Church Member Profile (CMP I) of these five denominations was conducted in 1972 and reported in Kauffman and Harder (1975). The results of the second (CMP II), conducted in 1989, were summarized by Kauffman and Driedger (1991). The methodological procedures are described in Appendix A.

14. The CMP II survey did not include any of the Amish or Old Order Mennonite groups, conservative and independent Mennonite groups, or bodies which have gradually departed from the Mennonite fold such as the Mennonite Brethren in Christ, and other similar groups.

15. The Evangelical Mennonite Church of midwestern United States should not be confused with the Evangelical Mennonite Conference of Mennonites in Canada which traces its roots back to Russia.

16. Robert S. Kreider has noted in personal conversations that one of the sources for the renewal of nonresistance in the Swiss-South German stream was the movement of acculturating members from the Old Order groups into the Mennonite Church. This "renewal from the right" was largely absent in the Dutch-Russian experience.

17. Personal correspondence of James C. Juhnke to Donald B. Kraybill, 7 October 1991. C. H. Wedel (1926) writing in 1903 said "that Jesus Christ, the Great Prince of peace, has called upon his followers to bring and establish peace on earth." In Wedel's (1910:247-48) last book he spoke not of nonresistance but of "Feindes liebe" (love of enemies) and "Vermeidung der Rache" (avoidance of revenge).

18. Robert S. Kreider notes that some GC congregations excommunicated members who entered the military and others did not. Such matters were congregational decisions and tended "to be handled more informally than in MC conferences."

19. MB statements on peace and nonresistance can be found in Janzen and Giesbrecht (1978), Loewen (1985), and Toews and Nickel (1986). The 1946 MB Catechism, *Fundamentals of Faith*, defines nonresistance as "love in action." Schmidt's (1981) dissertation traces continuity and change in the MB relations to the state between 1917 and 1979.

20. The BIC Statement of Doctrine (1961), for example, includes a special section on "Non-resistance" (Loewen, 1985: 239).

21. For examples see Burkholder (1857), Burkholder (1837), and *Herald of Truth* articles.

22. Written by Benjamin Hershey in 1775, "A Short and Sincere Declaration (to our honorable assembly, and all others in high or low station of administration, and to all friends and inhabitants of this country, to whose sight this may come, be they English or Germans)" was signed by a number of Elders and Teachers of the Society of Mennonists, and some of the German Baptists and presented to the Honorable PA House of Assembly on the 7th day of November, 1775. Early Correspondence and Papers Collection, Hist. Mss. 1-10, Box 3, File 5 entitled "1775," AMC.

23. See Hostetler (1987:157-164) for an extensive discussion of Godshalk's *New Creature*.

24. Emphasis added.

25. "Rules and Discipline of the Lancaster Conference" approved 7 October 1881, p. 2 of English variant found in the LMHS.

26. Numerous references to these terms can be found in the published *Minutes of the Indiana-Michigan Mennonite Conference 1864-1929*. Scottdale, Pa.: Mennonite Publishing House. AMC.

27. For descriptions and analysis of North American Mennonite involvement in military service consult MacMaster (1985) for the Revolutionary War, Schlabach (1988) for the Civil War, Juhnke (1989) for World War I, and Hershberger (1951) for World War II.

28. Brock (1991a:100) notes that prior to 1572 among Swiss, German, and Dutch Anabaptist congregations members who joined military forces were excommunicated. This practice continued in North America even beyond World War II among some Mennonites with a Swiss-South German heritage. It continues to the present among Old Order Mennonite and Old Order Amish groups.

29. Statements by the Evangelical Mennonite Church were not included in Peachey's (1980) compilation. Most of the MC, GC, and BIC statements which are cited throughout this volume can be found in Peachey's (1980) collation of official statements, letters, and telegrams issued between 1900 and 1979. Bert Friesen (1986) provides an index to peace and social concern statements by Mennonite and Brethren in Christ groups in Canada issued between 1787 and 1982. Peace statements within historic Mennonite confessions of faith are available in Loewen (1985). The appendix of Toews and Nickel (1986) includes key MB statements related to peacemaking. An analysis of MC peace statements issued between 1915 and 1966 was written by Detweiler (1968). Friesen (1982, ND) has analyzed peace and social concern statements issued by various Mennonite bodies between 1900 and 1980.

30. For examples see Kauffman (1898:217-218) and the 7 June 1923 minutes of the Indiana-Michigan Conference, p. 266, Indiana-Michigan Mennonite Conference Collection, II-5-1, "Minutes 1923," AMC.

31. Letter to Henry Neiss from six Lancaster County Mennonite leaders dated 29 August 1847 and reprinted in the *Mennonite Historical Bulletin*, April 1961, XXII No. 2 page 7.

32. Schlabach (1988) and Juhnke (1989) provide excellent discussions of Mennonite involvements and hesitations in political life in the nineteenth and early twentieth century respectively. Juhnke (1975) also describes the political acculturation of Kansas Mennonites.

33. The Mennonite Church issued a lengthy resolution on the flag salute

at the General Conference in Wellman, Iowa in August 1941. The statement was recorded in the proceedings of that year and also published in pamphlet form. Erb (1949) reports the actions of six local Mennonite conferences on the flag salute.

34. Erb (1949) identified two local conference actions opposing trespassing signs. Lancaster Mennonite High School was reluctant to post commercial "No Trespassing" signs on its property in the 1940s and 1950s. It was also reticent to press charges against vandals who trespassed on the school's property.

35. 31 October 1972, p. 883; 8 January 1985, p. 22.

36. For discussions of this ecumenical effort between Amish, Mennonite groups, Brethren in Christ, Old Order Dunkers, and Friends see Hershberger (1951:175) and Epp (1982:568).

37. For arguments and evidence of the strong association between sectarianism and pacifism see Martin (1966), Stark (1967), and Yinger (1970:466-472).

38. Approximately 11.8 percent of Brethren men entered Civilian Public Service or noncombatant military service as reported by the *BE* in a discussion of "World War II" on p. 1372. The equivalent number of Mennonites was 60.4 percent (Gingerich 1949:90). The Church of the Brethren acculturated more rapidly than the Mennonite Church in the first half of the twentieth century and the erosion of pacifist convictions accompanied the acculturation.

Chapter 2

1. For additional discussions of the Mennonite encounter with modernity consult Kauffman and Driedger (1991), Kraybill (1987 and 1988), Kraybill and Fitzkee (1987), Schlabach (1979), and Toews (1989).

2. Levy (1986) calls the use of "traditional" and "modern" the "fallacy of misplaced dichotomies," for their use implies that modern societies have no traditions. Thus he suggests it is more accurate to talk of modern and non-modern societies.

3. Discussions of individualism in American culture can be found in Bellah, et al. (1985) and Gergen (1991). Ainlay (1990) and Kauffman and Driedger (1991) analyze the impact of individualism in Mennonite communities.

4. Peter Berger discusses the concept of plausibility structures in Berger (1967:45-48), Berger (1977:173-174), Berger (1979:17-21), and Berger, et al. (1973:16).

5. For other discussions of the reconstruction of the Mennonite sacred canopy in the face of social change, consult Driedger (1988, chapter 3 and 1989, chapter 7) as well as Kauffman and Driedger (1991, chapter 7).

6. For a discussion of the delay see Kraybill (1988) and Driedger (1988).

7. This percentage is based on the 1936 Census of Religious Bodies (Bulletin No. 17 for Mennonite Bodies, U.S. Government Printing Office 1940) and refers to the location of the church building of Mennonite congregations. Buildings located in villages or townships with a population of 10,000 or more and population density of 1,000 or more per square mile were considered urban. The percentage of church buildings in rural areas by denomination were Mennonite Church (86%), General Conference (80%), and Mennonite Breth-

ren (77%). These are likely low estimates for the percent of rural members because some members may have attended urban churches even though they lived in rural areas.

8. The data for 1972 comes from the first Church Member Profile of five Mennonite denominations reported by Kauffman and Harder (1975).

9. The literature on the evolution of sects to denominations is abundant. Yinger (1970) provides one of the better discussions. In a recent analysis Calvin Redekop (1990:59-83) argues that the denominational label is inappropriate for Mennonites.

10. The GC Confessions of 1896, 1933, and 1941 all make explicit reference to nonconformity as does the BIC Confession of 1961 (Loewen, 1985). Nonconformity is less evident in the MB confessions, but was a dominant theme in MC confessions, conference disciplines, and other writings. The tie between nonresistance and nonconformity is perhaps weakest among MBs who stressed the former but not the later.

11. The references to nonresistance and nonconformity in close association are rife in disciplines, confessions of faith, theological writings, and denominational magazines. J. L. Burkholder (1951) in his master's thesis argued that nonresistance was a fundamental aspect of the Mennonite doctrine of nonconformity. Berkey (1953) found a close association between the twin "nons" in the actions of the Indiana-Michigan conference between 1864 and 1952. H. H. Janzen (1952:3) writing in *Mennonite Life* wrote, "the nonresistant Christian must also separate himself from the world, especially in his way of thinking. He cannot conform to the world in his thought life." J. C. Wenger (1954:42) in the same periodical described the two "nons" as, "the two most distinguishing tenets of traditional Mennonitism." The close association between the two is especially strong in the Swiss-South German heritage.

12. Major statements by the BICs in 1943, the MBs in 1943, and the MCs in 1937 made it clear that those who entered military service would disfellowship themselves or be excommunicated (Peachey, 1980). The GC polity placed these decisions more into the hands of local congregations, but as a whole GCs were more tolerant of members who entered military service than MCs.

13. For discussions of *Gelassenheit* consult Cronk (1981), Klaassen (1991), Kraybill (1989:25-36), and Redekop (1989:90-105).

14. The best discussions of the humility doctrine in the mid-nineteenth century can be found in Liechty (1980) and Schlabach (1988:95-105). For a description of the Mennonite personality see Redekop (1989:90-108). J. Denny Weaver has noted in personal conversation, that the term "quiet in the land" was almost always used pejoratively when a writer wanted to infer that a group lacked something which the writer considered important—revival meetings, holding political office, or organizing mission societies, etc.

15. Redekop (1989:90-105) reviews the literature on Mennonite personality. John R. Burkholder (1989) provides a brief discussion of the "psychology of nonresistance," and its relationship to *Gelassenheit* and humility.

16. Dueck (1988:203-224) describes some of the value conflicts between modern psychology and Mennonite values.

17. The petition, written by Ohio bishop John M. Brenneman in 1862, may have never been sent to President Lincoln. The petition and a discussion

of the circumstances surrounding it can be found in *The Mennonite Historical Bulletin* (October 1973, No. 4, pp. 1-3). The original documents are in the Nold/Yoder Collection, Hist. Mss. 1-422, Box 7, Files 4 & 5 entitled "J. M. Brenneman letter concerning petition to President Lincoln," and "Letter of President Lincoln," AMC.

Chapter 3

1. Although it is employed intermittently throughout the century, widespread use of the term peacemaking does not come into usage until the eighties. We use the term in this chapter and others in a rather generic manner to designate Mennonite efforts and concerns for peaceful human relations.

2. The eight themes we have identified are linguistic changes which are found in the public documents of the various time periods. To what extent they represent fundamental conceptual changes or alterations in the structure of consciousness needs further empirical exploration. Paul Toews, while acknowledging the changes in language suggests there may be fewer fundamental conceptual changes. He proposes a threefold evolutionary development: nonresistance, witness to the state, and responsibility. Personal correspondence of Paul Toews to Donald B. Kraybill and Leo Driedger, 24 June 1992.

3. Two important pamphlets written by Funk (1863) and Brenneman (1863) in the context of the Civil War criticized the war activities and called Mennonites to nonresistance. Funk's *Herald of Truth* published many articles on nonresistance in the 1860s and 70s.

4. Schlabach (1977; 1980:19-53; 1988:295-321) describes and assesses the "quickening" in several essays.

5. A copy of the tract and search warrant are in the Aaron Loucks Collection, Hist. Mss. 1-76, Box 4, File 4, AMC.

6. Unless otherwise indicated, all the statements and letters cited in this chapter can be found in the collection of *Mennonite Statements on Peace and Social Concerns* edited by Peachey (1980).

7. This statement cited in Juhnke (1989:212) was made in 1920 by S. K. Mosiman, chairman of the GC committee dealing with peace issues.

8. These phrases are found in the MC statements of 1915, 1917, 1919, and the GC statements of 1905, 1914, and 1917.

9. Toews (1986) offers an insightful and concise essay describing Mennonite peace theology between the wars. Other discussions of this period include Sawatsky (1973, 1977), Gingerich (1949), and Hershberger (1951).

10. "Opening Address" in *Report of Fourth All-Mennonite Convention*, September 6-7, 1992, p. 9, in MHL.

11. Letter to E. L. Harshbarger, 9 March 1939, written by Robert S. Kreider and signed by 10 Bethel College students. Copy in Kreider's personal file.

12. The exchanges between the fundamentalists and moderates within the Mennonite Church are traced by Hershberger (1967) and Sawatsky (1973 and 1977). Although Sawatsky (1973:179) argues that Fundamentalism "depoliticized" Mennonite nonresistance it might be more accurate to see the apolitical nonresistance articulated by the fundamentalists as one stream of influence seeking to redefine nonresistance between the wars. Mennonite nonresistance was hardly politicized at the turn of the century prior to the rise of Fundamentalism.

13. Personal correspondence of John A. Lapp to Donald B. Kraybill and Leo Driedger, 8 June 1992.

14. C. Norman Kraus in a 17 February 1992 interview with Donald B. Kraybill remembers hearing this assertion as a child.

15. The two-page undated document, written after 1937 (based on internal evidence) can be found in the Peace Problems Committee files: Mennonite General Conference Collection, Peace Problems Committee, H. S. Bender, Chair 1935-62, I-3-5.10, Box 55, File 6, AMC. A record of the charges and countercharges are discussed by Sawatsky (1977) and chronicled in the files of the Peace Problems Committee of the Mennonite General Conference, I-3-5, AMC and in Hershberger (1967).

16. The outpouring of Mennonite benevolence in the wake of World War I is traced by Juhnke (1986).

17. The formation of the Society is described in the *Bethel College Monthly*, Vol. 37, No. 3, 12 November 1931.

18. For the text of the statement endorsed by the 57 delegates and 24 visitors to the three-day meeting see Durnbaugh (1978:31-32).

19. This action is recorded in the minutes of the Peace Problems Committee 14 April 1937, Mennonite General Conference Collection, Peace Problems Committee, Guy F. Hershberger Files, Minutes and Reports, Box 59, AMC.

20. For other discussions of Hershberger's *War, Peace and Nonresistance* see Schlabach (1976) and Sawatsky (1977). A series of reflective essays commemorating Hershberger's work was edited by Burkholder and Redekop (1976).

21. Leo Driedger interviewed Guy F. Hershberger, 4 November 1989. The interview focused on the early development of the "Goshen School" and reactions of the MC constituency toward Hershberger's peace emphases. Hershberger was born in rural Iowa to Amish-Mennonite parents in 1896. In his formative years he lived through massive changes in the life of the church, including the shift from German to English, the beginning of Sunday schools, revival meetings, church publishing, and the establishment of colleges and mission boards (Schlabach, 1976:15).

After attending conservative Hesston College in Kansas, he joined the reorganized Goshen College faculty in 1925. Soon he became deeply involved as Executive Secretary of the Committee on Industrial Relations and the Peace Problems Committee of the Mennonite Church.

Robert Kreider (1976:66-69) summarizes his work as a scholar of the people. Anchored on the biblical record, he held a pragmatic concern, crossed disciplinary lines, and held considerable optimism for the future. He was a highly productive scholar, associated with many programs, often polarized by bitter controversies between fundamentalism and liberalism.

22. Goshen closed its doors for a year in 1923 over theological controversies when some faculty left for Bluffton College. As president of the young people's organization of the "Old" Mennonite Church in 1923, Bender left to study at Princeton and Heidelberg. As a young man he went to Goshen College where he and others later established the Mennonite Historical Society, Mennonite Historical Library, and the *Mennonite Quarterly Review*. A cluster of young scholars—Bender, Hershberger, Wenger, and Gingerich—introduced "the Anabaptist Vision" to the church. These young scholars stimulated and

encouraged each other at Goshen, hoping to avert another rift like the one which occurred between conservatives and progressives in 1923.

23. A 1991 printing of the 3rd (1969) edition contains "A Half-Century Perspective" by John R. Burkholder.

24. For a discussion of the misplaced contrast in ethical thought between compromise and suffering see John R. Burkholder (1976:152-3).

25. Leo Driedger recalls the expression Kermit Eby made about Guy Hershberger's *War, Peace, and Nonresistance*, when he attended Eby's classes at the University of Chicago in 1954. Eby thought it was a typical and simplistic Mennonite rural view of peace. Kermit Eby (1958) used the same imagery in a review of Hershberger's (1958) *The Way of the Cross in Human Relations*.

Hershberger's *War, Peace, and Nonresistance* was written during World War II, when thousands of Mennonite young men were serving in alternative service. At that time Mennonites were mostly living on farms and in small towns. Very few had moved to live and work in cities. Hershberger was teaching at Goshen College, located in the small town of Goshen. Hershberger, of Amish Mennonite parents, came from rural Iowa, so his perspective tended to be oriented to the largely Mennonite rural community. These conservative ethnic influences were reflected in his views on peace.

26. Donald B. Kraybill interview with Robert S. Kreider, 25 February 1992.

27. Personal correspondence of James Juhnke to Donald B. Kraybill, 2 June 1992. Juhnke goes on to note that Hershberger's booklet in the CPS series *Christian Relationships to State and Community* includes a two-chapter survey of "The Growth of the American Nation." After this positive narrative description of the development of Christian-influenced American democracy, Hershberger appeals for Mennonite rural community revitalization to help strengthen and restore American democracy to its original expression, which was then threatened by industrialism and imperialism.

28. Donald B. Kraybill interview with Robert S. Kreider, 25 February 1992.

29. The comments of Paul Toews in this section reflect his personal correspondence of 24 June 1992 with Donald B. Kraybill and Leo Driedger.

Chapter 4

1. This estimate is given in the introduction of the *Concern* pamphlet series No. 1., June 1954:3.

2. Moderator's address to the MC General Conference, program booklet, P. 19, 21-24 August 1951.

3. Some Mennonite high schools had been established in the forties and early fifties but the bulk of Mennonite students were attending public schools.

4. "Report of the MCC Peace Section Study Conference" held at Winona Lake, 9-12 November 1950, p. 69.

5. All the references in this section are from the Report of the MCC Peace Section Study Conference, Winona Lake, Indiana, 9-12 November 1950. The report, in the archives of MCC, contains the program, major addresses, a summary of discussions, and the statement. The Peace Section Newsletter for November-December 1991, Vol. 21 No. 6, contains the Winona Lake statement, reflections on it, as well as the draft of a proposed new inter-Mennonite statement which appears in Appendix B of this book.

6. Some younger scholars (e.g., John H. Yoder, Paul Peachey) who would form the Concern Group in a few years were in Europe and did not attend the conference.

7. Donald B. Kraybill interview with Bill Keeney, 10 March 1992.

8. Emphasis added.

9. Bender (1952) in an article on "the political and social implications of Christian faith" frequently uses the phrase "the way of love." The article explicitly addresses Niebuhr's charge of irresponsibility and Bennett's charge of social withdrawal. Bender proposes that "the way of love" rejects political action but assumes "full responsibility for the social order" by "securing individual Christians who will live in Christian love" (p. 2). The unpublished paper can be dated 1952 by internal evidence. It is found in the Peace Problems Committee files: Mennonite General Conference Collection, Peace Problems Committee, H. S. Bender, Chair 1935-62, I-3-5.10, Box 55, File 7 entitled "Peace Conference of 1935," folder 2, AMC.

10. An "Education and Political Responsibility" conference held at Bethel College in the spring of 1956 focused largely on Mennonite involvement in politics. The Peace Problems Committee of the Mennonite Church sponsored a conference on "Nonresistance and Political Responsibility" at Laurelville, Pa., in September 1956. Among other issues, it dealt with "Civic Affairs," "Litigation," and "Witness to Government."

11. Some of the articles and letters dealing with responsibility include Yoder (1954, 1955), Kaufman (1958), Neufeld (1958), Meyer (1958), and Habegger (1959). J. Lawrence Burkholder's (1958) Th.D. dissertation also focused on social responsibility.

12. Many of the source documents related to the ecumenical discussions in Europe can be found in Durnbaugh (1978). John H. Yoder provides a chronology of the ecumenical conversations in Europe (Gwyn et al., 1991). For an excellent article that summarizes the development of Mennonite concerns for responsibility in the fifties and especially the growing ecumenical conversations see Hostetler (1990).

A brief review of peacemaking issues in the 1950s can be found in John R. Burkholder (1977) as well as in Dula (1992). Bush's (1990) dissertation deals with the changing shape of church-state relations during this time. A master's thesis by Nisly (1992) charts the renewal and revision of peace theology in the Mennonite Church in the fifties and sixties.

13. The series of articles in *Mennonite Life* addressed the question of Mennonite responsibilities for political participation, Fretz (1956), Loewen (1956), Ediger (1956), and Stucky (1959).

14. A fifth position which was certainly alive in the fifties and beyond, but which we don't review, was the more traditional and somewhat fundamentalist and apolitical view of nonresistance ascribed to by some U.S. Mennonites—especially those sympathetic to the views of *The Sword and Trumpet* published in Virginia.

15. Guy F. Hershberger in his presentation on church-state relations at the MCC conference at Winona Lake in 1950 noted a few small booklets dealing with church-state relationships but concluded that "relatively little has appeared on this subject from the pen of Mennonite writers."

16. Members of the Concern Group included Irvin B. Horst, John W. Mill-

er, Paul Peachey, Calvin Redekop, David A. Shank, Orley Swartzentruber, and John H. Yoder. Toews (1990b) provides an excellent overview and analysis of the Concern Movement's origin and history in the spring 1990 (Vol. 8, No. 2) issue of the *Conrad Grebel Review* which is devoted to the Concern Movement. J. Lawrence Burkholder's "Concern Pamphlets Movement" in *MEV* (p. 177-180) offers a thoughtful assessment of the Concern Movement and its publications.

17. For a brief description of these conferences and some of the statements and papers see Durnbaugh (1978).

18. Paul Toews makes this point in personal correspondence with Donald B. Kraybill and Leo Driedger, 24 June 1992.

19. Unless otherwise indicated, the quotes from Burkholder in this chapter are derived from interviews conducted by Donald B. Kraybill on 25 August 1991 and 24 June 1992.

20. Some of Burkholder's (1992) autobiographical reflections are recorded in an informal and unpublished 63-page paper with the provisional title, "Some Background—Mostly Autobiographical."

21. Leo Driedger interview with Paul Peachey, 27 July 1991, and Leo Driedger interview with Calvin Redekop, 23 July 1991. The reasons for Hershberger's and Bender's reaction to Burkholder's dissertation are complex. Goshen scholars were suspicious of Reinhold Niebuhr's writings and Burkholder's use of "compromise" and "relativity" caused concern. Personality differences and community politics also added to the misunderstanding. Perhaps most centrally, Hershberger wanted to maintain pure New Testament ethics in rural ethnic enclaves, while Burkholder wanted more involvement in the larger society.

22. The incident illustrates how the power wielded by leaders in those days constrained young scholars such as Burkholder. Perhaps he needed a Concern Group. Few young scholars today would accept such a verdict by their elders. A product of a rural sectarian past, Burkholder yielded to the leaders of the fifties by not publishing his dissertation. Younger scholars today have more options and few would be willing to heed the counsel of their elders by putting their work on the shelf.

23. Telephone interview of Gordon Kaufman by Leo Driedger, 29 July 1992. For additional discussions of the "Russian Mennonite Trajectory" and basic differences between north and south Europeans, and between Dutch-Russian and Swiss Mennonites see Leo Driedger and Howard Kaufman (1982), and Howard Kaufman and Leo Driedger (1991). These historic differences tend to be perpetuated even today. Chapter seven of this volume traces the impact of some of these influences on peacemaking.

24. Handwritten comments on Burkholder's essay in Hershberger's personal copy of *Kingdom, Cross and Community,* now in the possession of Hershberger's descendants.

Chapter 5

1. Leo Driedger recalls that the meetings of the Southern Christian Leadership Conference in Shreveport, Louisiana, were moved to the various Baptist churches every half day to reduce attracting outside attention. Black voter registration was urgent, so they could influence political decisions more.

Driedger was the only white among the black participants, but because they welcomed and trusted Mennonites he was invited on a panel with King and others to discuss registration problems.

2. The General Conference Peace and Social Concerns Committee, including members like Gordon Kaufman, Robert Kreider, David Habegger, and Leo Driedger, tried to meet in larger cities, closer to some of the conflict situations. When King was assassinated they were meeting in New York, and that night several of them went to Times Square to observe the reaction to King's death. Violence did not break out in Times Square as it did in many other U.S. cities that night.

3. The Mennonite Biblical Seminary located on Woodlawn Avenue, Chicago, became a halfway house where students who attended seminary and the University of Chicago often boarded. Many who worked in the city stayed here also. Many ate together at the Main House at 4614 Woodlawn Avenue. Leo Driedger recalls that one group including Calvin Redekop, Elmer Neufeld, Leo Driedger, and others met once a month at the Mission House to discuss mutual problems related to Mennonite challenges and changes. Many participated in the Woodlawn Mennonite Church and its many programs, and many helped with summer recreation programs for black kids in the neighborhood. Others worked as janitors, painters, carpenters, and cleaners to supplement their incomes. These whites were very visible in a 99 percent black community.

4. In the latter fifties, when GC Mennonites debated whether to move MBS to the suburbs of Elkhart, Indiana, the lists of pros and cons were equally long. But the retreat to safer, quieter environs beckoned and "the land of Goshen" prevailed.

5. Technically speaking, the vote was on the authorization to negotiate the sovereignty of Quebec.

6. Overviews of the I-W program are provided by Eitzen and Falb (1980) and Juhnke (1980).

7. Bush (1990) provides one of the more creative social histories of the changing Mennonite stance toward the state from 1935-1973. For a series of recent essays on Mennonite views on church-state relationships, see the MCC *Peace Office Newsletter*, September-October, 1993.

8. The conference, organized around the theme "Christian Responsibility to the State," was held in Chicago on 15-16 November 1957 and attended by representatives from the major Mennonite bodies. A list of participants and the program are in the Mennonite Central Committee Collection, Data Files, IX-12-4, File entitled "Christian Responsibility to the State Conference," AMC.

9. This observation by Leo Driedger in his summary of the conference is cited by Bush (1990:211). Edgar Metzler recalls that "Neufeld's paper was an important statement in my own personal and intellectual development. I quoted from it dozens of times in speeches during the Vietnam debate." (Correspondence to Donald B. Kraybill, 3 September 1993.)

10. Unless otherwise indicated, the public statements cited in this chapter can be found in Peachey (1980).

11. The subcommittee met between September 1967 and May 1969. Their points of agreement and disagreement are summarized in the Proceedings of

the Mennonite Church General Conference, 15-19 August 1969 held in Turner, Oregon, pp. 41-42. John R. Burkholder (1985a) also summarizes the issues in a paper dealing with the Mennonite experience and the political order.

12. The entry in *MEV* titled "Lobbying," written by Delton Franz, describes the history and role of MCC's Washington office. Describing the motivation for the Washington office, Edgar Metzler said, "I was powerfully impressed with the hypocrisy of our investment in our own interests and lack of witness on behalf of others. That was a major motivation for the priority I gave to establishing a Washington office when I became Peace Section Secretary at Akron in 1962." (Correspondence to Donald B. Kraybill 3 September 1993.)

13. For a rhetorical analysis of the transformation of peacemaking in the Mennonite Church between 1951 and 1991, see Stutzman (1993).

14. Minutes of the Peace Problems Committee, 8 October 1959, p. 3. Mennonite General Conference Collection, Peace Problems Committee, Guy F. Hershberger File, Minutes and Reports, I-3-5.11, Box 59, File 36. Subcommittee members included Guy Hershberger, Albert J. Meyer, and Edgar Metzler. Meyer was responsible for drafting the bulk of the subcommittee's thirty-two-page report.

15. Minutes of the Peace Problems Committee 22-23 June 1960, p. 2. Mennonite General Conference Collection, Peace Problems Committee, Guy F. Hershberger File, Minutes and Reports, I-3-5.11, Box 59, File 36. During this two-day meeting the committee carefully reviewed the subcommittee's thirty-two page report, "Theses on the Christian Witness to the State," and began preparing a churchwide statement, "The Christian Witness to the State," based on the subcommittee's report.

The concept of the "lordship of Christ" was clearly a new idea. The committee agreed that the concept "may be used in our thinking from here on" but cautioned against public pronouncements, "so as to avoid any misunderstanding within the brotherhood as to our meaning" (p. 3). The use of the new concept worried some committee members, who feared that it would "baptize the unredeemed social order . . . thus removing the distinction between the two kingdoms."

Others argued that the lordship of Christ, "had not blurred the line between the two kingdoms" (p. 3). The subcommittee confessed that usage of the lordship concept was "not customary among American Mennonites, where it has rather been assumed that Christ is Lord only over the church" (p. 2 of the subcommittee report).

Harold Bender, who chaired the meeting, was "uncomfortable with the idea of the lordship of Christ because it wasn't traditional Mennonite thinking, but he accepted it—reluctantly dragging his feet—when Lancaster bishop Amos Horst and Franconia bishop John E. Lapp said, 'but Bro Bender the young men have brought us biblical teaching and we want to be biblical don't we?' " Donald B. Kraybill interview with Albert J. Meyer, 28 May 1992 and correspondence of 15 January 1993.

16. The statement, "The Christian Witness to the State," was approved at the MC General Conference held at Johnstown, Pa., 22-25 August 1961. It appears as exhibit A in the *Proceedings* of the conference as well as in Peachey (1980).

17. Emphasis is not in original text.

18. Emphasis in the original.

19. Consult Peachey (1980) for the text of these statements.

20. For a parallel discussion of the significance of the "lordship of Christ" concept which Bush (1990) calls a "theological breakthrough," see his dissertation, pages 209-217. The new conceptualization of the lordship of Christ can be traced to the four so called "Puidoux Conferences." The first one was held in Puidoux, Switzerland, 15-19 August 1955 and the last in the Netherlands in 1962.

These ecumenical conversations represented the first time in hundreds of years that representatives from Lutheran and Reformed Churches met with peace church scholars for serious theological discussions. The theme of the conferences focused on "The Lordship of Christ Over Church and State." Mennonites such as John H. Yoder, Paul Peachey, Harold Bender, and Al Meyer attended the sessions. A record of the Puidoux conferences and some of the significant addresses and statements have been edited by Donald F. Durnbaugh (1978).

21. Minutes of the MC Peace Problems Committee 22-23 June 1960, p. 3. Mennonite General Conference Collection, Peace Problems Committee, Guy F. Hershberger File, Minutes and Reports, I-3-5.11, Box 59, File 36. The authors of the subcommittee report are somewhat defensive about blurring the line between the two kingdoms. A footnote to their thirty-two page report (p. 2, fn 3) admits that historically the Mennonite Church viewed the lordship of Christ stretching only over the church. The authors contend that they are not trying "to minimize the distinction between the church and the world." The minutes of the full committee (22-23 June 1960) make it clear that the blurring of church-state lines by the new use of the lordship concept was a major issue of concern.

22. For a description of the campaign see Juhnke (1971).

23. An account of the Fort Detrick vigil as well as other examples of nonviolent direct action by a few Mennonites and especially other "radical" peace groups are described by Burkholder (1960).

24. While the concept of the lordship of Christ was ascending, the civil rights movement—triggered by the Montgomery bus boycott of 1956—was beginning to capture national attention. Hershberger, as noted before, had spoken to race relations in *War, Peace, and Nonresistance* already in 1944. The MC general conference and the GC general conference endorsed statements on race relations in 1955 and 1959 respectively that condemned discrimination.

25. A photo of Guy F. Hershberger and Martin Luther King, Jr., standing side by side at Goshen College in 1960 appears in the *Gospel Herald*, 3 March 1987, p. 146.

26. One account of the Turner meeting is provided in Miller and Shenk (1982:43-64). This book tells the story of ten Mennonite young men who refused to register for the draft during the Vietnam war.

27. The issue of noncooperation first came to the MB general conference meeting in Vancouver in August 1969. The conference did not address the issue directly because it hadn't come through the proper channels but called for a study of it. Noncooperation was explicitly rejected at the 1969 Pacific Dis-

trict Conference and in the 1969 Southern District Conference as well as at the U.S. MB conference in 1971 (Toews and Nickel, 1986:167-174).

28. *MEV* provides an overview of Mennonite war tax resistance in an article on "Taxes." The Peace Tax Fund received a hearing by a subcommittee of the U.S. House of Representatives Ways and Means Committee on 21 May 1992.

Chapter 6

1. See John R. Burkholder (1988) for a discussion of the ecumenical dialogue.

2. Interview with Hedy Sawadsky conducted by Donald B. Kraybill, 18 September 1992.

3. This account is taken from the MCC Peace office Newsletter, Vol. 22, No. 5, September-October 1992, p. 4.

4. This quote and a description of Friesen's pilgrimage can be found in the MCC Peace Office Newsletter , Vol. 22, No. 5, September-October 1992, p. 5. This volume of the Newsletter celebrates 50 years of peacemaking efforts by the MCC Peace Section and carries a number of portraits of Mennonite peacemakers.

5. The profile of Mary and Peter Sprunger-Froese was gathered in a telephone interview with Mary conducted by Donald B. Kraybill, 30 September 1992.

6. The story of the draft resistance in the eighties is told by Becker (1985:19-21).

7. Burkholder's story was constructed from his unpublished notes "Pilgrimage of a Reluctant Pacifist," a telephone interview conducted by Donald B. Kraybill, 17 September 1992, and personal correspondence to Leo Driedger and Donald B. Kraybill of 30 June 1992.

8. Personal interview with Bill Keeney conducted by Donald B. Kraybill, 21 September 1992.

9. Correspondence with Donald B. Kraybill, 3 September 1993.

10. For an excellent collection of stories that typify the importance of the MCC experience in the lives of many volunteers see Kreider and Goossen (1988).

11. John A. Lapp (1970b) describes the "Peace Mission of MCC" prior to 1970. One issue of the MCC Peace Office Newsletter celebrates fifty years of Peace Section's efforts, Vol. 22, No. 5, September-October 1992. Epp and Epp (1984) provide an abbreviated chronology of the development of the Peace Section. The Newsletters of the Peace Section published since 1970 offer a résumé of the Section's activities in the past two decades.

12. Personal interview with John K. Stoner conducted by Donald B. Kraybill, 18 September 1992.

13. Correspondence of Atlee Beechy to James S. Amstutz, 11 May 1992 in MCC archives.

14. Personal interview with Bill Keeney conducted by Donald B. Kraybill, 21 September 1992. For a history of the Washington and Ottawa offices see Kreider and Goossen (1988:320-330) as well as the entry of "lobbying" in *MEV*. For a recent dissertation that traces and analyzes the development of the Washington office, see Miller (1994).

15. Stoner (1983) makes this remark in a one-page unpublished paper "Demonstrations and Public Witness: Thoughts on Mennonite Participation." For a brief analysis of controversies in the Peace Section related to civil disobedience see John K. Stoner (1992a). Other articles and papers by Stoner dealing with public witness and civil disobedience can be found in Stoner (1980, 1981, 1983, 1985).

16. Personal interview with John K. Stoner conducted by Donald B. Kraybill, 18 September 1992.

17. Peace Office Newsletter, September-October 1992.

18. On 13 February 1992 the MCC in its annual meeting placed the work of the Peace Section under the MCC U.S. Board and incorporated its various program departments into Peace and Justice Ministries. Minutes 13 February 1992, Mennonite Central Committee U.S.

19. Personal correspondence from John A. Lapp to Donald B. Kraybill and Leo Driedger, 8 June 1992 and personal interview with John A. Lapp conducted by Leo Driedger, 30 September 1992.

20. Recent publications reflecting the historic peace churches include *A Declaration on Peace* (Gwyn, et al., 1991) and John K. Stoner's (1992b) *Called to Be Peacemakers*.

21. John H. Yoder's detailed chronology which traces some forty years of ecumenical dialogue between the historic peace churches and other major Protestant bodies appears as a thirteen-page appendix in *A Declaration of Peace* (Gwyn, et al., 1991). John R. Burkholder (1988) traces in narrative fashion the story of *Mennonites in Ecumenical Dialogue on Peace and Justice* in an MCC Occasional Paper No. 7, 25 pp.

22. Personal interview with C. Norman Kraus by Donald B. Kraybill, 17 February 1992.

23. Personal interview with Gene Stoltzfus conducted by Donald B. Kraybill, 11 September 1992. Among John H. Yoder's many works on Christian pacifism *The Original Revolution* (1971) is perhaps his most elaborate presentation of a nonviolent social ethic.

24. Paul Toews, in personal correspondence of 24 June 1992 to Donald B. Kraybill and Leo Driedger, suggests that Yoder in forging this middle ground was building upon and extending the work of Hershberger, thus providing continuity with the past.

25. The colloquium was held at St. Paul's School of Theology in Kansas City, 7-9 October 1976. John R. Burkholder's (1977) presentation was enlarged and published in a booklet.

26. Early references to justice in the context of racism appear in a 1965 GC statement on the "Freedom Movement" and in a 1965 MCC statement describing a voluntary service initiative in the Mississippi Delta. A BIC statement on racism passed in 1970 declared that the gospel is "opposed to social injustice in every form." The text of these statements can be found in Peachey (1980:180-181). John R. Burkholder (1988) traces the evolution of the Mennonite ecumenical dialogue regarding peace and justice.

27. This statement as well as other pre-1979 statements cited in this chapter are available in Peachey (1980).

28. The addresses were published in Peachey (1979). Peace and justice is the central theme in Urbane Peachey's preface to the publication.

29. For the text of this statement see (*Justice*, 1985). A significant milestone in viewing the use of the law for others as an expression of compassion came with the passage of a statement on *The Use of the Law* by the Mennonite church in 1981. This turnabout in thinking of the law viewed the use of the law on behalf of others as an expression of Christian service. For the full text, see *Use* (1982).

30. The Lancaster (MC) Conference Statement "Peace, Love and Nonresistance," adopted 19 September 1991, keeps nonresistance in the title but the text freely uses both nonresistance and peacemaking. The working draft of a new Mennonite Confession of Faith, sponsored by both the General Conference Mennonite Church and the Mennonite Church retains nonresistance in the title of a subsection, "Peace, Justice, and Nonresistance." Ruth-Heffelbower's (1991) *The Anabaptists Are Back* attempts to rehabilitate the word nonresistance by using it in an activist form.

31. See Stutzman (1993) for a discussion of the rise and fall of peace-related terminology in the *Gospel Herald* between 1951 and 1991.

32. "The Peacemaking Commitment," Akron, Pa.: Mennonite Central Committee, 1986, 12 pp. This pamphlet was written by Atlee Beechy.

33. The story of VORP is told in MCC's Peace Section Newsletter, January-February 1986, Vol. 16, No. 1 and in Kreider and Goossen (1988:343-351).

34. Ronald S. Kraybill (1980) describes the approach of MCS in *Repairing the Breach*. MCS publishes a *Conciliation Quarterly*.

35. John R. Burkholder's survey of Mennonite-related Peace Centers was summarized in a four-page 1984 paper titled "Mennonite Peace Centers" which includes an appendix with a brief description of all the centers. The report is available in the MCC archives.

36. More information about Christian Peacemaker Teams can be obtained by writing to them at 1821 W. Cullerton Street, Chicago, IL 60608.

37. For a history of the beginnings of the MCC Peace Section Task Force on Women in Church and Society see the July-August 1983 tenth year anniversary issue of *Report*, MCC, Akron, Pa.

Chapter 7

1. A special issue of the *Mennonite Quarterly Review* (Vol. 66, October 1992) is devoted to the Mennonite experience in World War II in both Canada and the U.S. Several articles deal with Civilian Public Service. Essays by Goossen (1992) and Roth (1992) describe the experience of women during the war.

2. William Janzen and Leo Driedger interviewed Peter J. Friesen on 9 November 1991, who himself served in the kitchen in the Headingly, Manitoba jail. Friesen claimed that there were at least 130 Mennonite COs in Headingly while he was there. William Janzen also came across many references in archival materials to "many men sent to prison" and he said during this interview that he felt there were more than thirty jailed.

3. The first sample of 3,591 respondents from 174 congregations of five denominations (Mennonite Church, General Conference Mennonite, Mennonite Brethren, Brethren in Christ, and Evangelical Mennonite) in the United States and Canada was collected in 1972. The second sample of 3,083 re-

spondents from 153 congregations of the same five denominations in the same two countries was collected in 1989. For more details on methodology for the 1972 study, see J. Howard Kauffman and Leland Harder (1975). For the methodology of the 1989 study see J. Howard Kauffman and Leo Driedger (1991). Appendix A contains details on sample selection, field procedures, and a profile of the characteristics of the respondents for both 1972 and 1989.

4. There are two Evangelical Mennonite Church conferences, one in Manitoba and a second headquartered in Indiana. The data we will use throughout this study represent the Indiana EMCs. The EMCs, formerly the Kleine Gemeinde Church, centered in Manitoba, were not part of this study.

5. The Anabaptist theological scale included items on the lordship of Christ, adult baptism, church discipline, swearing oaths, and combining deeds of mercy and evangelism. The religious Orthodoxy scale included items on the existence of God, the divinity of Christ, existence of miracles, the resurrection of Jesus, Jesus' return to earth, Satan as a personal devil, and life after death. The Fundamentalist scale contained items on the fundamentals of faith, biblical inerrancy, the virgin birth of Jesus, six-day creation of the universe, and eternal punishment. For more detailed information on these indicators see Kauffman and Harder (1975) and Kauffman and Driedger (1991).

6. The six indicators used for Associationalism included church attendance, serving the congregation, leadership in the church, attendance at church meetings, importance of the church, and Sunday school attendance. Devotionalism indicators were Bible reading, mealtime grace, frequency of prayer, family devotions, closeness of God, and divine guidance in decision-making. Religious life questions concerned discouragement in Christian life, consciousness of spiritual goals, doubts about salvation, quality of spiritual life, witnessing to the faith, and interest in serving others.

7. There are three service variables. The Mennonite Central Committee (MCC) support scale involved satisfaction with the work of MCC, the work of Mennonite Disaster Service (MDS), and with the Washington and Ottawa Offices. Serving Others included being at peace with others, treating others well, using resources for others, doing community and church volunteer work, and visiting the sick. Evangelism involved witnessing orally, inviting others to church, and leading others to Christ.

8. To study the impact of service experience we selected men between the ages of twenty-one and eighty, who would have had opportunity to enter service programs.

Chapter 8

1. Leo Driedger was present during some of these discussions. Conservative sectarians feared greater contacts with the state would lead to "compromise" and political action. Progressives (many of whom had served in MCC projects), were much more aware of extensive contacts with government officials overseas, and saw the need for similar more permanent contacts in Washington, D.C. A compromise was reached where an office would be established within a trial period as a "listening post" only, with no political action permitted. Later in 1975 such an office was also opened in Ottawa, Canada's capital, after similar discussions between conservatives and progressives in the MCC Canada board.

2. This is the language he uses for the article on "lobbying" in *MEV*. Such language would have been unacceptable in the 1960s.

3. As the strongest military power in the world, the U.S. with its large bureaucratic government becomes both complex and driven by power politics. While the same forces are at work in a much smaller democracy like Canada, everything is done on a smaller scale. Canada is also much less involved in world power politics, and fewer look to Canada for world-scale political diplomacy and power-posturing. A smaller proportion of Canada's budget goes into military spending. Economically, democratic socialism (New Democratic Party) has also modified the capitalist system greatly. NDP socialist governments have been in power in four of the ten provinces and presently hold power in Ontario, Canada's largest and most industrial province. Thus, government seems more friendly in Canada and more ready to consider the average citizen's concerns.

4. Epp was a Mennonite during much of his political career but no longer is affiliated with a Mennonite church.

5. Juhnke (1975) provides an extensive description of the political activities of Kansas Mennonites.

6. See a series of two articles in the *Mennonite Weekly Review* (22, 29 October 1992) for a listing of these political officeholders and a discussion of the growing participation of Mennonites in the political order.

7. Many of the Mennonites with graduate training who are living on farms may be living on small farms and earning their livelihood in professional work off the farm.

Chapter 9

1. "Inter-Mennonite Confession of Faith Committee Report: First Drafts," 28 March 1992, pp. 11-12.

2. As shown on Table 9.2 this particular witness item did not specifically deal with war and peace issues but general Christian witness to the nation. However, the next item in Table 9.2 which does deal with war and peace issues was supported by 68 percent of EMC members.

3. For recent discussions of Mennonite peacemaking commitments, see the special issue of the *Conrad Grebel Review*, Fall 1992 (vol. 10:3) which deals with Mennonite peace theology.

Chapter 10

1. Multiple regression analysis is a statistical technique which feeds a series of variables into an equation simultaneously and identifies the unique influence of each one. A positive value of .24 between Anabaptist theology and peacemaking means that as Anabaptism increases, peacemaking also increases, while other variables in the equation are simultaneously controlled. A negative value of -.13 between Anabaptism and political participation means that as Anabaptism increases, political participation decreases after the influence of other variables has been removed. Values which center around zero ranging between -.05 and .05 mean there is not a statistically significant relationship.

2. Wuthnow (1987, 1988, 1989b) has continued to pursue these issues in his recent writings.

3. Others (Sawatzky, 1992; Harder, 1993) have developed more complex modern types.

4. These themes are greatly expanded in Kauffman and Driedger (1991).

5. Duane Friesen (1986) has stimulated our thinking in this area with his five levels of social action for peacemaking but we have reconceptualized the material in new ways, suggesting a concern for ethos and structure in each of the six arenas.

6. Koontz' (1988) formulation is a revision of John H. Yoder's (1964) proposed middle level axioms for the ethical behavior of the state.

7. Emphasis added. This phrase from Menno Simons can be found in his complete works edited by Wenger (1956:198).

8. Written in 1539 these lines of Menno Simons can be found in his complete writings edited by Wenger (1956:307).

Epilogue

1. The question of "requiring" violence and/or its "necessity" is indeed complicated and one which we cannot address in depth in this provocative essay. For starters that deal with the question consult John H. Yoder (1971, 1983), Scriven (1988), Walsh (1989), Hauerwas (1990), and John R. Burkholder (1990b).

2. Many American Mennonites found public ways to protest the U.S. involvement in the Persian Gulf War. Various church bodies issued statements urging the U.S. not to use military means of intervention. Articles which criticized the military operations and called for nonviolent measures appeared in churchwide periodicals. The Christian Peacemaker Teams sent a delegation to Iraq.

An oral history project which tapped Mennonite responses to the war was conducted by the Oral History Institute at Bethel College. For a report of this project see *Mennonite Quarterly Review* (July 1992, News Note, p. 98). An excellent collection of essays written by Mennonites reflecting on the Persian Gulf War was edited by Duane Friesen (1991).

3. For a discussion of the relationship between church membership and peace convictions see J. Nelson Kraybill (1991) and Alghrim (1991). These two articles in the *Gospel Herald* stimulated a flurry of some sixty letters to the editor many of which are printed in the issue of November 5, 1991.

Appendix A

Sample Selection

Since the method of sample selection was identical to that of the 1972 survey, we refer the reader to the appendix in Kauffman and Harder (1975) for details. Here we report only the procedures for the 1989 sample selection process.

The sample was determined in two phases: (1) a selection of sample congregations, and (2) a selection of members within each sample congregation. In the first phase all congregations that were affiliated with a conference and had at least twenty-five members were listed alphabetically within each district conference. (Omitting congregations with fewer than twenty-five members removed only 2 percent of the total membership from the sampling frame.)

The number of members in each congregation was listed, and a procedure known as "probability of selection proportionate to size" yielded a total of 186 sample congregations. Five of these were found to be ineligible, either because they were disbanding or had recently disaffiliated from a conference. Of the 181 eligible congregations, 153 (85%) agreed to participate.

In the second phase, the pastor of each participating congregation submitted a membership list, from which a random sample of members was drawn: twenty-six for each MC congregation; twenty-eight, GC; thirty-one, MB; forty, BIC; and fifty, EMC. Each pastor was sent the sample list and asked to verify that the individual was still a member of the congregation, was at least thirteen years of age, could read English, was a resident in the community, and would be otherwise able to complete a questionnaire. All persons meeting these qualifications were sent a letter explaining the survey and inviting them to the church on a given evening to complete the questionnaire under the supervision of a research visitor.

Follow-up arrangements were made for all persons not present on the appointed evening. Absentees were provided later with a copy of the questionnaire to be completed at home and mailed to the research office in the envelope provided. An address was obtained for each sample member who did not reside in the community of his or her congregation, and a questionnaire with return envelope was mailed to all such persons.

Field Procedures

Forty "research visitors" assisted in the survey, each of them traveling from one to six congregations to administer the questionnaires. The project director met with these persons at various locations from eastern Pennsylvania to British Columbia, providing a research manual and reviewing the procedures to be used in carrying out the fieldwork and returning the questionnaires to the research office in Goshen, Indiana.

The fieldwork began in early March 1989 and was completed by the end of July. Depending on the respondent's speed, from one to three hours were required to fill out the twenty-five page questionnaire. The research visitors completed a report form for each congregation visited, indicating the persons present and persons absent (for follow-up), and giving addresses for all nonresident members. A total of 3,130 questionnaires were returned, of which 3,083 were usable, representing approximately 70 percent of all sample members eligible and able to complete a questionnaire.

Since the five denominations varied greatly in size, a different proportion of the total membership was obtained in the sample of each denomination. These proportions varied from less than 2 percent of the 102,150 members of the Mennonite Church in 1988 to approximately 12 percent of the 3,841 members of the Evangelical Mennonite Church.

Statistical adjustments were made when the data for all five denominations were combined, so that each denomination was represented in the combined data in proper proportion to each denomination's share in the total membership of the combined denominations. This adjustment is called weighting. Table A.1 reports—for each denomination—the total membership, the number of eligible sample congregations, the number of participating congregations, the number of usable responses, and the denominational weights. A profile of respondent characteristics for 1972 and 1989 is provided in Table A.2.

TABLE A.1
Profile of Sampling Results

Denomination	Members in 1988	Eligible sample congregations	Participating congregations	Usable responses	Denominational weights
Mennonite Church	102,150	58	50	888	1.57
General Conference	64,460	47	41	713	1.16
Mennonite Brethren	41,956	37	35	727	.77
Brethren in Christ	18,898	27	18	455	.56
Evangelical Mennonite	3,841	12	9	300	.17
Totals	**231,305**	**181**	**153**	**3,083**	

TABLE A.2
Profile of Respondent Characteristics by Year in Percent

	1972	1989
Denomination		
Mennonite Church	47	45
General Conference Mennonite Church	29	27
Mennonite Brethren	17	18
Brethren in Christ	6	8
Evangelical Mennonite Church	2	2
Gender		
Female	54	53
Male	46	46
Age		
under 25	22	11
26-45	35	41
46-65	32	31
66 and over	17	17
Residence		
Farm	34	22
Rural/Village	32	20
City of 2,500—250,000	26	35
City of 250,000 plus	9	12
U.S.	80	69
Canada	20	31
Occupation		
Farmer	11	7
Proprietor/Professional	21	36
Clerical/Craftsman	12	16
Housewife	32	25
Other	24	16
Education		
Elementary (grades 1-8)	24	12
Secondary (grades 9-12)	43	39
College (grades 13-16)	20	28
Graduate School (1 + years)	13	21

Appendix B

This statement was adopted by the Mennonite Central Committee (MCC) at its annual meeting in February 1993. MCC commended the statement to Mennonite and Brethren in Christ churches in North America for their study and adoption. The statement is the work of the Peace Committee, an advisory committee to the MCC Overseas Peace Office. The statement summarizes current understandings on peace within the North American Mennonite and Brethren in Christ conferences that make up MCC.

A Commitment to Christ's Way of Peace

Introduction

In 1950, delegates from Mennonite and Brethren in Christ church bodies in North America met at Winona Lake, Indiana, to consider their commitment to the biblical way of peace. Their "Declaration of Christian Faith and Commitment" stands as a testimony that has guided our churches in the past 40 years.

Much has changed in our world since 1950, and we as churches have also changed. While the people of God have given a strong witness to peace during this time, the forces of violence have not diminished. We have seen a vast growth in technological means of destruction, with the development of nuclear bombs and missile systems. We have experienced wars in which highly sophisticated weapons distanced many soldiers from seeing the enemy as human beings. While the East-West power struggle which led to a massive build-up in destructive capacity has ended, conflicts between rival groups threaten the hope for peace in many parts of our globe. People everywhere long for an end to war and strife.

As our congregations have reached out to become more diverse, we have grown in our awareness of the effects of sin and the need to be peacemakers. We have learned that violence can be done not only in warfare, but also through economic structures. We have seen the world's fragile ecosystem endangered by careless treatment of the natural environment. We have struggled against the effects of racism. We have come to realize that violence can reach into our churches and into our families.

As our churches have done at various points in history, we find it helpful to once again state clearly our convictions regarding the church's calling to be God's people of peace. We look toward the future with hope because of God's promise to be with us in all situations. We are committed to speaking clearly and courageously as messengers of the good news in a troubled world. Recognizing our own sinfulness, and relying on God's grace and strength, we make the following affirmations and commitments.

Our Convictions

1. We believe that God created the world and all its inhabitants as good. Despite human sin, God in Christ, through the Holy Spirit continues to offer forgiveness and reconciliation to all. As we personally acknowledge our sinfulness and repent, we are reconciled to God through Christ our Savior, united with the church community, and entrusted with the ministry of reconciliation. Acts 2; 2 Cor. 5.

2. We believe that through the life, death and resurrection of Jesus Christ, God has saved us and proclaimed peace to us. This message of peace is central to our witness to God's suffering love which is redeeming the world. Isa. 53; Luke 1-2; Matt. 5-7; Eph. 2.

3. We believe that God calls the church to demonstrate by its life the gospel of peace, which it has received through the reconciling work of Jesus Christ, the Prince of Peace. Nurtured by the Holy Spirit, the church gives this witness through expressions of love, peace and justice within its own community and beyond. We believe that God is creating a people—the church—as a sign of God's renewal of the world. 1 Cor. 12–14; 1 Peter 2-3; 1 John.

4. We believe that peace is the will of God, and that there is no peace without justice. God calls us to abandon hatred, strife and violence in all human relations, whether between individuals, within the family, within the church, among nations and races, or between religious factions, and to pursue a just peace for God's whole creation. Isa. 2:1-5; Rom. 12-14.

Our Commitments

We have chosen to follow Jesus as our Lord, and to serve him as disciples. As his representatives, we are called to be peacemakers. This call encompasses all of life, requiring certain attitudes, duties and commitments. We recognize that the strength to pursue these goals comes from God, as we together seek God's will in the context of a spiritual community. Asking for God's grace and guidance, we adopt these commitments as a definition of our path and direction.

1. We strive to share with all people the good news that the grace of God in Jesus Christ, experienced in forgiveness and discipleship, changes lives and enables us to be peacemakers. Our love and ministry reach out to all, regardless of race, religion or status, whether friend or foe.

2. We seek to build up the church as a community of love, which welcomes people of every race, class, sex and nation, uniting even those who were enemies. Though the church in its human expressions remains imperfect, it is the body of Christ, heralding the reign of God. Membership in this body which transcends national boundaries unites believers throughout the world in communion and witness.

3. We will contribute to the relief of human need and suffering by giving ourselves and our resources. The needs of our world and the cries of people in many places for justice call us to respond as Jesus did, with compassion. At the same time we recognize our own spiritual and moral poverty and seek to receive the gifts that others, some of whom may be materially poorer than we are, have to share with us.

4. We will live in relationships of love and mutual respect. We seek to model such relationships in our homes, churches and work places, and to refrain from behavior which violates and abuses others physically or emotionally. In the spirit of Christ, we will oppose and seek to correct abusive relationships within our church family.

5. We will pray for and witness to those in authority over our countries. We recognize that governing authorities have an ordering role in society. Some of us may be called to ministries or reconciliation, relief of human need and protection of the environment through service within governmental institutions. As Christians and citizens, we strive to live consistently according to the values of God's reign, and so we offer our witness to the state, reminding those in authority that they are called by God to use their power in ways that are constructive and life-giving rather than violent and life-destroying. As Christians we are keenly aware of our primary allegiance to follow the way of God which may at times conflict with the demands of government.

6. We will strive to show by our lives that war is an unacceptable way to solve human conflict. This calls us to refuse to support war, or to participate in military service. When war or war preparations lead to the conscription of ourselves, our money, or our property, we will seek alternative ways to serve humanity and our countries in the spirit of Christ. We support ministries of conciliation which search for peaceful resolution of conflicts. Recognizing the subtle ways in which our loyalties and resources can be conscripted in modern industrial states, we will strive to continually examine our complicity in systems which treat others as enemies.

7. We will resist evil and oppression in the nonviolent spirit of Jesus. Our stand against unjust treatment of people employs the "weapons" demonstrated by Jesus—love, truth, forgiveness and the willingness to suffer rather than inflict suffering. Our witness anticipates God's transformative power in human hearts and institutions. In loving resistance we will stand with people in their struggle against the power of sin, and proclaim the liberation and reconciliation which come with the rule of God.

8. We will work together to discern what God's reign means for our lifestyles and economic systems. As Christians we are called to be compassionate and just in our economic practices, domestically and internationally, and to critique all economic systems according to their impact on the poor. In our nations military expenditures are used to sustain and shape our economic systems. We seek to resist being trapped by the consumerism so prevalent in our societies, and to live modestly as witnesses against greed and militarism.

9. We will work to restore the earth which God has created. God made the earth good, and wills the redemption of the whole creation. The threats to the future of the creation posed by nuclear weapons and environmental degradation are the result of human sinfulness. We seek to live in sustainable ways as inhabitants of the earth, and to respect all of God's creation.

10. We submit ourselves to the study of Scripture, the giving and receiving of counsel, and the practice of prayer, as ways to receive the gift of God's peace. Our world is confronted with problems which are beyond the power of unaided human reason and resources to solve. Jesus relied on prayer in his ministry, and continues to intercede for us. In humility we confess that Christ shows us the way and provides strength, guidance and comfort as we walk in the way of peace.

Our Hope

We thank God for the many opportunities we find to learn from diverse peoples around the globe. We yearn to work together in the ministry of peacemaking with all Christians. We are grateful for the faithfulness of all God's people who have sought to follow the way of Jesus Christ, and for our own tradition which has affirmed Christ's way of love and nonresistance, expressed again in these declarations and commitments.

In humility we confess our failures in following this way, and our shortcomings in both demonstrating and proclaiming Christ's love. As we renew our commitment to Christ's way, we acknowledge our need for God's grace and each other's help in learning and obeying. With the hope that God gives us, we once more commit ourselves to live holy lives worthy of our calling and to discover anew Christ's message of reconciliation and peace for the world today.

Abbreviations

AMC	Archives of the Mennonite Church, Goshen, Indiana
BE	Brethren Encyclopedia
BIC	Brethren in Christ Church
EMC	Evangelical Mennonite Church
GC	General Conference Mennonite Church
LMHS	Lancaster Mennonite Historical Society
MB	Mennonite Brethren Church
MC	Mennonite Church
MCC	Mennonite Central Committee
ME	Mennonite Encyclopedia
MHL	Mennonite Historical Library, Goshen, Indiana

Bibliography

Ainlay, Stephen C.
1990   "Communal Commitment and Individualism." In Leo Driedger and Leland Harder, eds., *Anabaptist-Mennonite Identities in Ferment*. Elkhart, Ind.: Institute of Mennonite Studies.

Alghrim, Ryan
1991   "Should Pacifism be a Requirement for Church Membership?" *Gospel Herald* 37:5-7.

Archibald, Clinton
1988   "Parti Québécois." *The Canadian Encyclopedia*, Vol. 3, 2nd. ed., Edmonton: Hurtig Publishers.

Becker, Mark
1985   "Mennonite Resistance to Draft Registration." *Mennonite Life* 40:9-21.

Bellah, Robert N., Richard Madsen, William M. Sullivan, Ann Swidler, Steven M. Tipton.
1985   *Habits of the Heart*. Berkeley and Los Angeles: University of California Press.

Bender, Harold S.
1929   *Two Centuries of American Mennonite Literature, 1727-1928*. Goshen, Ind.: Mennonite Historical Society.
1944   "The Anabaptist Vision." *Church History* 18:3-24.
ca. 1952   "Political and Social Implications of Christian Pacifism." Unpublished paper found in the Peace Problems Committee files: Mennonite General Conference Collection, Peace Problems Committee, H. S. Bender, Chair 1935-62, I-3-5.10, Box 55, File 7, Folder 2, AMC.
1958   "Editorial." *Mennonite Quarterly Review* 32:82,110.

1959   "Seminaries, Mennonite Theological." *Mennonite Encyclopedia*
        4:499-500. Scottdale, Pa.: Mennonite Publishing House.
1960   "When May Christians Disobey the Government?" *Gospel
        Herald* 53:25-26.

Bender, Ross T. and Alan P. F. Sell, eds.
1991   *Baptism, Peace and the State in the Reformed and Mennonite Tradi-
        tions.* Waterloo: Wilfrid Laurier University Press.

Berger, Peter L.
1967   *The Sacred Canopy.* Garden City, N.Y.: Doubleday.
1977   *Facing Up to Modernity.* New York: Basic Books.
1979   *The Heretical Imperative.* Garden City, N.Y.: Doubleday.

Berger, Peter L., Brigitte Berger, and Hansfired Kellner
1973   *The Homeless Mind.* New York: Random House.

Berkey, Esther
1953   "Actions of the Indiana-Michigan Mennonite Conference: In
        Reference to Nonconformity and Nonresistance." Unpub-
        lished paper at the Mennonite Historical Library, Goshen Col-
        lege, Goshen, Ind.

Bohn, Stanley
1967   "Toward a New Understanding of Nonresistance." *Mennonite
        Life* 22:14-17.

Bonk, Jon
1988   *The World at War: The Church at Peace.* Winnipeg: Kindred
        Press.

Bowman, Carl
1987   *A Profile of the Church of the Brethren.* Elgin, Ill.: Brethren Press.

Braght, Thieleman J. van
1985   Comp. *The Bloody Theatre; or Martyrs Mirror.* 14th. ed. Scott-
        dale, Pa.: Mennonite Publishing House. Originally published
        in Dutch (Dordrecht, 1660).

Brenneman, John M.
1863   *Christianity and War: A Sermon Setting Forth the Sufferings of
        Christians.* Chicago: (MHL).
1873   *Pride and Humility.* Elkhart, Ind.: J. F. Funk & Bro.

Brock, Peter
1972   *Pacifism in Europe to 1914.* Princeton, N.J.: Princeton University
        Press.
1991a   *Freedom from Violence: Sectarian Nonresistance from the Middle
        Ages to the Great War.* Toronto: University of Toronto Press.

1991b   "Marcin Czechowic in Defense of Nonresistance, 1575." *The Conrad Grebel Review* 9:251-257.

Brunk, George
1929   "Pacifism-Nonresistance." *The Sword and Trumpet.* I, October, 6.

Burkholder, Christian
1857   *Christian Spiritual Conversation on Saving Faith, for the Young in Questions and Answers.* English Translation of the 1804 German edition. Lancaster, Pa.: John Baer and Sons. MHL.

Burkholder, J. Lawrence
1951   "An Examination of the Mennonite Doctrine of Nonconformity to the World." Unpublished Masters thesis, Princeton Theological Seminary.
1955   "Exercising the Ministry of Reconciliation." *Gospel Herald* 48, 721-722.
1958   *The Problem of Social Responsibility from the Perspective of the Mennonite Church.* Unpublished Th.D. dissertation, Princeton Theological Seminary.
1969   "Violence, Nonviolent Resistance, and Nonresistance in Revolutionary Times." *Canadian Mennonite.* June 27, 8-9.
1976   "Nonresistance, Nonviolent Resistance, and Power." In John R. Burkholder and Calvin Redekop, eds., *Kingdom, Cross, and Community.* Scottdale, Pa.: Herald Press.
1989   *The Problem of Social Responsibility from the Perspective of the Mennonite Church.* Elkhart, Ind.: Institute of Mennonite Studies.
1992   "Some Background—Mostly Autobiographical." Unpublished paper.

Burkholder, John R.
1960   "Radical Pacifism Challenges the Mennonite Church." Unpublished paper prepared for the meeting of the Mennonite Theological Study Group in Chicago.
1976   "A Perspective on Mennonite Ethics." In John R. Burkholder and Calvin Redekop, eds., *Kingdom, Cross, and Community.* Scottdale, Pa.: Herald Press.
1977   *Continuity and Change: A Search for a Mennonite Social Ethic.* Akron, Pa.: Mennonite Central Committee.
1985a   "Continuity and Change: An Analysis of the Mennonite Experience with the Political Order." Unpublished paper.
1985b   "Talking Back to Caesar: The Christian Witness to the State." Unpublished paper.
1988   "Mennonites in Ecumenical Dialogue on Peace and Justice." MCC Occasional Paper, No. 7. Akron, Pa.: Mennonite Central Committee.
1989   "The Mennonite Heritage and Conflict Management." Un-

published paper prepared for the Goshen College faculty. Goshen, Ind.

1990a   "Sociopolitical Activism." *Mennonite Encyclopedia* 5:837-838. Scottdale, Pa.: Mennonite Publishing House.

1990b   "Pacifist Ethics and Pacifist Politics." In Michael Cromartie, ed., *Peace Betrayed? Essays on Pacifism and Politics*. Washington, D.C.: Ethics and Public Policy Center.

1991a   "Can We Make Sense of Mennonite Peace Theology?" In John R. Burkholder and Barbara N. Gingerich, eds., *Mennonite Peace Theology: A Panorama of Types*. Akron, Pa.: Mennonite Central Committee Peace Office.

1991b   "Historic Nonresistance." In John R. Burkholder and Barbara Nelson Gingerich. eds., *Mennonite Peace Theology: A Panorama of Types*. Akron, Pa.: Mennonite Central Committee.

1992   "Mennonite Peace Theology: Reconnaissance and Exploration." *Conrad Grebel Review* 10:259-276.

Burkholder, John R. and Barbara Gingerich, eds.
1991   *Mennonite Peace Theology: A Panorama of Types*. Akron, Pa.: Mennonite Central Committee Peace Office.

Burkholder, John R. and Calvin Redekop, eds.
1976   *Kingdom, Cross, and Community*. Scottdale, Pa.: Herald Press.

Burkholder, Peter
1837   *The Confession of Faith of the Christians Known by the Name of Mennonites . . . Nine Reflections from Different Passages of the Scriptures, Illustrative of Their Confession, Faith & Practice*. Translated by Joseph Funk. Winchester, Va.: Robinson and Hollis. MHL.

Bush, Perry Jonathan
1990   *Drawing the Line: American Mennonites, the State, and Social Change, 1935-1973*. Unpublished Ph.D. dissertation, Carnegie-Mellon University.

Cromartie, Michael, ed.
1990   *Peace Betrayed? Essays on Pacifism and Politics*. Washington, D.C.: Ethics and Public Policy Center.

Cronk, Sandra
1981   "Gelassenheit: The Rites of the Redemptive Process in Old Order Amish and Old Order Mennonite Communities." *Mennonite Quarterly Review* 55:5-44.

Dayton, Donald W. and Robert K. Johnston, eds.
1991   *The Variety of American Evangelicalism*. Downers Grove, Ill.: InterVarsity Press.

Denlinger, Steven L.
1985   *Glimpses Past.* Lancaster, Pa.: Lancaster Mennonite Historical
        Society.

Detweiler, Richard C.
1968   *Mennonite Statements on Peace, 1915-1966.* Scottdale, Pa.: Her-
        ald Press.

Driedger, Leo
1975   "Canadian Mennonite Urbanism: Ethnic Villagers or Metro-
        politan Remnant?" *Mennonite Quarterly Review* 49:226-241.
1986   "Mennonite Community Change: From Ethnic Enclaves to
        Social Networks." *Mennonite Quarterly Review* 60:374-386.
1988   *Mennonite Identity in Conflict.* Lewiston, N.Y.: Edwin Mellen.
1989   "Urbanization of Mennonites in Post-War Canada." *Journal of
        Mennonite Studies* 7:90-110.
1990   *Mennonites in Winnipeg.* Winnipeg: Kindred Press.
1992   "The Peace Panorama: Struggle for the Mennonite Soul."
        Conrad Grebel Review 10:289-308.

Driedger, Leo and Leland Harder, eds.
1990   *Anabaptist-Mennonite Identities in Ferment.* Elkhart, Ind.: Insti-
        tute of Mennonite Studies.

Driedger, Leo and J. Howard Kauffman
1982   "Urbanization of Mennonites: Canadian and American Com-
        parisons." *Mennonite Quarterly Review* 56:269-290.

Dueck, Al
1988   "Psychology and Mennonite Self-Understanding." In Calvin
        W. Redekop and Samuel Steiner, eds., *Mennonite Identity*. Lan-
        ham, Md.: University Press of America, Inc.

Dula, Peter
1992   "Light or Leaven? Mennonite Discussion of the Christian Wit-
        ness to the State, 1952-1966." Unpublished Senior Thesis, De-
        partment of History, Eastern Mennonite College, Harrison-
        burg, Va.

Durnbaugh, Donald F., ed.
1978   *On Earth Peace.* Elgin, Ill.: The Brethren Press.

Dyck, Cornelius J., ed.
1985   "The Suffering Church in Anabaptism." *Mennonite Quarterly
        Review* 59:5-23.
1993   *An Introduction to Mennonite History.* Third edition. Scottdale,
        Pa.: Herald Press.

Eby, Kermit
    1958   "Square with the World." *The Christian Century* 22 October, 1211-1212.

Ediger, Elmer
    1956   "A Christian's Political Responsibility." *Mennonite Life* 11:143-144.

Eitzen, Dirk W. and Timothy R. Falb
    1980   "An Overview of the Mennonite I-W Program." Unpublished paper prepared for the Mennonite Central Committee, Akron, Pa.

Ens, Adolf
    1979   "Mennonite Relations with Governments: Western Canada 1870-1925." Unpublished Ph.D. dissertation, University of Ottawa.

Epp, Frank H.
    1968   "Mennonites and the Civil Service." *Mennonite Life* 23:179-182.
    1970   *I Would Like to Dodge the Draft Dodgers, But.* Winnipeg: Conrad Press.
    1982   *Mennonites in Canada, 1902-1940.* Scottdale, Pa.: Herald Press.

Epp, Frank H. and John Goddard
    1976   *The Palestinians: Portrait of a People in Conflict.* Toronto: McClelland and Stewart.
    1980   *The Israelis: Portrait of a People in Conflict.* Scottdale, Pa.: Herald Press.

Epp, Frank H. and Marlene G. Epp
    1984   *The Progressions of Mennonite Central Committee Peace Section.* Akron, Pa.: Mennonite Central Committee.

Erb, Delbert
    ca 1949   "Conference Resolutions of the Mennonite Church and its Area Conferences, 1835-1949." Unpublished paper. Mennonite Research Foundation Collection, Project #18, 1949-51, Index of Conference Minutes, AMC.

Franz, Delton
    1990   "Lobbying." *Mennonite Encyclopedia* 5:528. Scottdale, Pa.: Mennonite Publishing House.

Fretz, J. Winfield
    1956   "Should Mennonites Participate in Politics?" *Mennonite Life* 11:139-140.

Friesen, Bert
  1986   *Where We Stand: An Index of Peace and Social Concerns Statements
            by the Mennonites and Brethren in Christ in Canada, 1787-1982.*
            Winnipeg: Mennonite Central Committee.

Friesen, Dorothy
  1990   "The Mennonite Peace Witness Tomorrow." *Mennonite World
            Handbook.* Carol Stream, Ill.: Mennonite World Conference.

Friesen, Duane K.
  1986   *Christian Peacemaking and International Conflict: A Realist Pacifist
            Perspective.* Scottdale, Pa.: Herald Press.
  1982   *Mennonite Witness on Peace and Social Concerns: 1900-1980.*
            Akron, Pa.: Mennonite Central Committee U.S. Peace Section.
  1991   ed. *Weathering the Storm: Christian Pacifist Responses to War.*
            Newton, Kan.: Faith & Life Press.
  ND   *Teachings on Peace and Social Concerns: Mennonite and Brethren in
            Christ Churches in the United States: 1900-1980.* Unpublished
            manuscript.

Friesen, Lauren
  1991   "Culturally Engaged Pacifism." In John R. Burkholder and
            Barbara N. Gingerich, eds., *Mennonite Peace Theology: A Panora-
            ma of Types.* Akron, Pa.: Mennonite Central Committee.

Funk, John F.
  1863   *Warfare. Its Evils, Our Duties.* Chicago: Chas, Hess.

Gergen, Kenneth J.
  1991   *The Saturated Self.* New York: Basic Books.

Giddens, Anthony
  1987   *The Nation-State and Violence.* Berkeley and Los Angeles: Uni-
            versity of California Press.

Gingerich, Barbara
  1991   "Radical Pacifism." In J. Richard Burkholder and Barbara
            Gingerich, eds., *Mennonite Peace Theology: A Panorama of Types.*
            Akron, Pa.: Mennonite Central Committee.

Gingerich, Melvin
  1949   *Service for Peace.* Akron, Pa.: Mennonite Central Committee.
  1955   "Alternative Service Work Camps." *Mennonite Encyclopedia*
            1:76-78. Scottdale, Pa.: Mennonite Publishing House.

Godshalk, Abraham
  1838   *A Description of the New Creature.* Doylestown, Pa.: William M.
            Large.

Goossen, Rachel Waltner
    1992   "The 'Second Sex' and the 'Second Milers': Mennonite Wom-
            en and Civilian Public Service." *Mennonite Quarterly Review*
            66:525-538.

Gwyn, Douglas, George Hunsinger, Eugene F. Roop, and John Howard Yoder
    1991   *A Declaration on Peace: In God's People the World's Renewal Has
            Begun.* Scottdale, Pa.: Herald Press.

Habegger, David
    1959   "Nonresistance and Responsibility." *Concern*, A Pamphlet Se-
            ries for Questions of Christian Renewal. Scottdale, Pa.: Herald
            Press.

Harder, Leland
    1993   *Doors to Lock and Doors to Open: The Discerning People of God.*
            Scottdale, Pa.: Herald Press.

Hauerwas, Stanley
    1990   "Pacifism: A Form of Politics." In Michael Cromartie, ed.,
            Peace Betrayed? Essays on Pacifism and Politics. Washington,
            D.C.: Ethics and Public Policy Center.

Haury, Samuel S.
    1894   *Die Wehrlosigkeit in der Sonntagsschule.* Dayton: United Brethren
            Publishing House.

Hershberger, Guy F.
    1940   *Can Christians Fight? Essays on Peace and War.* Scottdale, Pa.:
            Mennonite Publishing House.
    1944   *War, Peace, and Nonresistance.* Scottdale, Pa.: Herald Press. Sub-
            sequent editions 1953, 1969.
    1950   "The Disciple of Christ and the State." Unpublished paper, pp.
            53-58 in Report of the MCC Peace Section Study Conference,
            Winona Lake, Ind.
    1951   *The Mennonite Church in the Second World War.* Scottdale, Pa.:
            Mennonite Publishing House.
    1957   ed. *The Recovery of the Anabaptist Vision: A Sixtieth Anniversary
            Tribute to Harold S. Bender.* Scottdale, Pa.: Herald Press.
    1957   "Nonviolence." *The Mennonite Encyclopedia* 3:908.
    1958   *The Way of the Cross in Human Relations.* Scottdale, Pa.: Herald
            Press.
    1960   "Nonresistance, the Mennonite Church, and the Race Ques-
            tion." *Gospel Herald* 53:577-579.
    1967   "Questions Raised Concerning the Work of the Committee on
            Peace and Social Concerns (of the Mennonite Church) and its
            Predecessors," Unpublished manuscript, 87 pp. as found in
            the Guy F. Hershberger Collection, Hist. Mss. 1-171, Box 54,
            File 9, AMC.

1976 "Our Citizenship Is in Heaven." In John R. Burkholder and Calvin Redekop, eds., *Kingdom, Cross, and Community: Essays in Honor of Guy F. Hershberger.* Scottdale, Pa.: Herald Press.

1979 "Comments on Sawatsky's Thesis: The Influence of Fundamentalism on Mennonite Nonresistance 1908-1944." Unpublished paper, 145 pp., Guy F. Hershberger Collection, Hist. Mss. 1-171, Box 57, File 3, AMC.

Hershey, Benjamin
1775 "A Short and Sincere Declaration, to Our Honorable Assembly, and All Others in High or Low Station of Administration, and to All Friends and Inhabitants of This Country, to Whose Sight This May Come, Be They English or Germans." As found in the Early Correspondence and Papers Collection, Hist. Mss. 1-10, Box 3, File 5 entitled "1775," AMC.

Hillerbrand, Hans J.
1958 "The Anabaptist View of the State." *Mennonite Quarterly Review* 32:83-110.

Horsch, James E., ed.
1992 *Mennonite Yearbook.* Scottdale, Pa.: Mennonite Publishing House.

Horst, Irvin B., ed. and trans.
1988 *Mennonite Confession of Faith.* (Dordrecht) Lancaster, Pa.: Lancaster Mennonite Historical Society.

Hostetler, Beulah Stauffer
1986 "Midcentury Change in the Mennonite Church." *Mennonite Quarterly Review* 60:58-82.

1987 *American Mennonites and Protestant Movements.* Scottdale, Pa.: Herald Press.

1990 "Nonresistance and Social Responsibility: Mennonites and Mainline Peace Emphasis, ca. 1950 to 1985." *Mennonite Quarterly Review* 64:49-73.

1992 "The Formation of the Old Orders." *Mennonite Quarterly Review* 66:5-25.

Hunter, James D.
1987 *Evangelicalism: The Coming Generation.* Chicago: University of Chicago Press.

Jackson, Dave and Neta Jackson
1989 *On Fire for Christ.* Scottdale, Pa.: Herald Press.

Janzen, A. E. and Herbert Giesbrecht, comps.
1978 *We Recommend . . . Recommendations and Resolutions of the General Conference of the Mennonite Brethren Churches.* Fresno, Calif.:

The Board of Christian Literature of the General Conference of Mennonite Brethren Churches.

Janzen, H. H.
1952   "Strengthening the Peace Witness." *Mennonite Life* 7:3-4.

Janzen, William
1990   *Limits on Liberty: The Experience of Mennonite, Hutterite and Doukhobor Communities in Canada.* Toronto: University of Toronto Press.

Janzen, William and Frances Greaser
1990   *Sam Martin Went to Prison: The Story of Conscientious Objection and Canadian Military Service.* Winnipeg: Kindred Press.

Juhnke, James C.
1971   "A Mennonite Runs for Congress." *Mennonite Life* 26:8-11.
1975   *A People of Two Kingdoms: The Political Acculturation of the Kansas Mennonites.* Newton, Kan.: Faith & Life Press.
1980   "The Response of Christians to Conscription in United States History." *Mennonites and Conscientious Objection in 1980.* Akron, Pa.: Mennonite Central Committee U.S. Peace Section.
1986   "Mennonite Benevolence and Revitalization in the Wake of World War I." *Mennonite Quarterly Review* 60:15-30.
1988   "Mennonite History and Self-Understanding: North American Mennonitism as a Bipolar Mosaic." In Calvin Redekop and Samuel Steiner, eds., *Mennonite Identity.* Lanham, Md.: University Press of America, Inc.
1989   *Vision, Doctrine, War: Mennonite Identity and Organization in America, 1890-1930.* Scottdale, Pa.: Herald Press.
1991   "Limited War in a Century of Total War." In Duane Friesen, ed., *Weathering the Storm: Christian Pacifist Responses to War.* Newton, Kan.: Faith & Life Press.

Justice and the Christian Witness
1985   Newton, Kan.: Faith & Life Press and Scottdale, Pa.: Mennonite Publishing House.

Kauffman, Daniel
1898   *Manual of Bible Doctrines.* Elkhart, Ind.: Mennonite Publishing Co.
1914   *Bible Doctrine.* Scottdale, Pa.: Mennonite Publishing House.

Kauffman, J. Howard and Leland Harder
1975   *Anabaptists: Four Centuries Later.* Scottdale, Pa.: Herald Press.

Kauffman, J. Howard and Leo Driedger
1991   *The Mennonite Mosaic: Identity and Modernization.* Scottdale, Pa.: Herald Press.

Kaufman, Donald D.
1969   *What Belongs to Caesar?* Scottdale, Pa.: Herald Press.

Kaufman, Edmund G.
1931   *The Development of the Missionary and Philanthropic Interests Among the Mennonites of North America.* Berne, Ind.: Berne Book Concern.

Kaufman, Gordon D.
1958   "Nonresistance and Responsibility." In *Concern, A Pamphlet Series of Christian Renewal.* Scottdale, Pa.: Herald Press.
1961   *The Context of Decision.* New York: Abingdon Press.
1979   *Nonresistance and Responsibility, and Other Mennonite Essays.* Newton, Kan.: Faith & Life Press.

Keim, Albert N.
1990a   "Alternative Service." *Mennonite Encyclopedia* 5:18-19. Scottdale, Pa.: Mennonite Publishing House.
1990b   *The CPS Story: An Illustrated History of Civilian Public Service.* Intercourse, Pa.: Good Books.
1990c   "Military Participation." *Mennonite Encyclopedia* 5:587-588. Scottdale, Pa.: Mennonite Publishing House.
1992   "Mennonites and Selective Service in World War II: An Ambiguous Relationship." *Mennonite Quarterly Review* 66:508-524.

King, Martin Luther, Jr.
1958   *Stride Toward Freedom; the Montgomery Story.* New York: Harper.
1964   *Why We Can't Wait.* New York: Harper & Row.

Klaassen, Walter
1962   "The Biblical Basis of Nonresistance." *Mennonite Life* 17:51-52.
1991   "Gelassenheit and Creation." *The Conrad Grebel Review* 7:23-35.

Klippenstein, Lawrence, ed.
1979   *That There Be Peace: Mennonites in Canada and World War II.* Winnipeg: Manitoba CO Reunion Committee.

Koontz, Theodore J.
1988   "Mennonites and the State: Preliminary Reflections." In Willard Swartley, ed., *Essays on Peace Theology and Witness.* Occassional Papers No. 12. Elkhart, Ind.: Institute of Mennonite Studies.
1990   "Church-State Relations." *Mennonite Encyclopedia* 5:159-162. Scottdale, Pa.: Mennonite Publishing House.

Kraus, C. Norman
1956   *Christians and the State.* Scottdale, Pa.: Herald Press.

1968a   "Toward a Theology of Revolution." Unpublished paper pre-
         sented at Intercollegiate Peace Fellowship Conference, Wash-
         ington D.C.
1968b   "A Theology for Action." *Gospel Herald* 16:538-540.
1969   "Jesus and Nonresistance—Toward a Theology of Involve-
         ment." Unpublished paper presented at Canadian Mennonite
         Bible College.
1970a   "Confronting Revolutionary Change." *Gospel Herald* 63:566-
         567.
1970b   "The Nature and Causes of Revolution." *Gospel Herald* 63:582-
         583.
1970c   "Why Political Revolution?" *Gospel Herald* 63:602-603.
1970d   "A Christian Perspective on Revolution." *Gospel Herald*
         63:618-619.

Kraybill, Donald B.
1976   *Our Star-Spangled Faith.* Scottdale, Pa.: Herald Press.
1987   "At the Crossroads of Modernity: Amish, Mennonites, and
         Brethren in Lancaster County in 1880." *Pennsylvania Mennonite
         Heritage* 10:2-12.
1988   "Modernity and Identity: The Transformation of Mennonite
         Ethnicity." In Calvin Redekop and Samuel Steiner, eds., *Men-
         nonite Identity.* Lanham, Md.: University Press of America.
1989   *The Riddle of Amish Culture.* Baltimore, Md.: The Johns Hopkins
         University Press.
1990a   "Modernity and Modernization." In Leo Driedger and Leland
         Harder, eds., *Anabaptist-Mennonite Identities in Ferment.* Elkhart,
         Ind.: Institute of Mennonite Studies.
1990b   *The Upside-Down Kingdom.* Revised edition. Scottdale, Pa.: Her-
         ald Press.

Kraybill, Donald B. and Donald R. Fitzkee
1987   "Amish, Mennonites, and Brethren in the Modern Era." *Penn-
         sylvania Mennonite Heritage* 10:2-11.

Kraybill J. Nelson
1991   "When Soldiers Want to Become Mennonites." *Gospel Herald*
         37:5-7.

Kraybill, Ronald S.
1980   *Repairing the Breach: Ministering in Community Conflict.* Scott-
         dale, Pa.: Herald Press.

Krehbiel, H.P.
1931   *What Is a Pacifist?* Newton, Kan.: Herald Publishing Co.
1937   *War, Peace and Amity.* Newton, Kan.: The author.

Kreider, Alan F.
1984   "The Servant Is Not Greater Than His Master: The Anabap-

tists and the Suffering Church." *Mennonite Quarterly Review* 57:5-29.

Kreider, Elizabeth Weaver
1991   *A Christian Peacemaker's Journal.* Intercourse, Pa.: Good Books.

Kreider, Robert S.
1953   "The Relation of the Anabaptists to the Civil Authorities in Switzerland, 1525-1555." Unpublished Ph.D. dissertation, University of Chicago.
1957   "The Anabaptists and the State." In Guy F. Hershberger , ed., *The Recovery of the Anabaptist Vision.* Scottdale, Pa.: Herald Press.
1976   "Discerning the Times." In John R. Burkholder and Calvin Redekop, eds., *Kingdom, Cross, and Community.* Scottdale, Pa.: Herald Press.
1991   "The 'Good Boys of CPS.' " *Mennonite Life* 46:4-11.

Kreider, Robert S. and Rachel Waltner Goossen
1988   *Hungry, Thirsty, A Stranger: The MCC Experience.* Scottdale, Pa.: Herald Press.
1989   *When Good People Quarrel.* Scottdale, Pa.: Herald Press.

Kremer, Russell
1974   "Nonresistance to Nonviolence: The Mennonite Story." Unpublished paper, 12 pp. MHL.

Lapp, John A.
1969   ed. *Peacemakers in a Broken World.* Scottdale, Pa.: Herald Press.
1970a   "The New Militarism Makes Its Harsh Demand." In Frank H. Epp, ed., *I Would Like to Dodge the Draft Dodgers But. . . .* Waterloo: Conrad Press.
1970b   "The Peace Mission of the Mennonite Central Committee." *Mennonite Quarterly Review* 54:281-297.
1992   "If I Were Writing the History of MCC Peace Testimony." *Peace Office Newsletter* 22:2.

Levant, Victor
1988   "Vietnam War." *The Canadian Encyclopedia*, Volume 4, Second edition. Edmonton: Hurtig Publishers.

Levy, Marion J., Jr.
1986   "Modernization Exhumed." *Journal of Developing Studies* 2:1-11.

Lichdi, Diether Götz, ed.
1990   *Mennonite World Handbook: Mennonites in Global Witness.* Carol Stream, Ill.: Mennonite World Conference.

Liechty, Joseph C.
1980   "Humility: The Foundation of Mennonite Religious Outlook in the 1860s." *Mennonite Quarterly Review* 53:5-31.

Linteau, Paul-André
1988   "Quebec Since Confederation." *The Canadian Encyclopedia,* Volume 3. Second edition. Edmonton: Hurtig Publishers.

Littell, Franklin H.
1962   *From State Church to Pluralism.* New York: Doubleday Anchor.

Loewen, Esko
1956   "Church and State." *Mennonite Life* 11:141-142.

Loewen, Howard John
1985   *One Lord, One Church, One Hope, and One God.* Elkhart, Ind.: Institute of Mennonite Studies.

Loewen, Jacob A.
1986   "The German Language, Culture and Faith." A paper read at the Mennonite Brethren Bible College, Winnipeg, November 15, 1986, p. 20.

Lowry, James W.
1990   "The *Martyrs Mirror,* A Mirror of Nonresistance." *Mennonite Life* 45:36-44.

MacMaster, Richard K.
1985   *Land, Piety, Peoplehood.* Scottdale, Pa.: Herald Press.

Marsden, George M.
1991   *Understanding Fundamentalism and Evangelicalism.* Grand Rapids, Mich.: Eerdmans.

Martin, David A.
1966   *Pacifism: An Historical and Sociological Study.* New York, N.Y.: Schocken Books.

Mennonite Encyclopedia, The
1955   Five vols. Scottdale, Pa.: Mennonite Publishing House. Volume five published in 1990.

Metzler, Edgar
1959   "Another Alternative for Draft-Age Youth." *Gospel Herald* 52:977-978.

Meyer, Albert J.
1958   "A Second Look at Responsibility." In *Concern,* A Pamphlet Series for Questions of Christian Renewal. Scottdale, Pa.: Herald Press.

Miller, Keith Graber
   1994   "Wise as Serpents, Innocent as Doves: American Mennonites Engage Washington." Unpublished Ph.D. dissertation, Emory University.

Miller, Larry
   1993   "Global Mennonite Faith Profile: Past, Present, Future." *Mennonite Weekly Review* 36:1-2.

Miller, Levi
   1992   "Why I Sat Out the Gulf War." *Gospel Herald* 85, 1-3.

Miller, Melissa and Phil M. Shenk
   1982   *The Path of Most Resistance.* Scottdale, Pa.: Herald Press.

Miller, Orie
   1926a   "Aggressive Peace Work." *Gospel Herald* 18:858-859.
   1926b   "Our Peace Message." *The College Record: Review Supplement.* 27:23-28.
   1929   "Our Peace Policy." *Mennonite Quarterly Review* 3:26-32.

Mumaw, John R.
   1944   *Nonresistance and Pacifism.* Scottdale, Pa.: Mennonite Publishing House.

Neufeld, Elmer
   1957   "Christian Responsibility in the Political Situation." Paper read at a conference on Christian Responsibility to the State, held in Chicago, 15-16 November, 1957.
   1958   "Christian Responsibility in the Political Situation." *Mennonite Quarterly Review* 32:141-162.

Neufeld, Mark
   1988   "Critical Theory and Christian Service: Knowledge and Action in Situations of Conflict." *Conrad Grebel Review* 6:249-262.

Neufeld, Tom Yoder
   1992   "Varieties of Contemporary Mennonite Peace Witness: From Passivism to Pacifism, From Nonresistance to Resistance." *Conrad Grebel Review* 10:243-257.

Niebuhr, H. Richard
   1951   *Christ and Culture.* New York: Harper.

Niebuhr, Reinhold
   1937   "Japan and the Christian Conscience." *The Christian Century* 54:1391.
   1945   *Interpretation of Christian Ethics.* New York: Harper.

Nisly, Hope
1992   "Witness to a Way of Peace: Renewal and Revision in Menno-
         nite Peace Theology 1950-1971." Unpublished Master's the-
         sis, Department of History, University of Maryland.

Oyer, John S. and Robert S. Kreider
1990   *Mirror of the Martyrs*. Intercourse, Pa.: Good Books.

Parsons, Talcott, ed.
1947   *Max Weber: The Theory of Social and Economic Organization*. New
         York: Oxford University Press.

Peachey, Paul
1954   *Die soziale Herkunft der Schweizer Täufer in der Reformationszeit:
         Eine religionssoziologische Untersuchung*. Karlsruhe: Verlag
         Schneider.
1957   "Nonviolence in the South." *Gospel Herald* 50:177.
1963   *The Church in the City*. Newton, Kan.: Faith & Life Press.

Peachey, Titus and Linda Gehman Peachey
1991   *Seeking Peace*. Intercourse, Pa.: Good Books.

Peachey, Urbane, ed.
1979   *The Kingdom of God and the Way of Peace*. Lombard, Ill.: Menno-
         nite World Conference.
1980   *Mennonite Statements on Peace and Social Concerns, 1900-1978*.
         Akron, Pa.: Mennonite Central Committee.

Ramseyer, Robert L., ed.
1979   *Mission and the Peace Witness: The Gospel and Christian Dis-
         cipleship*. Scottdale, Pa.: Herald Press.

Rawlyk, George A., ed.
1990   *The Protestant Experience, 1790-1990*. Burlington, Ont.: Welsh
         Publishing.

Redekop, Calvin W. and Samuel Steiner, eds.
1988   *Mennonite Identity: Historical and Contemporary Perspectives*. Lan-
         ham, Md.: University Press of America, Inc.

Redekop, Calvin W.
1989   *Mennonite Society*. Baltimore, Md.: The Johns Hopkins Univer-
         sity Press.
1990   "Sectarianism and the Sect Cycle." In Leo Driedger and Le-
         land Harder, eds., *Anabaptist-Mennonite Identities in Ferment*.
         Elkhart, Ind.: Institute of Mennonite Studies.

Redekop, John H.
1972   *Making Political Decisions: A Christian Perspective*. Focal Pam-
         phlet 23. Scottdale, Pa.: Herald Press.

1976   "The State and the Free Church." In John R. Burkholder and
            Calvin Redekop, eds., *Kingdom, Cross, and Community: Essays
            on Mennonite Themes in Honor of Guy F. Hershberger.* Scottdale,
            Pa.: Herald Press.
1983   "Mennonites and Politics in Canada and the United States."
            Journal of Mennonite Studies 1:79-105.
1984   *Two Sides: The Best of Personal Opinion.* Winnipeg: Kindred
            Press.
1986   "Why is Christian Nonresistance Weakening Among the
            Mennonite Brethren?" *Mennonite Brethren Herald.* November
            14, 1986, p. 10.
1987   *A People Apart: Ethnicity and the Mennonite Brethren.* Winnipeg:
            Kindred Press.
1988   "A Reassessment of Some Traditional Anabaptist Church-
            State Perspectives." In Willard M. Swartley, ed., *Essays on
            Peace Theology and Witness.* Elkhart, Ind.: Institute of Mennonite
            Studies, pp. 61-72.
1990a   "Politics." *Mennonite Encyclopedia* 5:711-714. Scottdale, Pa.:
            Mennonite Publishing House.
1990b   "Theory and Theology of Government." *Mennonite En-
            cyclopedia* 5:349-351.
1990c   *The Christian and Civil Disobedience.* Winnipeg: Board of Faith
            and Life, Canadian Conference of Mennonite Brethren
            Churches.
1991   "A Perspective on Anabaptism in Canada." In John R. Burk-
            holder and Barbara Nelson Gingerich, ed., *Mennonite Peace
            Theology: A Panorama of Types.* Akron, Pa.: Mennonite Central
            Committee.

Regehr, Ernie
    1975   *Making a Killing: Canada's Arms Industry.* Toronto: McClelland
                and Stewart.
    1980   *Militarism and the World Military Order: A Study Guide for
                Churches.* Toronto: World Council of Churches.

Regehr, T. D.
    1992   "Lost Sons: The Canadian Soldiers of World War II." *Menno-
                nite Quarterly Review* 66:461-480.

Roth, Lorraine
    1992   "Conscientious Objection: The Experiences of Some Canadi-
                an Mennonite Women During World War II." *Mennonite Quar-
                terly Review* 66:539-545.

Ruth, John L.
    1984   *Maintaining the Right Fellowship.* Scottdale, Pa.: Herald Press.

Ruth-Heffelbower, Duane
    1991   *The Anabaptists Are Back.* Scottdale, Pa.: Herald Press.

Sanders, Thomas G.
1964   *Protestant Concepts of Church and State.* New York: Holt, Rine-
          hart and Winston.

Sawatzky, Rodney J.
1973   "The Influence of Fundamentalism on Mennonite Nonresis-
          tance, 1908-1944." Unpublished Master's thesis, University of
          Minnesota.
1977   "History and Ideology: American Mennonite Identity Defini-
          tion Through History." Unpublished Ph.D. dissertation,
          Princeton University.
1992   "The One and the Many: The Recovery of Mennonite Plural-
          ism." In Walter Klaassen, ed., *Anabaptism Revisited: Essays on
          Anabaptist/Mennonite Studies in Honor of C. J. Dyck.* Scottdale,
          Pa.: Herald Press.

Schipani, Daniel
1991   "An Emerging Neo-Sectarian Pacifism." In John R. Burk-
          holder and Barbara Nelson Gingerich, eds., *Mennonite Peace
          Theology: A Panorama of Types.* Akron, Pa.: Mennonite Central
          Committee Peace Office.

Schlabach, Theron F.
1976   "To Focus a Mennonite Vision." In John R. Burkholder and
          Calvin Redekop, eds., *Kingdom, Cross, and Community.* Scott-
          dale, Pa.: Herald Press.
1977   "Reveille for Die Stillen im Lande: A Stir Among Mennonites
          in the Late Nineteenth Century," *Mennonite Quarterly Review*
          51:213-226.
1979   "Mennonites, Revivalism, Modernity—1683-1850." *Church
          History* 48:398-415.
1980   *Gospel Versus Gospel: Mission and the Mennonite Church, 1863-
          1944.* Scottdale, Pa.: Herald Press.
1988   *Peace, Faith, Nation.* Scottdale, Pa.: Herald Press.

Schmidt, Henry Jake
1981   *Continuity and Change in an Ethical Tradition: A Case Study of
          North American Mennonite Brethren Church-State Rhetoric and
          Practice 1917-1979.* Unpublished Ph.D. dissertation, University
          of Southern California.

Schroeder, David
1991   "Social Responsibility." In John R. Burkholder and Barbara
          Nelson Gingerich, eds., *Mennonite Peace Theology: A Panorama
          of Types.* Akron, Pa.: Mennonite Central Committee Peace Of-
          fice.

Scriven, Charles
1988   *The Transformation of Culture: Christian Social Ethics After H.
          Richard Niebuhr.* Scottdale, Pa.: Herald Press.

Shank, J. Ward
    1970   "Militant Nonresistance." Editorial in *The Sword and Trumpet* 38,1:7-9.
    1988   *The View from Round Hill: Selected Writings of J. Ward Shank.* Edited by Paul L. Kratz. Harrisonburg, Va.: The Sword and Trumpet.

Sider, Ronald J.
    1979   *Christ and Violence.* Scottdale, Pa.: Herald Press.
    1987   *Completely Pro-Life: Building a Consistent Stance.* Downers Grove, Ill.: InterVarsity Press.
    1989   *Non-Violence, the Invincible Weapon?* Dallas: Word Publishing.
    1990   *Rich Christians in an Age of Hunger.* Dallas: Word Publishing.

Simons, Menno
    1956   *The Complete Writings of Menno Simons.* Translated by Leonard Verduin and edited by John C. Wenger. Scottdale, Pa.: Herald Press.

Smith, C. Henry
    1938   *Christian Peace: Four Hundred Years of Mennonite Principles and Practice.* Newton, Kan.: Peace Committee of the General Conference of Mennonites.

Snyder, Arnold C.
    1984   "The Relevance of Anabaptist Nonviolence for Nicaragua Today." *Conrad Grebel Review* 2:123-137.

Stark, Werner
    1967   *The Sociology of Religion.* Bronx, N.Y.: Fordham University Press.

Stayer, James M.
    1976   *Anabaptists and the Sword.* New Edition. Lawrence, Kan.: Coronado Press.

Stayer, James M., Werner Packull, and Klaus Depperman
    1975   "From Monogenesis to Polygenesis: Historical Discussion of Anabaptist Origins." *Mennonite Quarterly Review* 49:83-121.

Steiner, Susan Clemmer
    1982   *Joining the Army That Sheds No Blood.* Scottdale, Pa.: Herald Press.

Stoltzfus, Gene
    1990   "A Call to Peacemaking." *Mennonite World Handbook.* Carol Stream, Ill.: Mennonite World Conference.

Stoner, John K.
1980   "Take the Message to Jerusalem." *Sojourners* August.
1981   "Herod's Fear: The Spiritual Roots of Effective Political Ac-
           tion." Unpublished paper.
1983   "Civil Disobedience in the Peace Church Tradition." Unpub-
           lished paper.
1985   "If I Am Asked About Civil Disobedience." Unpublished pa-
           per.
1992a   "Is it Lawful?" Unpublished paper.
1992b   *Called to Be Peacemakers*. Akron, Pa.: New Call to Peacemaking.

Stucky, Harley J.
1959   "Should Mennonites Participate in Government?" *Mennonite
           Life* 14:34-38.

Stutzman, Ervin R.
1993   "From Nonresistance to Peace and Justice: Mennonite Peace
           Rhetoric, 1951-1991." Ph.D. dissertation, Temple University.

Suderman, Robert J.
1991   "Liberation Pacifism." In John R. Burkholder and Barbara Nel-
           son Gingerich, eds., *Mennonite Peace Theology: A Panorama of
           Types*. Akron, Pa.: Mennonite Central Committee.

Swartley, Willard M., ed.
1988   *Essays on Peace Theology and Witness*. Elkhart, Ind.: Institute of
           Mennonite Studies, Occasional Papers No. 12.

Swartley, Willard M. and Cornelius J. Dyck, eds.
1987   *Annotated Bibliography of Mennonite Writings on War and Peace:
           1930-1980*. Scottdale, Pa.: Herald Press.

Thiesen, John D.
1990   "Civilian Public Service: Two Case Studies." *Mennonite Life*
           45:4-12.

Toews, John A.
1959   *Alternative Service in Canada During World War II*. Winnipeg: Ca-
           nadian Conference of the Mennonite Brethren Church.

Toews, John B.
1982   *Czars, Soviets and Mennonites*. Newton, Kan.: Faith & Life Press.

Toews, John E.
1985   "Theological Reflections." *Direction* 14:66-68.

Toews, John E. and Gordon Nickel, eds.
1986   *The Power of the Lamb*. Winnipeg: Kindred Press.

Toews, Paul
    1986   "The Long Weekend or the Short Week: Mennonite Peace Theology, 1925-1944." *Mennonite Quarterly Review* 60:15-30.
    1989   "Mennonites in American Society: Modernity and the Persistence of Religious Community." *Mennonite Quarterly Review* 63:227-246.
    1990a   "Will a New Day Dawn from This?" *Mennonite Life* 45:16-24.
    1990b   "The Concern Movement: Its Origins and Early History." *Conrad Grebel Review* 8:109-126.

Troeltsch, Ernst
    1960   *The Social Teaching of the Christian Churches.* New York: Harper and Brothers.

Use of the Law, The
    1982   Adopted by Mennonite Church General Assembly. Scottdale, Pa.: Mennonite Publishing House.

Walsh, Brian J.
    1989   "The Transformation of Culture: A Review Essay." *The Conrad Grebel Review* 7:253 -267.

Weaver, J. Denny
    1987   *Becoming Anabaptist.* Scottdale, Pa.: Herald Press.

Weber, Max
    1947   *The Theory of Social and Economic Organization.* New York: Free Press.
    1958   "Politics as a Vocation." In H. H. Gerth and C. Wright Mills, trans. and ed., *Max Weber: Essays in Sociology.* New York: Oxford University Press.

Wedel, C. H.
    1910   *Meditationen zu den Fragen und Antworten unseres Katechismus.* A commentary on the Elbing catechism.
    1926   *Words to Young Christians.* Written 1903, translated by Theodore O. Wedel. Berne, Ind.: Mennonite Book Concern.

Wenger, John C.
    1954   "Basic Issues in Nonconformity." *Mennonite Life* 9:42-44.
    1956   ed. *The Complete Writings of Menno Simons.* Scottdale, Pa.: Herald Press.
    1968   *Pacifism and Biblical Nonresistance.* Scottdale, Pa.: Herald Press.

Wuthnow, Robert
    1981   "Two Traditions in the Study of Religion." *Journal for the Scientific Study of Religion* 20:16-32.
    1987   *Meaning and Moral Order.* Berkeley, Calif.: University of California Press.

1988   *The Restructuring of American Religion.* Princeton, N.J.: University of Princeton Press.
1989a   *Communities of Discourse: Ideology and Social Structure in the Reformation, the Enlightenment, and European Socialism.* Cambridge, Mass.: Harvard University Press.
1989b   *The Struggle for America's Soul: Evangelicals, Liberals, and Secularism.* Grand Rapids, Mich.: Eerdmans Publishing.

Yinger, J. Milton
1970   *The Scientific Study of Religion.* New York: The Macmillan Company.

Yoder, Edward
1943   *Must Christians Fight?* Akron, Pa.: Mennonite Central Committee.

Yoder, John H.
1954   "The Anabaptist Dissent." *Concern* 1:45-68. Scottdale, Pa.: Herald Press.
1955   "Reinhold Niebuhr and Christian Pacifism." *Mennonite Quarterly Review* 29:101-117.
1963   "Review of *Context of Decision.*" *Mennonite Quarterly Review* 37:133-138.
1964   *The Christian Witness to the State.* Newton, Kan.: Faith & Life Press.
1971   *The Original Revolution.* Scottdale, Pa.: Herald Press.
1972   *The Politics of Jesus.* Grand Rapids, Mich.: Eerdmans Publishing.
1973   translater and ed., *The Legacy of Michael Sattler.* Scottdale, Pa.: Herald Press.
1983   *What Would You Do?* Scottdale, Pa.: Herald Press.
1984   *The Priestly Kingdom: Social Ethics as Gospel.* Notre Dame, Ind.: University of Notre Dame Press.
1992   *Nevertheless: The Varieties and Shortcomings of Religious Pacifism.* Revised edition. Scottdale, Pa.: Herald Press.

Zorrilla, Hugo
1988   *The Good News of Justice.* Scottdale, Pa.: Herald Press.

Index

Matthew, Gospel of, 21-22, 30, 150, 157, 259
McSorley, Richard, 143
Mediation, 248-249, 253
Mennonite Biblical Seminary (MBS), 111, 285
Mennonite Brethren Church (MB), 16, 25, 27, 70, 129, 166, 184, 186, 198, 215-217, 233-234, 245-246, 261, 276-277, 279, 287-288, 290, 295, 297-298, 304
Mennonite Central Committee (MCC), 16, 31, 67, 70, 72, 84, 87, 89-90, 92, 115, 117-118, 120-121, 135, 137-138, 140-142, 149-150, 154-157, 177-178, 181, 184, 213, 243-244, 251-252, 261-262, 270, 283, 285, 288-291, 304
Canada, 141, 184-185, 291
Ottawa office, 135, 143, 184-186, 217-218, 251, 288, 291
Peace Section (office), 51, 113, 115, 117, 120-121, 128-129, 135, 140-145, 149, 155, 184, 282, 288-290
support of, 176-179, 185, 241, 291
Washington office, 112, 118, 135, 140, 143, 184-186, 217-218, 251, 286, 288, 291
Mennonite Church (MC), 24, 26-27, 29, 31-32, 49-50, 52, 57, 63-64, 66-67, 69-71, 78, 83, 85, 87, 110, 117-119, 121, 123, 128, 131, 141, 148, 151-152, 166-168, 170, 191-192, 214-217, 221, 231-233, 244, 246, 276-282, 286-287, 290, 295-298, 304
peace statements, 58, 65, 68
Mennonite colleges, 25
Mennonite Conciliation Service (MCS), 51, 135, 155, 213, 252. *See also* International Conciliation Services
Mennonite Confession of Faith, 290, 292
Mennonite Disaster Service (MDS), 155, 252, 291
Mennonite Encyclopedia, 304
Mennonite history. *See* Anabaptist history

Mennonite identity, 14, 21, 35, 44, 49, 177, 233-234, 238, 246, 272. *See also* Ethnic identity
Mennonite migration. *See* Migrations
Mennonite-related peace centers. *See* Peace centers
Mennonite World Conference, 126, 150-151, 156, 260
Metzler, Edgar, 16, 126, 140-141, 147, 286
Meyer, Albert J., 16, 283, 286-287
Migrations, 26
Militarism, 138, 151, 158, 214, 246, 258
Military, 20, 177, 229. *See also* Alternatives to military service
armed service, 30, 46-47, 50, 58, 64-65, 68, 71, 73, 83, 128, 163-164, 166-169, 171-181, 214-216, 218, 279
conscription, 20, 126, 161, 243
draft, 57, 147, 163, 165, 171-173, 176, 181, 214
exemption, 188
noncombatant service, 65, 162-163, 166-174, 180, 278
service options, 163, 169, 171, 173-175
Millenarian, 80
Millennium, 73
Miller, John W., 284
Miller, Levi, 271, 287
Miller, Orie, 67-69
Miller, Terry, 191
Missions. *See* Evangelism
Mobility, 41-42, 46-48, 71, 73, 83-84, 134-136, 181, 225, 261
Modernist pacifism. *See* Pacifism
Modernist/fundamentalist controversy, 69, 281
Modernity, 39-44, 46, 48, 52-55, 59, 64, 67, 73, 75, 79, 84-85, 94, 96, 106, 133-134, 136, 152, 157-158, 216, 221, 224-225, 238, 245, 272, 278
Modernization, 14-15, 39-40, 42, 45-48, 50-51, 56, 62-63, 79, 83, 109, 134, 171-172, 175-177, 179-180, 208-209, 216, 221-222, 225, 238,

O
Oaths, swearing of, 167, 291
Obedience, 58, 66, 76, 90, 99, 101, 104
Occupational status, 47-48, 171, 173-174, 176-177, 179-180, 183-184, 223, 298
Officeholding. *See* Political officeholding
Old Order Amish, 25, 44, 49, 62, 78-79, 170, 250, 269-270, 276-278, 282
Old Order Mennonites, 24, 44, 49, 53, 62, 78-79, 84, 276-277
Oppression, 253, 259-261, 263, 265
Original Revolution, The, 289
Orthodoxy scale, theological, 176, 179, 209, 227-229, 291
Ottawa office. *See* Mennonite Central Committee
Oyer, John S., 111, 275

P
Pacifism, 20-21, 27, 30, 36-37, 70-71, 76-78, 91, 97, 100, 104, 126-128, 137, 145-146, 153, 172, 227, 235, 238, 254, 256, 259, 268-269, 278, 288
liberal, 36, 69-70, 72, 74
political, 70, 73-74
religious, 254
sectarian, 36
Pacifist. *See* Pacifism
Palestinians, The, 141
Pantex plant, 137-138
Parks, Rosa, 110
Partisan issues, 194
Party preference. *See* Political party affiliation
Patriotism, 19-20, 65, 113, 136
Pawley, Howard, 190
Peace, 67. *See also* Mennonite Central Committee (MCC); Peace statements, official
education, 140
issues, 234
literature, 32, 62-63, 71, 154, 157, 169
tax fund, 131, 143, 252-253, 288

witness, 67-68, 76-77, 79, 85-86, 88, 136, 138, 223, 225, 236, 246
Peace and justice, 150-151, 157, 250-251, 253, 256, 289
Peace and Social Concerns Committee (GC), 111
Peace centers, 135, 155, 290
Peace churches, historic, 70, 145-146, 162, 164, 180, 254
Peace Problems Committee (MC), 71-72, 110, 119, 281, 283, 286-287
Peace statements, official, 27, 31-32, 57, 62, 65, 68, 85, 129, 135, 150, 213, 221, 276-277, 282
social concerns, 277, 280
Peace tax. *See* Peace
Peace Theology Colloquium, 149
Peaceable kingdom, 28
Peacemaker Workshops, 133
Peacemakers in a Broken World, 133, 141
Peacemaking, 76-78, 85, 152, 154, 213, 218, 254, 263, 271, 293. *See also* Activism; Christian Peacemaker Teams
arenas, 247-249, 251
convictions, 271-272
dimensions of, 154, 213-214, 217, 222, 235-236
history of, 67-68, 133, 151-153, 280
scale (composite), 213, 219-222, 224-226, 228-232, 234-237, 240-241
Peacemaking scales
activism scale, 218-219, 221, 225-228, 230-232, 236
composite scale, 221, 223
nonresistance scale, 215-216, 221-222, 226, 228, 230-233, 235-236
separatism scale, 235
witness scale, 217, 221, 226-228, 230-232, 236
Peachey, Linda Gehman, 16
Peachey, Paul, 16, 87, 125, 170, 194, 244-245, 283-284, 287
Peachey, Titus, 16
Peachey, Urbane, 58, 83, 128, 277, 279-280, 285, 287, 289

Authors

Leo Driedger is professor of sociology at the University of Manitoba in Winnipeg, Manitoba, where he has taught for twenty-five years. His teaching and research specialties are in minority relations, urban sociology, and the sociology of religion.

Driedger has published extensively in most scholarly sociological journals in North America and has published a dozen books. Recent publications include *Ethnic Canada* (Copp Clark Pitman, 1987), *Aging and Ethnicity* (with Chappell, Butterworths, 1987), *Mennonite Identity in Conflict* (Mellon, 1988), *The Ethnic Factor* (McGraw-Hill, 1989), *Mennonites in Winnipeg* (Kindred, 1990), *Anabaptist-Mennonite Identities in Ferment* (IMS, 1990), *Ethnic Demography* (with Halli and Trovato, Carleton, 1990), *The Urban Factor* (Oxford, 1991), and *The Mennonite Mosaic* (with Kauffman, Herald Press, 1991).

Driedger was executive secretary of the General Conference Mennonite Church Peace and Social Concerns Committee (1957-1961) and a member of the Mennonite Central Committee (MCC) Peace Section. He served on the MCC Canada board for sixteen years, on the International MCC, and chaired MCC Manitoba. He has served on the executive board of the Canadian Conference as well as of the General Conference and its service, peace, and social concerns committees.

Darlene (Koehn) and Leo Driedger have two children. They have lived for almost thirty years in Winnipeg, where they are deeply involved in local Mennonite congregational life and service. They are members of the Charleswood Mennonite Church.

Donald B. Kraybill is professor of sociology at Elizabethtown (Pa.) College, where he also directs the Young Center for the Study of Anabaptist and Pietist Groups. He is the author of many articles and a dozen books dealing with Anabaptist groups, including *The Upside-Down Kingdom* (Herald Press, 1990) and *The Riddle of Amish Culture* (Hopkins University Press, 1989).